THE NEW INVESTMENT FRONTIER II

THE NEW INVESTMENT FRONTIER II

A Guide to Exchange Traded Funds for Canadians

Howard J. Atkinson
with Donna Green

INSOMNIAC PRESS

Edited and designed by Mike O'Connor
Copy-edited by Jan Barbieri and Adrienne Weiss

National Library of Canada Cataloguing in Publication Data

Atkinson, Howard J., 1958-
    The new investment frontier II : a guide to exchange traded funds for
    Canadians / Howard J. Atkinson with Donna Green. -- 2nd ed.

ISBN 1-894663-38-1

1. Exchange traded funds. 2. Stock index futures. I. Green, Donna H. II. Title.

HG6043.A85 2003   332.63'228   C2003-900252-7

The publisher and the author gratefully acknowledge the support of the Canada Council, the Ontario Arts Council and the Department of Canadian Heritage through the Book Publishing Industry Development Program.

Printed and bound in Canada.

Insomniac Press, 192 Spadina Avenue, Suite 403,
Toronto, Ontario, Canada, M5T 2C2
www.insomniacpress.com

THE CANADA COUNCIL | LE CONSEIL DES ARTS
FOR THE ARTS | DU CANADA
SINCE 1957 | DEPUIS 1957

ONTARIO ARTS COUNCIL
CONSEIL DES ARTS DE L'ONTARIO

For my parents, who continue to make the investment of a lifetime.

Acknowledgements for the First Edition

The biggest challenge in writing this book was laying hands on data. Thanks go to Norman Rothery of *www.stingyinvestor.com* for his invaluable research and number crunching, and to Morningstar Canada's J. Stephen Burnie for making their extensive mutual fund data available and putting it in a useful form.

I also want to thank all the people who agreed to be end-of-chapter interviews: Nate Most, Bill Fouse, John Bogle, Duff Young, Steve Rive, Paul Mazzilli, Gavin Quill. Special thanks to Dan Hallett who also contributed throughout the book and read the entire manuscript.

There were many others who also gave generously of their time. I'd like to thank Peter Haynes at TD Newcrest for his explanation of the ETF market making activity and his tour of TD's ETF trading area; Janice Russell, investment tax specialist with PricewaterhouseCoopers for reviewing the tax related information and explaining the intricacies of Canadian tax legislation; Mark Rubinstein, the unrecognized inventor of ETFs, who went well out of his way to explain the history of modern financial markets; Eric Kirzner who was a help in the early history of TIPs, along with Gord Walker and Bruce Thompson.

Thanks go to Lea Hill, closed-end fund specialist, for some statistics; Glenn Doody at S&P Canada and Jim Nevler at Dow Jones Indexes in New Jersey for explaining the technical aspects of indices; and thanks to Rudy Luukko for rummaging through his basement one glorious weekend on a fruitless quest for some hard-to-find numbers.

A number of financial advisors volunteered information on the way they work with ETFs: John De Goey, Keith Matthews, and John Hood. Paul Morse at Charles Schwab Canada and Craig Ellis, Portfolio Manager, took a good part of their day to explain their Core and Explore approach in Canada.

Much of the information on U.S. ETFs was drawn from the excellent ETF research reports written by Morgan Stanley, Goldman Sachs, and Salomon Smith Barney. I salute their hardworking ETF analysts. Sarah Thompson and John Mountain at Investment Funds Institute of Canada answered more than their share of questions.

Steve Geist and Stephen Hoffman at TD Financial Group read some of the manuscript and promptly responded to questions and requests for information. Jean Dumoulin and Louis Basque at State Street Global Advisors were similarly helpful.

A very special thanks to the team at Barclays Global Investors Canada Limited (BGI); Gerry Rocchi, Steve Rive, Linda Brillante, Warren Collier, Ruby Velji, Barb Clapham and Ed Hughes for their support on this project.

I am indebted to Brad Zigler, Adam Gebler and Jeannie Somsen from

BGI's head office in San Francisco, for ensuring that this work continued no matter which side of the border I was on.

Erica O'Keeffe, assistant extraordinaire, has been and continues to be invaluable in holding even projects like this together. I am grateful a hundred times over for her untiring help.

I hope Deb, who painstakingly reviewed the manuscript, and my three children, Sydney, Garrett and Olivia (who think that ETF stands for "Extremely Tardy Father") realize that a few missed dinners and fatherless baseball games doesn't mean I love them any less.

And finally, my sincerest appreciation to Donna Green. Without her tireless effort and forgiving nature, these words would not have made it to paper.

The night is late and I hope that if there is anyone I have inadvertently left out, know that it isn't due to a shortcoming of gratitude, but only to the feebleness of memory.

Howard Atkinson
Oakville
July, 2001

My warmest thanks to Howard Atkinson whose vision made this book possible and whose generosity and good nature sustained the effort. Thanks to Anne Papmehl for suggesting me to Howard; Tim Whitehead for starting me on this path in the first place; and to Jane Sembera, in keeping with a very old promise and in gratitude for an even older friendship that showed itself again on a long gloomy night of revisions. Love and thanks to my unceasingly supportive husband, Arthur, and my very understanding children.

Donna Green
Oakville
July, 2001

Acknowledgements for the Second Edition

The success of the first edition of this book, which saw two printings, owed a lot to the enthusiastic support of my colleagues at BGI Canada. I am most grateful to Rajiv Silgardo for his comments on the second edition. I am doubly indebted to Gerry Rocchi and Steve Rive for once again investing many hours in order to provide sound feedback.

This edition was helped by the invaluable research of Norman Rothery, Ph.D. of *www.stingyinvestor.com*, and Phillip Whitter, CFA, CIM who squeezed in my requests on top of his already hectic workload. I'd also like to thank J. Stephen Burnie at Morningstar Canada who always had time for Donna's inquires and even made access to U.S. Morningstar data possible through Haywood Kelly.

Thanks go again to Steve Geist and Stephen Hoffman at TD Financial Group for their kind cooperation. Similarly, I'd like to thank Lea Hill at CIBC World Markets, Glenn Doody at Standards & Poor's, and Dan Hallett at Sterling Mutuals.

Gordon Lang, Dean Alexander, John De Goey, Kevin Dehod and John Hood were generous with their time and their knowledge.

Jamie Golombek, Deborah Fuhr, and Kevin Ireland were good sports about doing the end-of-chapter interviews which takes much more time than is apparent.

Erica O'Keeffe is responsible for the detailed ETF information in the appendices which she did in her spare time, along with much help in formatting charts and text. Everyday I am the beneficiary of her cheerful professionalism.

A big thanks to Donna Green for working with me yet again and to Mike O'Connor and his team at Insomniac Press, who weren't frightened away after the first edition.

Kudos go to Deborah Kimsa (again) and David Ward who each volunteered to provide complete copy edits for the second edition.

And finally, to my family, the biggest thank you of all.

Howard J. Atkinson
Oakville
September 2002

Table of Contents

Author's Foreword

Twelve years ago when I was a stockbroker in London, Ontario, I passed a billboard every day on the way to work that carried this message: "The 90s, the decade of mutual funds." Little did I know how prophetic that billboard was.

I bought my first mutual fund in 1986, Templeton Growth Fund, with a gift from my grandmother. The fund had a 9% front end sales commission, a good deal for my broker. Less than two years later I sold it with a 50% profit, a really good deal for me.

Those days are gone. A 9% sales charge on a mutual fund is the personal finance equivalent of smoking in a pharmacy. Sales charges have become competitive and front end funds, when they're sold at all, don't often go above 2% in sales commissions. Even mutual funds with deferred sales charges, where sales commissions are paid only when you redeem the fund within a specified period, are growing less popular.

Investors know the days of regular double digit returns are likely over for a good while and usurious investment commissions and costs are an insult to both our intelligence and our returns. It makes no sense for investors to put up 100% of the capital and get only 50% of the return because of the corrosive effects of sales charges and management fees. The insult becomes greater as expected returns shrink, and increasingly sophisticated investors are now hungry for low-cost alternatives.

That's why I believe the next ten years will be the decade of exchange traded funds (ETFs). The concerted downturn in the market has been devastating for the mutual fund industry while being something of a boon to exchange traded funds. According to Investor Economics, a Canadian financial industry consultancy, 60% of Canadian mutual fund companies (non-deposit-taking institutions) have more redemptions than sales in their long-term funds as of June 2002. Yet ETFs everywhere continue to grow in number and assets.

The reason for this is simple. ETFs are refreshingly low cost and enviously tax efficient. They have the prudent diversification of mutual funds but with razor-thin management fees and completely disclosed holdings. In addition, they trade on a stock exchange, so are bought and sold with the speed, ease and price transparency of an ordinary stock.

Today, about 75% of ETF assets are held in institutional accounts. ETFs are "the funds the fund managers use," but there's no reason you and I shouldn't be sowing our investments with the same tools the professionals use.

I believe ETFs will continue to evolve and change the way people invest. ETFs are a fundamentally better way of delivering a diversified portfolio than conventional mutual funds, and I'm thrilled once again to be bringing knowledge of these productive tools to Canadian investors.

How to Use This Book

The New Investment Frontier II is divided into four sections. Part One explains what ETFs are and how they work, and explores the concept of indexing and the alternatives to ETFs for implementing an indexing approach. Part Two explores investment strategies using ETFs, their tax implications and tax saving strategies. Part Three looks to the past and future of ETFs. Where did they come from and what will they evolve into? Mutual funds are going to rise to the competitive threat and you'll be best equipped to understand the new products that will inevitably spring forth by knowing a little bit of history and stealing a peek at the future. Part Four is an aggregation of vital statistics on ETFs, their universe, and related information sources. Part Four on its own is an invaluable ETF resources centre. Feel free to skip around to the chapters that most interest you. This material, and ETFs themselves, should be used to complement existing investment strategies or help to develop new ones, whether you invest on your own or with the aid of an advisor. For the second edition, I've updated information throughout the text in keeping with new products and developments, and added substantial new material to the investing chapter and the chapter devoted to using ETFs with an advisor.

It's easy to forget that financial products are invented and run by people, people who often face obstacles in making their product come alive. To capture this human dimension, there's an interview at the end of each chapter with product pioneers or industry experts intimately in touch with the birth pangs—like Bill Fouse who invented the first index fund and whose patriotism was questioned for doing so, or John Bogle, the founder of the world's largest index fund company who has made it his mission to challenge the fund industry to justify their management costs. This is an unusual element in a personal finance book but one I'm particularly proud of.

When you close the covers of this book, the story will be far from over. As I write, many more ETFs are in development and the prospect of a new breed of (actively managed) ETFs seems close. ETFs will continue to evolve and so should our consciousness of their benefits. May you reach your goals, and if ETFs can help get you there this book should be of service.

Howard J. Atkinson
Oakville
December, 2002

Disclaimer

The author is National Marketing Manager for iUnits in Canada and a principal with Barclays Global Investors Canada Limited.

The opinions expressed in this book are exclusively his and do not necessarily reflect those of Barclays Global Investors.

While every effort was made to ensure the accuracy of the information herein, the author and the publisher assume no responsibility for errors, omissions or inconsistencies, and they disclaim any liability arising from the use of information in this book. Every investor's situation is different and it is always prudent to consult qualified financial professionals.

Part One

The Powerful Case for ETFs

Part One

Chapter One

What Are ETFs?

Exchange traded funds (ETFs) are the investment world's equivalent of a nectarine—part mutual fund, part stock but a marvellous improvement over both. Simply, an ETF is a portfolio of securities that trades on a stock exchange. As a basket of investments, ETFs offer the broad diversification of mutual funds but at a fraction of their cost. And, because they are traded rather than redeemed, ETFs are more tax efficient than mutual funds.

The differences between ETFs and mutual funds are significant because they can have a big effect on the overall cost of your investments and, as a result, your returns. So here's a rundown of the similarities and differences between mutual funds and their more delectable hybrid, ETFs.

How are Conventional Mutual Funds Different from ETFs?

A mutual fund is a basket of securities owned by a number of investors but managed by a professional money manager. Because the fund holds a basket of different investments, you spread your risk among a plentiful number of bets. Both mutual funds and ETFs enjoy the single biggest advantage of funds—their broad diversification, but the two diverge in a number of ways.

Buying, Selling and Pricing

Once a day, after the close of trading, a mutual fund's assets are priced and the mutual fund is given its daily value. When the fund has been priced, all fund unit buy and sell orders that have been queuing up throughout the day are transacted by the mutual fund company. (The mutual fund company does the redeeming and selling of its fund units.) This pricing arrangement doesn't allow you to know beforehand just what price you are going to get when you place an order to buy or sell a mutual fund.[1]

ETFs, on the other hand, trade on an exchange exactly like a stock. They are priced continuously, based on the value of their underlying portfolio, and can be bought and sold any time the market is open. That means you can know exactly what is going to end up going into or coming out of your pocket when you execute a trade. It also means that all the devices used for stock trading can be applied to trading ETFs: price limit orders, stop loss orders, short selling, margining, and in some cases even option strategies.

Because ETFs trade on an exchange, a brokerage commission applies on their sale or purchase. That's different from most mutual funds which usually impose no transaction fees to do a sale or purchase, though such transactions can trigger "loads." A load is a sales commission payable to an advisor and his company. Front-end load funds pay the sales commission on purchase of the fund directly from your investment money. Back-end load funds ding you for a sales commission on the sale of the fund if you redeem before some specified holding period—usually six or seven years.

If you buy or sell a mutual fund through a discount broker, you may have to pay a flat transaction fee. Don't confuse this transaction fee with loads or charges from the mutual fund company. A transaction fee in this case is imposed by the brokerage and has nothing to do with the mutual fund company itself.

Conventional Mutual Funds are Actively Managed— ETFs are Not (Yet).

A conventional mutual fund uses a manager to select the fund's investments. The manager actively buys and sells securities in hopes that he or she can outperform the market. The sad truth is that the cost of active management is frequently greater than the value that management adds to a fund's return. As a result, most fund managers don't often surpass their benchmark indices—especially over the long haul. That sticky little fact has prompted many investors to turn to a passive style of management in which a fund manager simply replicates the market he's in—with the more modest ambition of merely keeping pace with the market. This is called "passive management," and so far, all ETFs are passively managed. But then, so are index mutual funds. So what's the difference?

ETFs Most Resemble Index Mutual Funds

ETFs don't have all that much in common with actively managed funds but they are very similar to index mutual funds. An index mutual fund is one whose portfolio is intended to track a target index. An index is a collection of stocks or bonds that reflects the movement of a broader market. The S&P/TSX 60 Index, for instance, is a collection of 60 of Canada's largest and most widely traded stocks. The movement of those 60 stocks is indicative of the broader Canadian market as a whole—or at least the larger companies that make it up.

Index fund managers generally buy the same stocks in the same proportion as the index they are tracking, put their head in their hands and watch it work. Good index funds will mimic the performance of their index, minus the management expenses. That's pretty well how ETFs work. The difference is that ETFs do it better. ETFs can track an index with bloodhound precision because they are burdened with very small management fees compared to index mutual funds, and they positively scoff at the bloated management fees of actively managed funds.

ETFs are More Cost Efficient than Mutual Funds

ETFs are renowned for their low management fees. This is a critical advantage in an industry that pays itself out of the investor's returns whether those returns are positive or negative. Obviously, the lower the management expense, the more closely any index product will track its target.

The management expense ratio (MER) is a standard measure of fund costs. It is an annualized figure that captures a fund's operating expenses and management fees, stated as a percentage of the fund's assets. The bigger this number, the less of the fund's return you see. The median Canadian diversified equity fund carries an MER of 2.72% (or 272 basis points). Although it varies, as much as 40 to 50 of those basis points goes to paying the manager for investment research and decisions. A much larger portion typically finances sales and distribution.

Index funds, free of the expense of active management though not always entirely free of paying sales commission, typically shoulder a much lighter MER. Canadian equity index funds have a median MER of 0.95% because all they've got to do is hold on to an index.[2] That may seem like a bargain until you see the parsimonious MER of their rival ETFs.

Each ETF tracks a specific index, domestic or foreign, and they do it even more cheaply than index funds. Canadian-based ETF MERs range from 0.17% to 0.55%, a fairly ascetic lot. Canada's most popular ETF, the i60 Fund, has a sporty MER of 0.17%. 3

Why Costs are So Important

If you don't think saving 1 or 2% in MERs over the lifetime of your investments is anything to worry about, consider the chart below. It shows the difference of a few percentage points on what you get to keep of your own returns. It's chilling.

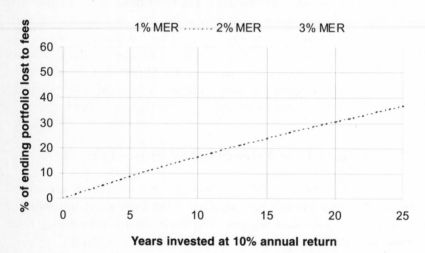

What Funds Keep (fig. 1)

Source: www.stingyinvestor.com

After 20 years, a 2% MER consumes 30% of what your portfolio value would have been without the MER.

In an interview for this book, John Bogle, the famous U.S. pioneer of low cost index investing, didn't mince words: "Take a look at the difference between 10% and 9% over an investment lifetime of 50 years. Just that little 1%. The difference is staggering. A dollar at 10% is going to be worth $117 and a dollar at 9% is going to be worth $74. If you want to put $10,000 around that it's $1,170,000 vs. $740,000 to the investor at a 1% difference. That's $430,000 to the croupier. At a 1% difference. Think of that. A third of the return is taken by the croupiers. The investor puts up 100% of the capital and takes 100% of the risk but gets two-thirds of the returns."

Fat MERs and back-end load commissions are the Black Jack dealers here. Your financial advisor's commission on a back-end load fund (otherwise known as a deferred sales charge fund or DSC) is around 5% of the value of your investment, and typically another 0.5% annually (on equity funds) for providing on-going service. That commission, though not paid directly by you, is financed through your fund's MER. The economics work because the MERs are high enough to make it work, and if you should have to redeem your fund before your declining sales charge schedule has run its course, you'll think ETFs, even with their trading commission costs, a real bargain.

As long as you hold a back-end load fund for the full course of its declining sales charge schedule, usually about seven years, you don't pay any sales charge on redemption. Most fund companies do allow 10% free annual redemptions and free switches among funds in the same fund company, but should you want to move your money out of the fund company altogether before the DSC schedule has run its inexorable course, you pay a "back-end load" that starts as high as 7% of your investment and declines over the schedule.

Back-end Load Charges vs. Trading Commissions. Which Do You Prefer?

Compare having a percentage of your assets clawed back on the redemption of a back-end load fund to the flat fee cost of selling an ETF at a discount broker for $25 a trade.

A $10,000 ETF sale with a commission of $25 = 0.25% (or 25 basis points).
A $10,000 fund redemption with a load of 3%* = 3% (or 300 basis points).
*insert any number from 7-0 here depending on holding period

$300 - $25 = $275 savings

You can avoid a back-end charge by purchasing front-end load funds. These are the second most popular commission option through full service and discount brokers. Under the front-load arrangement, your advisor's sales commission comes immediately and directly out of your invested dollars. You can often negotiate this charge to zero especially for large accounts, but the MER doesn't budge, and front-end MERs are not much different from their back-end twins.

Why are front-end MERs so high when front-end funds don't have to finance the advisor's commission? Well, front-end load funds are paying out a sweet 1% annual trailer to your advisor (on equity funds). So with either front-end or back-end option, one whole percentage point of your MER is going to pay advisor compensation in one form or another.

No-load funds, those that have neither front nor back-end charges, will spare you hurtful sales charges, but they will not let you escape high MERs. With a few exceptions, no-load fund companies charge MERs comparable to their load counterparts.

Index mutual funds, sold almost exclusively as no-load funds, have MERs that are also hard to justify, at least compared to ETFs. Bank index funds easily range from 50 to 90 basis points higher than a comparable ETF. Many insurance company index fund MERs are right off the chart with MERs well over 2%.

Once you understand the destructive impact these charges have on your returns over time, it's hard to feel indifferent to them. You must decide if you are receiving value commensurate with the cost.

Canadian Equity Fund vs. Index Fund vs. Index (fig. 2)

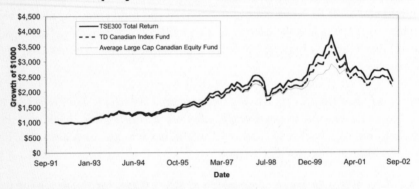

The longer management costs compound, the harder it is to beat the index
Note: MER on Cdn large cap fund, 2.3%, MER on TD Canadian Index Fund, 0.85%.

Source: www.stingyinvestor.com

ETFs are More Tax Efficient than Mutual Funds

Active managers sell securities at a profit, which is their job after all, but that has the unfortunate consequence of generating capital gains. The more active a fund manager is, the more likely she is to be racking up a tax bill for you at the end of the year (unless your holdings are in a tax-sheltered account like an RRSP.) The average equity fund manager turns over 80% of their portfolio in a year. The S&P/TSX 60 Index turns over its holdings on average about 8% a year.[4] Capital gains from these changes must be passed on, at least annually, to the fund investor. Not only is this likely to result in a tax bill, but sometimes you can find yourself paying tax on gains the fund made before you even owned it.

The less a portfolio trades, the fewer capital gains are realized and ultimately distributed. Since an index manager is most often sitting passively on her portfolio doing little more than trying to keep her portfolio as similar to the target index as possible, passively managed funds generally are more tax efficient than actively managed funds. Sure, a change to the underlying index will trigger a buy or sell within an index fund or ETF, but these changes are seldom momentous.

This isn't to say that index mutual funds and ETFs have the same potential tax liabilities. They don't, and the difference is in how they deal with redemptions. Imagine a popular index, like NASDAQ, suffering a severe and prolonged downturn. Push your imagination even further, and imagine that NASDAQ fund investors decided to flee to safer ground, redeeming their units in droves. The index fund manager would be forced to liquidate some portfolio holdings to get the cash to buy back the redeemed units. This could lead to some unwanted capital gains distributions for the remaining loyal unit holders who went on to see the value of their holdings diminish as the bear market continued to maul their index and their fund manager. Nobody wants a tax bill on top of a disastrous year.

ETF investors don't have to stay up late worrying about redemption runs because retail investors can't redeem their shares; they can only buy and sell them to other parties. These transactions on the secondary market don't directly affect the underlying portfolio and so have no tax consequences to other fund investors. This is the main reason ETFs should be more tax-efficient than index mutual funds. U.S.-based ETFs are decidedly more tax efficient than U.S.-based index funds. In Canada the jury is still out because up until recently there hasn't been an ETF to compare to an index fund tracking the same index. There's reason to believe, though, that the tax efficiency difference between index funds and ETFs may not be as pronounced as it is for U.S. products. As we'll discuss later, institutional clients can cash in large ETF positions for their underlying securities. In the U.S. this redemption does not trigger tax calculations. In Canada it does.

Nevertheless, in general, ETF index investors have greater control over their own tax liabilities than their counterparts with mutual funds. Actively managed fund unit holders are at the mercy of the manager's selling activity. Index mutual fund owners are at the mercy of the redeeming millions.

What Mutual Funds have that ETFs Don't

Mutual funds do have some attractive features that ETFs don't share. For one thing, mutual funds can be bought with small minimum investments—often as little as $500, and it is easy to arrange small regular monthly purchases (commonly known as a pre-authorized chequing plan, or PAC). ETFs, in contrast, are generally bought and sold in lots of 100 shares. This fall, i60s were trading around $38 a share. Based on 100 shares, (a "board lot"), that's a $3,800 minimum investment plus brokerage commission. Of course it is possible to buy less than 100 shares, an "odd lot," but the minimum brokerage commission still applies to these smaller orders which makes them less cost effective than a board lot purchase.

While ETFs have a trading commission associated with them, there is usually no transaction cost to buy or sell a mutual fund. The mutual fund company typically executes these transactions for free. Remember, of course, that mutual funds often have front or back-end loads and even no-load funds, and discount brokers can charge small transaction fees.

Another nice feature of mutual funds is the ease with which dividends can be reinvested. Mutual fund owners can elect to have their dividends and other distributions sent to them in cash or reinvested into units of the fund automatically. ETF investors have to take the cash—unless their brokerage house has a private dividend reinvestment plan in place. At the time of printing, only two institutions in Canada had dividend reinvestment programs for ETFs. RBC Investments allows its clients to reinvest i60 cash dividends and Canadian ShareOwner Investments Inc. permits reinvestment on all iUnits. Don't be surprised to see others offer this convenient service in the future.

For those interested in taking out an investment loan or using your investments for collateral, keep in mind that ETF distributors do not issue certificates. Your ETF holding is noted electronically and no physical certificate is required or produced. Most mutual fund companies, on the other hand, will provide share certificates upon request for a small fee. This permits you to hold the investments in a safety deposit box or to pledge them at a bank for a loan.

ETFs and Closed-end Mutual Funds

A basket of securities trading on a stock exchange is not a radically new idea. A certain kind of mutual fund has always traded on a stock exchange. Known as "closed-end" funds, these are not to be confused with ETFs.

Closed-end funds issue a fixed number of units which trade on a stock exchange or over-the-counter. Unlike conventional mutual funds which continually issue and redeem shares (hence "open-end"), closed-end funds do not regularly issue or redeem shares after the initial offering. That means investors in closed-end funds must find someone else to buy their shares when they wish to sell, just as they would for a stock.

Closed-end funds may sound like a good idea but in practice they have one stiff disadvantage. They frequently trade at less than the value of their underlying assets. This practice is called "trading at a discount." (If they were to trade at more than their net asset value, they would be trading at a premium.) The average discount for closed-end funds in Canada was running at 2.7% for the 12 months ending August 2002, a narrowing from the 5% discount of some previous years.[5] It's not entirely clear why there is a discount and why it is occasionally of considerable magnitude. Some have suggested that discounts arise because of concerns about liquidity—the ease with which the investment can be sold.

In any event, though similar to closed-end funds in some respects, ETFs don't suffer their familiar disadvantage. ETFs trade close to the value of their underlying portfolio and there's a good reason for this. With a sufficiently large number of units, ETFs can be redeemed for their underlying securities. This requisite chunk is called a "creation/redemption unit" and generally consists of 50,000 shares. (The exact number varies from ETF to ETF). The ability to distill an ETF into its constituent securities keeps ETFs trading close to their net asset value (NAV).

This redemption mechanism sets ETFs apart from closed-end funds. It also distinguishes them from conventional open-end mutual funds. These sell and redeem their shares daily for cash which is why the price of open-end mutual fund units is strictly related to the value of the underlying assets without variance.

The first closed-end fund in Canada was the Economic Investment Trust, launched in 1928. In the past year, closed-end funds have had something of a resurgence, going from $6.7 billion in assets in 2001 to $8.1 in 2002.[6] ETFs, which have been around for only 12 years, have already collected $5 billion in assets. You'll often see closed-end funds grouped with ETFs and referred to as exchange traded funds. The contemporary crop of ETFs is then distinguished by the fetching phrase, "index-linked" exchange traded funds. Closed-end funds might like to think of themselves as ETFs, but they're a generation behind, and even now not all contemporary ETFs are index-linked.

Fund Structure Comparison (fig. 3)

Features	Index-Linked ETFs	Closed-End Funds	Open-End Funds
Management Style	Passive	Actively Managed	Passive/Active
Management Fees	Very Low	Low	Moderate to High
Pricing	Intraday	Intraday	End of Day
Investment Restrictions on Illiquid Securities	No	No	Yes
Ability to Leverage	No	Yes	No
Premium/Discount Risk	Low	High	None
Tax Efficiency	High	Moderate	Moderate
Redemption Feature	Yes	No	Yes
Ability to Short	Yes	Yes	No
Transparency of Portfolio	Yes	No	No
Marginable	Yes	Yes	No
Limit Orders	Yes	Yes	No

How ETFs Stay Close to the Value of their Underlying Securities

Simply having some way to convert ETF shares to their underlying investments and vice versa, means that ETFs almost always trade close to the full value of their assets. It's the beauty of "arbitrage" at work and here's how it's done.

If the market price for an ETF share is cheaper than the proportional portfolio value, an investor with enough shares to form a creation unit, usually an institutional investor, can redeem the shares for the underlying securities. Since the securities are worth more than the ETF share, the investor then sells the individual securities and pockets the profit. That's basic arbitrage and it works in reverse just as well. Should the ETF shares be selling for more than the value of the underlying portfolio, an investor can independently buy up the individual securities and hand them over to the ETF administrator who will issue shares in the ETF. The investor can turn a profit by immediately selling those ETF units.

So arbitrage in simple terms is buying cheap and simultaneously selling what's dear and pocketing the difference after your costs. If you are arbitraging identical or nearly identical investments, there is little risk to this strategy provided you can execute your orders instantaneously.

As a retail investor you'll never have to do this arbitrage, but the fact that somebody else can, and is willing to, keeps the price of the ETF shares cozily close to the value of the underlying investments. That's what really matters.[7]

Arbitrage Mechanism Results in Low Premium/Discount (fig. 4)

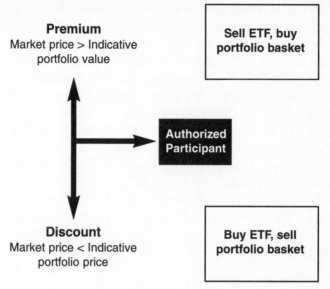

Premium
Market price > Indicative portfolio value

Sell ETF, buy portfolio basket

Authorized Participant

Discount
Market price < Indicative portfolio price

Buy ETF, sell portfolio basket

Source: Michael Porter, ETF Analyst, Salomon Smith Barney

"I've never seen a product as good at tracking their bogey as this one," says Steve Elgee, Executive Managing Director, Equity Derivative Products, with BMO Nesbitt Burns Inc., referring to the i60 Fund. Nesbitt Burns is one of the designated brokers for the i60, and as such, is responsible for ensuring an efficient, liquid and orderly market for iUnits. "There are a lot of eyes on this," he says. "We are always watching for price discrepancies greater than a dime because that presents arbitrage opportunities."

Arbitrage is made possible by two important features of ETFs—transparency and interchangeability. ETFs are transparent because their portfolio holdings are known at all times. Contrast that with the portfolio disclosure of mutual funds. Conscientious mutual fund investors know how hard it is to get current positions in a conventional mutual fund portfolio. The information is at best a month old by the time it is public, and quite frequently, because the law permits this, as old as six months. With average actively managed portfolio turnover of 80% a year, that means that almost half of a mutual fund's portfolio is different from the six month old snapshot—hardly a satisfactory state of affairs for those who would prefer to know exactly what they're buying.

ETFs are also interchangeable with their underlying securities and vice versa. You will sometimes see ETFs referred to as "fungible." This is another way of saying they are interchangeable, and it's the creation/redemption mechanism that makes this possible.

Even with this creation/redemption mechanism, however, ETFs do sometimes experience a premium or discount—most often towards the end of the trading day. The price discrepancies are most often minor; nevertheless, it's best to trade ETFs while the market for their underlying securities is open. In the U.S., that means avoiding that tempting period from 4 p.m. to 4:15 p.m. when many ETFs still trade. For ETFs pegged to foreign markets, that means coordinating your trades with time zone considerations.

How can you be sure you are getting a fair price? With U.S. ETFs it's easy since the American Stock Exchange, where almost all U.S. ETFs trade, calculates the value of the underlying portfolio of securities every 15 seconds—as well as supplying real time quotes for ETFs themselves. The Toronto Stock Exchange doesn't have a similar NAV calculator so, if you're inclined, get your calculator ready for Chapter Seven where we'll lift the hood and take a good look at how ETFs run and how they're priced.

But before that fun, meet the foot soldiers of the new investment frontier.

Getting to Know ETFs

With the exception of two Canadian bond ETFs, all current ETFs are related to an index. Name an index and it's likely there is an ETF corresponding to it. ETFs are easy to use and make it simple to gain exposure to just about any geographical area, economic sector, or market segment. The sheer number of ETFs testify to this. As of November 30, 2002, there were 132 ETFs trading in North America—116 in the U.S. and 16 in Canada. The global ETF population is booming at 281 and counting.

The Varieties of ETFs

There's an ETF for all major indices: S&P 500, the Dow Jones Industrial Average, the Fortune 500, NASDAQ 100, S&P/TSX 60, and MSCI EAFE (Europe, Australasia and the Far East.) Then there are ETFs for just about every industry sector known to analysts: Financial, Industrial, Technology, Utilities, Internet, Business-to-Business Internet, Biotechnology, Pharmaceuticals, Regional Banks, you name it. Global sector ETFs are also proliferating. (For a complete list of ETFs and their indices see the appendices.)

And if sectors aren't enough, there are ETFs to suit your taste in market capitalization and/or investment style. There's a U.S. ETF series based on the Dow Jones Index broken down according to a combination of capitalization and investment style. You can invest in a large cap value ETF, a small cap growth ETF and many variations in between. Closer to home, Canadians can now select a growth or value ETF tied to a Canadian equity index.

In the U.S., you'll also find ETFs for a broad range of developed and developing countries, too, from humble Malaysia to languorous Brazil—21 country ETFs in all—each one trying to track their respective country's broad market. There are even ETFs that track the movement of real estate investment trusts (REITs), and ETFs that track U.S. bond indices. Most recently, ETFs have been introduced that track American Depositary Receipts (ADRs) Indices. ADRs are certificates that trade on American markets but which represent shares of companies that trade on foreign markets. ADRs allow North American investors to have a direct interest in foreign corporations while still having the protection and convenience of dealing with a U.S. exchange. These products are well-established and are now being bundled into ever versatile ETFs.

In Canada, two 100% RRSP eligible ETFs based on foreign indices are available, and their relatively low MERs look positively athletic in comparison to the overweight MERs most 100% RRSP eligible, foreign mutual funds carry.

Although ETFs have found a comfortable niche in indexing, the ETF structure and concept lend themselves easily to other investments. Two Canadian ETFs, for instance, hold one bond each to be exact. BGI Canada's iG5 Fund holds one Government of Canada five-year bond which changes periodically to maintain a five-year maturity. Similarly, the iG10 Fund holds one ten-year Government of Canada bond.

Beyond indices and bonds you'll find actively managed ETFs. These are exchange traded baskets of investments the contents of which are actively bought and sold by a fund manager—exactly like a conventional actively managed mutual fund—just one that trades like a stock on an exchange. There aren't any of these in North America yet but it's likely that actively managed ETFs will make their appearance here in the next few years. When that happens, the whole mutual fund industry will be looking over its shoulder, if it's not already.

What's in a Name?

For all their conceptual elegance, exchange traded funds have a nomenclature easy to confuse with a spoonful of vegetable soup. Take, for example, streetTRACKS DJ U.S. Smallcap Value, or even the simpler i60C Fund. Generally some letter or word in the name indicates the company that constructs and administers the fund. That company is known as the fund sponsor. "streetTRACKS" is the general product name for a number of ETFs offered by State Street Global Advisors, a U.S. investment firm. The rest of the name identifies the particular index the ETF is associated with, in this case the Dow Jones U.S. Small Cap Value Index, an index that consists of stocks in companies with small market capitalization and which are considered undervalued and longer-term holds—value plays in other words.

The i60C Fund has a similar name structure. The "I" stands for "index" and is the distinctive indicator of "iUnits," the brand name for all of Barclays Global Investors Canada Limited's ETFs. (iShares are Barclays' U.S. and global product.) The "60" refers to the S&P/TSX 60 index consisting of Canada's biggest and most frequently traded companies. The "C" stands for "capped." A capped index sets limits on how large a percentage any one stock in an index can obtain—typically no more than 10% which is the case with the i60C Fund. Capped indices became respectable when Nortel Networks Corp. made up a third of the TSE 100 in early 2000. So great was its concentration on the index that it was said when Nortel sneezed, the whole index shivered. When Nortel caught pneumonia and investors and investment managers realized the appeal of limiting index concentrations.

TD Asset Management has an ETF based on a capped index also, the "TD S&P/TSX Capped Composite Index Fund." It's important not to confuse "capped" with "cap"—a short form of "market capitalization." There are small, mid and large cap ETFs all of which have "cap" in their name but are not necessarily "capped" in terms of their investment weightings. "Cap" refers to the size of companies that make up the fund's core holdings or emphasis. "Capped" means the fund has a limit on the percentage that any one company can represent in the fund.

Here's a list of all Canadian ETFs and their sponsors as of December 1, 2002.

Canadian Exchange Traded Funds (fig.5)

Fund	Description	Symbol	Sponsor
i60	Oldest and biggest ETF in Canada. TIPS35 and TIPS 100 merged with i60s in 03/2000. Based on S&P/TSX 60 Index.	XIU	BGI Canada
iG5	5-year Government of Canada Bond	XGV	BGI Canada
iG10	10-year Government of Canada Bond	XGX	BGI Canada
i60C	Based on S&P/TSX 60 Capped Index (weights capped at 10%).	XIC	BGI Canada
iMidCap	Based on S&P/TSX MidCap Index (The next 60 companies by market cap after the i60 companies).	XMD	BGI Canada
iEnergy, iIT, iGold iFinancial iREIT	Five funds: Energy, Information Technology, Gold, Financials, REITs Based on respective S&P/TSX sector indices	XEG XIT, XGD XFN XRE	BGI Canada
i500R	Based on S&P 500 Index 100% RRSP eligible.	XSP	BGI Canada
iIntR	Based on MSCI EAFE Index 100% RRSP eligible.	XIN	BGI Canada
TD S&P/TSX Composite	Based on the S&P/TSX Composite Index	TTF	TDAM
TD S&P/TSX Capped Composite	Based on the S&P/TSX Capped Composite Index (weightings limited to 10%)	TCF	TDAM
TD Select Canadian Growth	Based on the Dow Jones Canada TopCap Growth Index	TAG	TDAM
TD Select Canadian Value	Based on the Dow Jones Canada TopCap Value Index	TAV	TDAM

BGI Canada: Barclays Global Investors Canada Ltd.; TDAM: TD Asset Management Inc.,owned by TD Bank Financial Group.

Canadians can also buy any of the 100+ U.S.-listed ETFs. For a complete list of U.S. ETFs, please refer to the Appendix. The 10 largest U.S.-based ETFs are listed below.

Popular U.S. Exchange Traded Funds (fig.6)

See Appendix for complete list of all ETFs

Fund	Description	Ticker	Sponsor
Standard & Poor's Depositary Receipt	Abbreviated as SPDR Based on the S&P 500 Index. Oldest and biggest U.S. ETF.	SPY	SSgA
NASDAQ 100	Often called "Qubes." NASDAQ 100 Index. Most heavily traded U.S. ETF.	QQQ	BoNY
MidCap SPDR	S&P MidCap 400 Index	MDY	BoNY
DIAMONDS	Based on the Dow Jones Industrial Average	DIA	SSgA
iShares S&P 500	Based on S&P 500 Index	IVV	BGI
iShares Russell 2000	U.S. Small Cap Index	IWM	BGI
iShares MSCI EAFE	Based on MSCI Europe, Australasia, Far East Index	EFA	BGI
iShares Corporate Bond	Follows Goldman Sachs Investop Index	LQD	BGI
iShares Russell 3000	U.S. Broad Based Benchmark	IWV	BGI
Vanguard Total Market VIPERs	Based on the Wilshire 5000	VTI	Vanguard

SSgA: State Street Global Advisors; BGI: Barclays Global Investors Ltd.; BoNY: Bank of New York

Just to avoid confusion, note that in Canada mutual funds and ETFs are sold in "units." In the U.S., they are sold in "shares." We'll be using the terms similarly in this book.

Sponsors, Index Providers, and Distributors

The company that constructs and administers an ETF is known as the ETF sponsor. Sponsors must pay an index provider for the rights to use an index. The i60 Fund, for instance, uses the S&P/TSX 60 Index which is administered by Standard & Poor's, the index provider. Index providers charge a licensing fee to fund sponsors. Continuing our example, BGI Canada, the originator and sponsor of the i60 Fund, must pay Standard & Poor's for the use of its index. (As you might expect fights over licensing fees have kept a number of ETFs from market—especially an S&P 500 VIPER from U.S. index fund giant, Vanguard Group.)

And just to make things complicated, in the U.S., the company that sponsors the ETF is not the same company that distributes them. BGI manufactures the iShares series but they are distributed by a separate company, SEI Investment Distribution Co. Ltd. This isn't terribly relevant for ETFs in Canada but knowing this can avoid some confusion when you're looking at U.S. ETFs.

Are ETFs the Death of Mutual Funds?

A major U.S. mutual fund industry intelligence company did a study in 2000 on the effect ETFs would have on mutual funds. Financial Research Corporation's (FRC) study, "The Future of Exchange Traded Funds—An Emerging Alternative to Mutual Funds," had some interesting projections about the growth of ETFs and their threat to mutual funds.

Gavin Quill, Senior Vice President with FRC and Director of Research Studies, co-authored the study. In an interview he said he was optimistic about the long-term prospects of ETFs, but that "optimism is built more around the successful introduction of actively managed ETFs than around the long-term substantial growth of the index-based versions."

Even with optimistic growth projections for the current crop of ETFs, Quill says they won't eliminate index mutual funds even though they're a clearly superior product: "There is a compelling superiority to ETFs versus index mutual funds in most cases. Nevertheless, you're not going to see the elimination of index mutual funds. In the real world, there is substantial inertia to investor behaviour. They stick with what's working well enough."

As long as ETFs are not a threat to index funds, they're certainly not going to be sucking the lifeblood out of actively managed equity mutual funds with U.S.$3.5 trillion in assets.

Quill believes the competitive threat will heat up substantially when actively managed ETFs become available. "People like actively managed funds—rationally or irrationally. Once you move to an actively managed option, now you've got a viable competitor to the mutual fund industry," he says. "We have been forecasting in the first five years from the first actively managed ETF, that we would get to about $200 billion in the U.S. Even under the very best case, that's only a small fraction of equity mutual funds and it would clearly still not annihilate the mutual fund industry. It would just be a respectable complement to the mutual fund giant."

Until the introduction of actively managed ETFs, Quill says ETFs will have their strongest growth overseas. "They're exploding in Europe, Australia and Asia," he observes.

"I expect over the next decade we will see ETFs, mutual funds and folios all thrive together in the U.S., Canada and around the globe," continues Quill. "Growing wealth, increasing pools of financial assets, retirement privatization, and low interest rates will create a prosperous environment with plenty of opportunity for each of these vehicles to grow at a healthy pace without having to kill off one of the others to succeed."

Meet the First Spider Man

Now that you have a good understanding of ETFs and their prospects, meet the man most responsible for bringing the first and biggest ETF to American investors.

An Interview with Nathan Most—Father of "SPDRs"

A man who earned a living trading coconut oil in the sixties was the driving force behind the first successful ETF in the U.S., the now famous SPDRs. Nathan Most, now 88, had been responsible for the international trading of coconut and palm oil for a San Francisco company, Pacific Vegetable Oil.

When the company closed because of a falling out between the owners, Most was approached by the Bank of America to start up a futures exchange in San Francisco to trade western commodities. It opened in 1970 and as Most says with disarming casualness, he "finally ended up running it."

Then, says Most, there was a worldwide draught in 1974 that sent the price of coconut oil soaring. "Our principal contract was trading coconut oil from the Philippines. The price went from 13¢ a pound to 56¢ a pound in six months and I had a lot of millionaires on my trading floor who thought they knew something about coconut oil."

"When the crop began to come back in," he recalls, "we got a market reversal that wiped out half my trading floor. Then the brokerage houses that were clearing for my floor traders said they weren't going to clear it anymore so I had to shut it down."

That was in early 1976. Before he could dust off a pair of bell-bottom jeans he was invited to Washington as technical assistant to the first chairman of the Commodities Futures Trading Commission.

Very soon thereafter, the American Stock Exchange (AMEX) asked him to help them put together a futures exchange, the AMEX Commodities Exchange. This was subsequently sold to the New York Stock Exchange and now runs as the New York Futures Exchange.

Most stayed on with AMEX, however, as head of new products. It was a splashy title but Most admits he "pretty much made it as I went." His job was to build AMEX's then languishing trading volume, and his first thought was to get mutual funds to trade on the exchange.

He approached Jack Bogle, founder of Vanguard Group, and famed advocate for low-cost index funds. Bogle didn't have any interest in putting his funds on an exchange. The trading in and out of the fund that would result, he believed, would drive up fund costs. Most was aware of other attempts to trade baskets of securities, but he liked best an idea hearkening back to his commodities days, a warehouse receipt. With such a receipt commodities are bought and sold innumerable times without ever leaving the warehouse and with no additional expenses. Most applied that principle to a basket of securities, namely those in the S&P 500 Index—hence **S**tandard & **P**oor's **D**epositary **R**eceipt**s**, SPDRs. To actually implement them, Most created an investment company as a modified Unit Investment Trust and then spent three years and a million dollars of AMEX's money in legal expenses to break down the regulatory barriers.

Standard & Poor's Depositary Receipts, more affectionately known as "spiders," was launched in January 1993, and what was originally just a way to build trading volume has become an internationally popular investment vehicle.

Asked if the launch of SPDRs was a particularly gratifying personal moment, Most says, "When you work on something that long it is sort of an anticlimax." But Most, still in the game as a board member for iShares Trust for BGI and Chairman Emeritus, says the gratification is coming now. "Looking where it's gone it is almost unbelievable. They are spreading around the world very rapidly. It is just incredible."

Notes

1) With mutual funds, the price you buy or sell at is determined only at the end of the trading day and after you've placed your buy or sell order. The only exception is with some money market funds: their value stays constant at $1 or $10 a unit.

2) MERs in the U.S. are considerably lower than in Canada. According to *www.Morningstar.com*, the median actively managed U.S. large cap equity fund had an MER of 1.38% as of August 31, 2002. The most popular ETFs in the U.S., SPDRs and Qubes, have a positively ascetic MER of 0.12% and 0.18% respectively. The median MER for Canadian equity index funds was derived from information on *www.Globefund.com* as of July 31, 2002. Only bank no-load equity index funds were included in the calculation. Insurance company index funds were excluded because their extremely high MERs from 1.09% to 3.06% would have made the median MER too high to be representational of the overall retail market. The median diversified Canadian equity fund MER number came from Morningstar Canada's PALTrak as of August 31, 2002.

3) Coming in at the incredible bantam weight of a mere 0.08% was StateStreet Global Advisor's Dow Jones Canada 40 ETF. That ETF was phased out in November, 2002.

4) Michael Thorfinnson and Jason Kiss, "The Overlooked Piranha," *Canadian Investment Review,* fall, 1996, pp. 17-21, cites 80% as a best guess for the average Canadian equity mutual fund turnover. The 8.2% for the TSE 300 turnover was based on their historical research.

5) As per Lea Hill, closed-end fund specialist and Executive Director, CIBC WorldMarkets in Toronto, as of September 19, 2002.

6) As above.

7) This is how arbitraging works in principle. In actual practice, however, ETF arbitraging in Canada benefits from additional tools without redeeming fund units. What regularly happens by sophisticated players is arbitraging between the i60 and an index future on the S&P/TSX 60 index. When the future is cheaper, arbitrageurs will buy the future and sell the corresponding ETF, and vice versa. Since both investments have claim to the identical assets, the S&P/TSX 60 index, it is an easy and fairly risk free way to make money and help the market keep the price of the i60 in line with its underlying asset value.

Chapter Two

Why Index?

Exchange traded funds are almost all related to an index. You've got to be convinced that tracking the market is a good and noble pursuit, or ETFs, at least in their current incarnation, will have little appeal. Fortunately the argument for indexing is very easy to make. The simple truth is that for most asset classes, indexing gives better investment returns over the long haul than active management, but somehow the perverse gambler in us all urges us to forsake the certain for the extraordinary. Here's why you shouldn't.

It's Too Hard to Pick this Year's Top Funds

Ask yourself just how many times you've had one of the top 25 performing mutual funds of the year—the year they were in the top. If you're like most, chasing yesterday's star means making a bed for today's tired dog.

A study done in 2001 by Financial Research Corporation (FRC) found that on average, funds do about 20% better than most fund investors in those very same funds. How is that possible? It's the phenomenon of chasing returns. Most investors jump into a fund after it has made most of its gains so a fund can have, say, a 15% return yet most of its investors will see only a 12% gain—or less. It's long been known that investors don't hold their funds long enough and have a nasty habit of investing just after a fund's top performing quarter when most of the gains have been made.

The FRC study found on a three-year rolling return basis from January 1990 to March 2000, the average U.S. mutual fund's mean three-year return was 10.9%, while the average invested dollar gained only 8.7%. FRC also reports that American fund investors hold their funds for about 2.9

years. Four years ago their patience lasted 5.5 years.[1] There's no reason to think the Canadian experience is much different.

"Investors (in aggregate) have poor timing and tend to *underperform* the very funds in which they are invested," says Dan Hallett, a mutual funds analyst based in Windsor, Ontario in a report he wrote for FundMonitor.com Corp. in 1999.[2] Hallett's study looked at two popular specialty funds with big sales and redemptions, AIC Advantage I and AIC Advantage II. He tracked the money going in and out of them and timed these cash flows to the fund's actual performance. Combining the figures for these two funds together, nearly 70% of the money in these funds to the end of September 1999 was invested in just the 36 months before. During those 36 months, Hallett says, "investors earned an aggregate annualized return less than one-seventh of the funds's own published performance numbers." This means that most of the money came into the funds after the funds had already made their gains and left before the funds got back on track.

Jumping around among funds is a form of market timing. It's ironic that mutual funds should have this problem since one reason investors have flocked to them is in acknowledgement that they can't time the market—yet investors continually try to time their mutual fund purchases. Clearly market timing is just as difficult to do with mutual funds as it is with stocks. (If you're going to try to time the market, the best way is to invest in the market itself, and ETFs are absolutely the best way to do that. But more on that later.)

Winners Don't Stay Winners

Even if you are lucky enough to have picked a winner just before its glory, only a small fraction of today's stars stay in the top quartile of funds the next year. After three years, your chances of having a fund still in the top quartile are wispy. In 1996 there were 31 Canadian equity funds in the top performance quartile. Of those winners, only one was consistently a top quartile performer in each subsequent year including 1999. By 2000 not a single one was still a top quartile performer. They don't just quietly slip down into the second quartile either. In 1998, 10 of them, 32%, had tumbled into the fourth quartile. [3]

Durability of Performance (fig. 7)

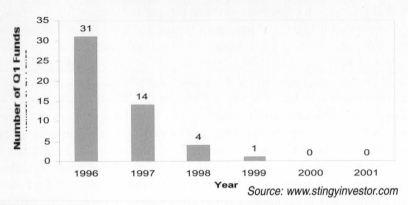

Source: www.stingyinvestor.com

First Quartile Funds in 1996 that Remained First Quartile in All Subsequent Years.

Where the First Quartile 1996 Funds Landed in 1998 (fig. 8)

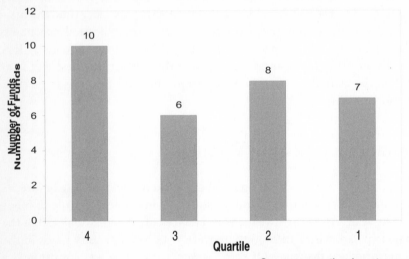

Source: www.stingyinvestor.com

Top performing funds don't stay that way for long. Of 31 first quartile funds in 1996, only seven were first quartile performers after two years.

The more outstanding the fund, the worse its chances of remaining outstanding, too. FundMonitor.com Corp., a financial advisory support company based in Toronto, has discovered something they playfully call the "newspaper effect." They tracked the performance of funds from the first time they were advertised in one newspaper's mutual funds supplement. A staggering 92% of these funds did not subsequently match their advertised three-year record, and 45% of these funds went on to do at least 10 percentage points less the year following the ad.[4]

This is called "reversion to the mean," and it is an unattractive reality as it is an English phrase. Sooner or later returns gravitate to the historical levels of their asset class. Of course a few exceptionally brilliant managers have index-breaking ten-year records, but as their funds grow ever larger, their chances of continued success seem to diminish all the faster.

Although it's possible to beat the index— and to do so over a substantial period—it is unlikely, and it is even more unlikely that you are going to be fortunate enough to own the fund that does it. You need to ask yourself, to use Dirty Harry's famous words, "Do you feel lucky?" Do you think your luck will steer you to the winning active manager this year, and the one after, and the one after until retirement? Chances are your funds will have more mediocre years than exceptional ones, and a mediocre year with an actively managed mutual fund usually means getting returns below the benchmark index.

After Tax, Where's the Advantage?

Having an excelling fund does not necessarily mean it beat the index, especially after taxes. Fund returns are always quoted after management expenses are deducted, but take no consideration of the after-tax return. Because the average Canadian equity fund sells 80% of its holdings in any given year, a normal portfolio turnover rate for actively managed funds, there are usually taxes to pay. Too few investors scrutinize their after-tax returns. If they did they'd realize holding a hot fund outside a registered account can be, if not a Pyrrhic victory, sometimes an uncomfortable one. Of course everyone would prefer to pay tax if that means they're making money. The trouble comes when the outperforming fund becomes just a mediocre fund while its old, formerly winning trading habits continue kicking out tax liabilities.

Using their proprietary software, PALTrak, Morningstar Canada surveyed a broad range of mutual fund categories to show the impact of taxation on average fund returns. Their chart is an eye-opener. An abbreviated version is reproduced here.

1 YEAR

IFSC Category	# Funds*	Avg Return	Avg After-tax Return	Percentage Lost to Tax	% of Returns Lost to Tax
CdnBal	103	-2.03	-2.63	0.60	29.43
CdnBond	140	6.50	4.55	1.95	30.04
CdnDivdnd	17	2.97	1.01	1.96	65.94
CdnEquity	153	-9.57	-9.65	0.08	0.81
CdnLgCap	55	-12.57	-12.57	0.00	0.01
CdnSmCap	80	0.31	0.02	0.30	95.16
CdnTAA	15	-4.14	-4.57	0.43	10.31
GlobalEq	256	-17.70	-17.74	0.04	0.21
Sci&Tech	120	-43.83	-43.83	0.00	0.00
USEquity	180	-22.78	-22.80	0.02	0.07

3 YEAR

IFSC Category	# Funds*	Avg Return	Avg After-tax Return	Percentage Lost to Tax	% of Returns Lost to Tax
CdnBal	151	2.55	1.39	1.16	45.51
CdnBond	101	5.43	3.32	2.10	38.79
CdnDivdnd	36	7.17	5.39	1.78	24.79
CdnEquity	99	3.73	2.88	0.85	22.83
CdnLgCap	41	3.53	2.29	1.24	35.13
CdnSmCap	62	5.16	4.34	0.82	15.95
CdnTAA	24	3.03	1.67	1.36	44.98
GlobalEq	51	-2.68	-3.18	0.50	18.74
Sci&Tech	6	-20.77	-20.77	0.00	0.00
USEquity	35	-6.01	-6.81	0.79	13.16

5 YEAR

IFSC Category	# Funds*	Avg Return	Avg After-tax Return	Percentage Lost to Tax	% of Returns Lost to Tax
CdnBal	91	2.86	1.28	1.58	55.13
CdnBond	74	4.96	2.53	2.43	49.02
CdnDivdnd	32	5.98	4.28	1.71	28.56
CdnEquity	69	2.85	1.90	0.95	33.47
CdnLgCap	32	2.95	1.56	1.39	47.03
CdnSmCap	39	1.91	1.06	0.86	44.77
CdnTAA	21	2.50	0.98	1.53	61.03
GlobalEq	41	3.08	1.69	1.39	45.25
Sci&Tech	2	2.30	1.65	0.65	28.26
USEquity	40	2.57	1.04	1.53	59.55

Source: Morningstar Canada

Assumed tax rates: interest 50%, capital gains 25%, Canadian dividends 34%.

*Morningstar does not calculate a tax efficiency ratio for a given period if the fund return is negative unless efficiency would be 100% (ie. no distributions and no tax).

Taxes can take a big bite out of the returns you're paying a manager to get for you. A seminal paper in *Canadian Investment Review* calculated the performance penalty due to taxes on a Canadian equity portfolio with 80% turnover at a painful 4 percentage points.[5] Since that study, tax rates have gone down and although the calculations haven't been redone, it's reasonable to estimate the tax bite is now closer to 2 percentage points of return. To overcome the taxes you have to pay on an actively managed fund with average portfolio turnover, your mutual fund will have to outperform an index by 2 percentage points, after management fees, every single year you own the fund. Just how likely do you think that is? That's why high turnover mutual funds, the ones that inevitably generate capital gains, should, at the very least, be held in a tax sheltered account like an RRSP.

After Tax Returns (fig. 10)

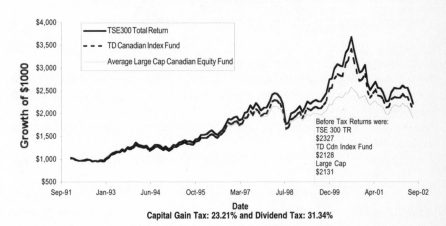

Capital Gain Tax: 23.21% and Dividend Tax: 31.34%

An index and index products will usually have better after-tax returns than actively managed mutual funds. *Source: www.stingyinvestor.com*

Management Fees Are Corrosive

If all your money is safely tucked away from the worrying touch of Canada Customs and Revenue, and you're reasonably content with consistent but not stellar funds, why should you consider indexing? For one thing, you'll still make more money in the long run with an indexing strategy because the large fees required to keep an actively managed fund going are corrosive. Over time these fees will eat into your returns as surely as battery acid on aluminum.

No doubt fees played a big part in keeping two-thirds of U.S. active equity managers from surpassing their benchmark in the ten years between 1991 to 2001.

Active Managers vs. their Benchmarks

Percent of actively managed funds in the U.S. that underperformed their benchmark index from 1991-2001.* (fig. 11)

	Large Cap	Mid Cap	Small Cap
Growth	56% (82%)	58% (88%)	9% (30%)
Blend	76% (94%)	63% (89%)	21% (57%)
Value	84% (93%)	56% (85%)	74% (97%)

Pre-tax (After-tax)

Most managers cannot do better than their benchmark index.
Benchmarks: S&P 500, BARRA Large Cap Growth, BARRA Large Cap Value, S&P 500 MidCap 400, BARRA MidCap Growth, BARRA MidCap Value, Russell 2000, Russell 2000 Growth, Russell 2000 Value.
*Ten-year data through December 31, 2001 except for MidCap Growth and MidCap Value which use five-year data.

Source: BGI analysis of Morningstar (U.S.) data

Except for the small cap growth sector, active U.S. equity managers struggled and mostly failed to outwit the index in the ten years from 1991 to 2001. That's the battery acid at work, not stupidity.

The Canadian long-term experience is hardly different. In the race for returns, the index wins the marathon mostly because fund management fees are a big obstacle for even talented fund managers to consistently overcome. Where a median MER for an actively managed Canadian large cap equity fund is 2.63%, the average MER for a Canadian equity index mutual fund is 0.95% . The MER on a Canadian equity index-based ETF is 0.25% or less. Those little numbers make a big difference.[6]

Not only does the average fund underperform the index over long stretches, but the majority of funds do, too. Of the 33 large cap Canadian equity funds existing from August 31,1992 to August 31, 2002, only four beat the S&P/TSX 60 Total Return Index (backrun), and only one beat the S&P/TSX 60 Capped Total Return Index. Of Canadian equity funds in general, 40 out of 74 (54%) beat the S&P/TSX Composite's total return of 8.96%. Only 22% (16 funds) beat the S&P/TSX Capped Composite total

Distribution of Returns and Cost, 7% annual return (fig. 12) *

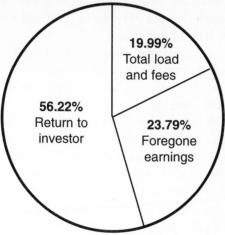

56.22%
Return to
investor

19.99%
Total load
and fees

23.79%
Foregone
earnings

Source: Ontario Securities Commission

Distribution of Returns and Cost, 10% annual return (fig. 13) *

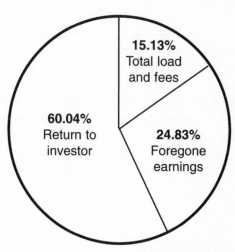

60.04%
Return to
investor

15.13%
Total load
and fees

24.83%
Foregone
earnings

Source: Ontario Securities Commission

* Assumes holding a no-load mutual fund with a MER of 2.34% for 20 years.

return of 10.49%.[7] That's a remarkable indictment of active management when you think that all those funds gasping for breath behind the Canadian index had the octane of up to 30% foreign stocks in their holdings—a benefit the indices don't have.[8]

The miracle of compounding makes sure the longer these fees eat away at your returns, the greater the damage they do. You can find an MER impact calculator on the iUnits site at *www.iunits.com* or use the older calculator devised by the Ontario Securities Commission at *www.osc.gov.on.ca*, under "tools." Both calculators show the damaging effect of MERs on returns. Let's look at just one example from the OSC site.

An MER of 2.34% in a no-load mutual fund held for 20 years and earning an annual return of 10% will eat up 15% of your total returns. The absence of that money over the years ends up costing 24.8% in foregone earnings so that your final return is only 60% of what it would have been without any MER at all. At a 7% annual return you end up with only 56% of what should have been the total return. The smaller the returns, the more proportional damage the fees do, so every bit of return counts as does every bit of MER.

Are Actively Managed Funds Better in a Down Market?

The long-term superiority of indexing doesn't mean there aren't bursts when active managers come into the fore. Last year was a prime example. In 2001, the median Canadian equity fund manager beat the TSE 300 Index by 2.2%. Her counterpart in U.S. equities underperformed the S&P 500 by 3.5%.[9] A similar pattern held the previous year. By historical standards, 2000 and 2001 were exceptional years for professional Canadian equity money managers. The market was also busy tanking.

No accident you might say—active funds protect against a falling market. That, at least, is the popular belief, but one that isn't supported by history. Yes, active funds did protect investors from the precipitous fall of the major markets beginning in 2000, but they haven't always and there's not much reason to think they will do so with any more consistency in the future.

What Protection in a Down Market? (fig. 14)

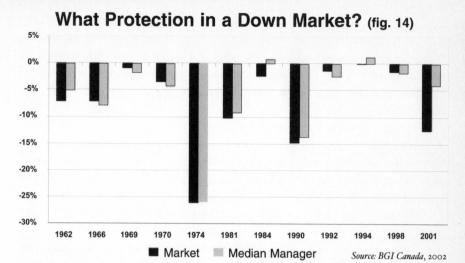

Market ■ **Median Manager** ■

Source: BGI Canada, 2002

This chart shows the performance of institutional money managers in 12 down markets from 1962.

Even institutional managers, as shown in the chart, have trouble beating their benchmark indices in bad times. If anything, the collective performance of pension fund managers will be better than collective performance of mutual fund managers because their management fees are much lower. As you can see, these active managers did better than the market in seven of those periods but in most cases they eked out only a minor differential. In five periods they did substantially worse.

It's often said that the cash component of an actively managed fund will pad the fall of a bad market. In fact, active managers are seldom prescient enough to throw a sizable chunk of money into cash at the right times.

Ted Cadsby, one of Canada's foremost indexing advocates, took a look at cash levels in actively managed mutual funds during the 1998 bear market in his book, *The Power of Index Funds* (revised edition). He found barely a difference in cash holdings throughout that dreadful year when the TSE 300 dropped a painful 25%. In fact, the average Canadian equity fund went into the 1998 bear market with less cash than it started out with, though not by much (9.5% vs. 10.2%) which shows the managers didn't see what was coming. Overall, the percentage of Canadian equity funds with 15% or more in cash *decreased* immediately before the downturn (from 19.4% to 18.2%). Clearly fund managers can't see into the future any better than anyone else.

In 2000 it wasn't cash that saved fund managers' bacon, but legal fund restrictions that saved them from themselves. At the beginning of 2000 Nortel Networks Corp.'s huge price run up had rocketed it to 36% of the

TSE 300. But because Canadian equity fund managers are not permitted to buy a position that costs more than 10% of their assets, Nortel and its stunning growth was under-represented in Canadian equity fund portfolios. Managers were banging on security regulator doors to increase or eliminate the threshold because they were getting creamed by the TSE 300 index heavy with Nortel.

Regulators did not acquiesce for actively managed funds, though they did allow funds to exceed 10% in cases of spin-offs and they did loosen the threshold for index funds. As you might expect, when Nortel plummeted later in 2000, the actively managed funds suddenly looked pretty smart in spite of themselves (though it didn't salvage their ten-year records).

It wasn't active management that served investors well in 2000, it was securities regulation. But one good benefit of the Nortel experience was the general acceptance of capped indices—as benchmarks for mutual funds and as indices for investment products like index funds and ETFs. Investors who want to index but still see the prudence of moderation, can now buy a capped index product in which no single component of the index exceeds 10%.

You might think the amount of cash managers have in their portfolios would say something about their market outlook—a bearish outlook leading to more cash and a bullish outlook resulting in less cash, but it seems cash levels are mostly just a reflection of money coming into or out of a fund. In actual practice, a mutual fund's cash levels are more a function of investor behaviour than manager savvy. Cash often results from an influx of new money into a fund that can't be invested fast enough, or it can indicate that the manager is expecting a rush of redemptions.

You've also got to wonder why you want to pay a manager a high MER to manage your portfolio's cash position. Frequently money managers plow excess cash into an ETF so as not to be handicapped by low interest rates. That means cash may not even stay cash for long. Determining your cash allocation is a basic and critical asset allocation decision you should be making and not deferring to a portfolio manager who knows nothing of your overall portfolio, investment objectives or risk tolerance. Cash, too, is notoriously easy to manage at little or no cost so why is a pricey equities portfolio manager managing it?

Indexing Provides Better Portfolio Diversification

One of the biggest advantages of mutual funds is their diversification. Owning a great number of stocks diminishes the investment risk of a few stocks getting into trouble. In actively managed funds, the fund manager selects on those stocks she likes. It's a fairly select universe, and investors have to hope her wisdom isn't flawed. In general, index funds and ETFs are more diversified than actively managed funds because they hold more stocks and in proportion to an index—not in proportion to the manager's favourites. The result is more portfolio diversification and less active manager risk.

Asset Allocation

The equity component of a well-constructed mutual fund portfolio will be diversified according to investment styles, capitalization, industry sectors, geographical regions, countries and so on. Trouble is mutual funds don't always stay true to their original colours and this throws off those prudently assembled portfolios.

Active managers come and go but funds stay long beyond them. With each change of fund manager the fund can undergo an investment-style change. It doesn't happen all the time, but it is common. A large cap fund can start taking on more small cap, for instance, or a fund with a predominantly value orientation can start getting more aggressively growth-oriented. Even a continuing manager can feel pressure to adjust her style to prevailing market conditions to enhance performance. That's something called "style drift" and it was common during the tech run up when value got left in the dirt and Warren Buffett was being called yesterday's man. Plenty of value style funds bought Nortel Networks, the prototypical growth play in 2000 just so as not to be left out of the party.

The issue of style purity is particularly complicated by the fact that mutual fund investors rarely know current portfolio holdings. Fund managers disclose their entire portfolio only semi-annually and even that disclosure can be dated before it is made public. Looking for style drift or manager signature in an actively managed mutual fund portfolio is a little bit like looking through fog for treasure.

Style purity and manager drift are never an issue with an index product. With a portfolio of index investments your asset allocation will be affected by only one thing—the changing proportional values of the indices themselves. The S&P/TSX 60 may go up relative to the S&P 500 and require you to rebalance your portfolio, but you'll never have to worry that your large cap index is slipping into small cap territory, or that your value index is slowly letting in more growth plays.

Index products also allow you to design exact asset allocations in your portfolio. Mutual funds are a mix of cash, and quite often, foreign stocks. These are not pure asset pools. Furthermore, the percentage of cash and foreign equities can vary considerably without timely disclosure. Using mutual funds for asset allocation allows you only an approximation, but with an index product your allocation will be surgically precise.

A Zero Sum Game

Perhaps the simplest argument for indexing is William F. Sharpe's famous one from logical first principles. Sharpe is a Professor of Finance at the Stanford University Graduate School of Business and a Nobel Laureate. He argues that the average actively managed dollar will equal the return on the average passively managed dollar, but after costs the return on the average actively managed dollar will be less than that of the average passively managed dollar.

He begins with the self-evident observation that the market return will be a weighted average of the returns on all the securities within the market. Since each passive manager will obtain the market return (before costs), then it follows that the return on the average actively managed dollar must equal the market return. The market is a closed system, thus

Before Costs
Average passive return = market return
Average active return = market return

Therefore: the average passive return must equal the average active return (before costs).

If the average active dollar outstripped the passive dollar, then the total market return would be increased—which isn't the case because it is a closed system. The market return is unchanged whether active or passive managers are plying their trade. Therefore, collectively, active managers cannot beat out passive managers.

However, our returns in the real world are after costs. Since active management costs are higher than passive management costs, then,

After Costs
Average passive return > Average active return

Sharpe naturally acknowledges that some active managers do beat the market, sometimes even after costs, but the trick is to find them just before they do it. Despite the great difficulty identifying these stars, and their greater difficulty staying stars, most people still place the majority of their money on active managers. No small reason for that is the shamelessly self-serving practice mutual funds have of comparing themselves to each other rather than to an index benchmark. Standard Canadian fund comparisons rank funds by their peer group performance—all large cap Canadian equities, for instance, or mid-cap U.S. equities, or balanced funds. If none of the funds managed to trounce their relevant index, being first among a group of underperformers is better than nothing, but do you want your money there?

As of early 2001, Canadian securities regulators have required mutual funds to identify every fund's benchmark index so investors can compare the fund's returns with that of an appropriate index. This is a good first step but appropriate benchmarking still has a way to go. Nevertheless, once it is understood that the real race is not for the best fund out of all funds, but rather for the best return relative to the proper index, indexing will seem less a counsel of despair and more a strategy of choice.

Ultimately there are only two ways for a fund manager to beat their benchmark index: buy investments that aren't in the benchmark index; or overweight or underweight benchmark positions. If you find a manager who has successfully outperformed and you believe it will continue, you should own that manager—and not tell anyone else about it lest money rush into the fund and handicap your manager's performance. In mutual funds, success really can lead to an embarrassment of riches—for the manager.

As CIBC's Cadsby says, the decision to index is a trade-off. You trade off "the *low possibility* of doing better than the index, for the *high probability* of doing better than most other funds."[10] If the evidence has any sway, the probability of the index outperforming your active manager is a lot greater than your possibility of picking a winning fund. Add to that the tax burden of so many actively managed funds, and it seems anything but an index play is a gambler's folly. Overall, indexing is cheaper, more tax efficient, less risky, better suited for fine tuning asset allocation, and gives more consistent returns than actively managed mutual funds. It's hard to do much better than that.

The Origin of Indexing and the Efficient Markets Hypothesis

You might think indexing as an investment strategy would be as old as the invention of a stock index, but indexing is actually a latecomer. The first stock index was invented by Charles Henry Dow in 1884 and was originally computed by adding up the price of 11 big U.S. stocks (most of them railroads) and dividing them by the number of stocks. The index was revised to 12 stocks on May 26, 1896 for an average of 40.94. Today the Dow, which includes 30 blue chip companies like Wal-Mart and General Electric (the only remaining original Dow component) now stands at about 7,500. Of course many more indices have followed, almost all of them weighted by market capitalization rather than the straight price average of Mr. Dow.[11]

For a long time indices were used simply as a shorthand for broader market movement, rather like how a wind-sock indicates the direction and strength of the prevailing wind. But then in the 1940s an academic, Harry Markowitz, began to scrutinize index returns for what it could reveal about the risk/return tradeoff among asset classes. His paper in 1952 lead to what is called "Modern Portfolio Theory," and the now widely accepted practice of asset allocation.

It's Modern Portfolio Theory (MPT) that says investors should pay more attention to getting their asset allocation right for their desired level of risk and leave market timing and individual security selection as secondary considerations. An ideal asset allocation gives an investor the optimal mix of investments with the potential to get the return they need with the least fluctuation in their portfolio's total value. This is achieved by mixing together asset classes that react to market conditions in different ways.

Asset classes whose performance diverge under similar market conditions have what's known as a low correlation with each other. Real estate, for instance, goes up during periods of high inflation. On the other hand, bonds tend to wither away under those conditions. This counterbalancing of risk and return through asset class diversification (especially with low correlations) is the hallmark of asset allocation. According to MPT, diversification has a far greater impact on portfolio returns than smart investment selection or psychic market timing, and this wisdom is the foundation of all portfolio management today. Dr. Markowitz subsequently took home a Nobel Prize for his insights.

Around the time Modern Portfolio Theory was being propounded in the early 1960s, another market theory was taking hold—the Efficient Markets Hypothesis (EMH). EMH says that stock prices reflect all past and present public information about a stock. In other words, the market is perfectly efficient and immediately factors all relevant information into a stock price. As a result, you cannot expect extraordinary returns from a stock. You may get extraordinary returns, but if you do it is purely a fluke. Don't bother doing detailed fundamental analysis—it won't pay off. There are three versions of this theory—weak, semi-strong and strong.

The weak version says you can't predict future stock price moves by studying past movements—so technical analysis is pointless. The semi-strong version puts the kibosh on fundamental analysis, too. It says that the current market price of a stock reflects all publicly available information about a stock and that scrutinizing annual reports, financial statements and economic forecasts will not lead to consistent superior returns. The strong form of EMH holds that the market price of a stock reflects absolutely all information—including insider information. This means that even those trading on insider information will not be able to make superior returns.

Trading on insider information happens to remain illegal. A number of its practitioners have failed to make a profit from it not so much because the market's utter efficiency defeated them but because they ended up in jail. Despite market regulators' skepticism about EMH, the weaker forms of EMH had some popularity for a number of years and was one of the philosophical foundations of indexing. If the market is indeed as perfectly efficient as the theory purports, there's not much point in trying to beat it—you might as well join it by indexing.

However, there have been, a number of demonstrated, legal contradictions to the weaker forms of EMH, such as the Value Line stock selection system, the January Effect, and the tendency of low price to earnings (P/E) multiple stocks to do better than expected. It seems then that no market is perfectly efficient—some are efficient most of the time while others are efficient only some of the time.

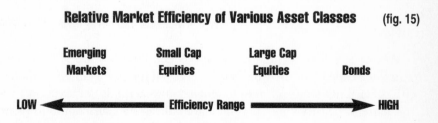

Relative Market Efficiency of Various Asset Classes (fig. 15)

| Emerging Markets | Small Cap Equities | Large Cap Equities | Bonds |

LOW ⬅️ Efficiency Range ➡️ HIGH

Asset classes vary by the efficiency of their markets.

Indexing: Is It Just for Efficient Markets?

You may hear it said that indexing works best in efficient markets and active management works best in inefficient markets. This may be true. At least it makes sense from first principles. Those poor, beleaguered active managers do have a better track record outpacing certain international and Canadian and U.S. small cap indices. Small caps and emerging market stocks trade within a wider band of fair market value than more actively followed stocks like large cap blue chips. This wider margin gives active managers an opportunity to add value.

Even still, it is devilishly hard for even the majority of managers in these less dense waters to overleap their respective indices. A quick look at the chart below reveals the embarrassing truth.

The Number of Canadian Fund Managers Who Beat Their Benchmarks on "Inefficient" Markets Over One Year (fig. 16)

Global Equity	International Equity	U.S. Mid & Small Cap
221 out of 571	45 out of 205	15 out of 78
MSCI World	MSCI EAFE	Russell 2000

Source: www.globefund.com for one year ending August 31, 2002

If you think things might improve over the longer term, they do a little but the odds aren't stacked in your favour.

The Number of Canadian Fund Managers Who Beat Their "Inefficient" Benchmarks Over Ten Years (fig. 17)

Global Equity	International Equity	U.S. Mid & Small cap
5 out of 34	3 out of 10	3 out of 8
MSCI World	MSCI EAFE	Russell 2000

Source: www.globefund.com as of August 31, 2002

Part of the reason these ratios are as good as they are is because of something called "survivorship bias." The bad funds are closed or merged with other funds so the class of long-lived mutual funds decreases in a way that flatters the survivors. Limited data indicates a Canadian fund failure rate of about 9% a year. Recent U.S. numbers point to a similar story with about 8% of funds failing since the bear market began.[12]

Markets are not inherently efficient and what efficiency they get is owed to an army of bright analysts identifying and acting on any mispricings. As markets continue to develop through regulation, increased competition among investment managers and robust security analysis, the opportunity to extract value diminishes. It gets to the point where the research costs start plundering the value added. The market may still be inefficient, but the inefficiency can't be exploited without self-defeating costs.

It isn't easy to know when inefficiencies will become difficult to exploit in any given market, though the proliferation of large actively managed funds in any one market might be a harbinger. The EAFE Index (Europe, Australasia and the Far East) was long considered easy to beat, but the proliferation of funds, increased competition among fund managers and better index methodologies by MSCI's index designers, has made EAFE less of a pushover now.

A skilled manager stays skilled just so long as she can capture the inefficiencies and as long as that happens, active funds should have a place in even a predominantly indexed portfolio. Actively managed funds aren't all bad, they're just a lot less useful than you've been led to think. In the next chapter we'll look at the various ways to do indexing—with ETFs, index mutual funds, index-linked GIC, and futures.

Although indexing seems as though it should have sprung up immediately with the introduction of an index, it took almost 90 years and some determined personal conviction to bring the first index fund into existence. Bill Fouse is the one who did it.

The Inventor of Passive Investing:
An interview with Bill Fouse

Back in the early days of indexing, William Fouse's advocacy put even his patriotism into question. An investment research company, the Leuthold Group, copied the famous "'Uncle Sam Wants You' poster that reads 'Indexing is un-American.' They sent these posters everywhere. Most trading rooms in money management organizations had one of those posters over the Marilyn Monroe poster," recalls Fouse.

He's laughing now but in the early 1970s the feelings were much closer to the nerve.

"It was just like an atheist trying to set up an operation in Baptist country," says Fouse on his attempts to introduce the notion of passive investing. "It was an emotionally charged thing."

His boss at Mellon Bank in Pittsburgh where Fouse had worked for 18 years was positively hostile to Fouse's suggestion that they start an index fund. The boss' reaction was just the first of many similar responses.

"It's an anti-establishment product," says Fouse, "because it doesn't square with the beliefs and intuitions and emotions of either the majority of plan sponsors or the investment bankers, brokers, traditional analysts and portfolio managers. It attacks their fantasy system."

In 1970 Fouse found a more receptive employer and moved camp to Wells Fargo Bank in San Francisco. There he started a quantitative group and in July 1971 gained the pension account for the luggage manufacturer, Samsonite Corporation. That was, by all accounts, the first passive portfolio to be implemented. Fouse characterized it as an above average risk index account replicating an equal-weighted New York Stock Exchange Index. He says it had about a 10% higher risk than the NYSE capitalization-weighted index, and in 1972 and 1973 it did just what it was supposed to do: it lost money like the rest of the market.

In 1972 Wells Fargo started an S&P 500 index fund, originally funded by the bank's own pension fund. The next year they got their second client, Illinois Bell Telephone Company, an account they still retain. Together the two accounts totalled US$10 million.

Eventually, Samsonite switched to the less volatile S&P product, too.

Fouse's study of market pricing and the efficacy of analysts' recommendations firmed his conviction that returns were random and that indexing was the surest way to consistently good performance. Thirty years later a lot of people agree with him although he complains that the pension management consulting community still gives little more than lip service to indexing. "It is certainly inimical to their interests. Through luck or through skill they've been able to classify indexing as a style so logically you wouldn't put all your money in one style, would you?" In his mind, indexing rises above and encompasses all styles. They can't very well say, he remarks, "Put all your money in an index fund and go fishing and then you don't have to pay us any more."

Asked why investors should put money into index products in a bear market, Fouse replies, "Historically, active managers have usually done worse in falling markets than the index funds and where they have done better by raising cash, let's say, they typically miss the market when it recovers. So there is no hard evidence that you're protected in a market decline by being with an active manager. I would say the only protection you can conjure up is a valid tactical asset allocation approach where you take a look at the alternative values in the marketplace between stocks, bonds and cash."

The company Fouse co-founded, San Francisco-based Mellon Capital Management, does just that for over US$30 billion. At 74, the man who graduated in 1952 from the University of Kentucky with an MBA in industrial administration says he wouldn't hire himself today. It's a good thing Wells Fargo did because Fouse and other indexing pioneers revolutionized modern investing. Far from being un-American, Fouse says "It's Yankee ingenuity to take advantage of all the hard work and effort expended by others to make the market efficient and get a free ride." Mellon Capital still has the Samsonite account. BGI bought Wells Fargo Investment Advisers in 1995.

Notes

1) FRC study as reported by Jim MacDonald "Mutual Fund Investors Lose the Performance Chase: Study," in *www.advisor.ca*, April 30, 2001.

2) Dan Hallett, CFA, CFP is now Senior Investment Analyst with Sterling Mutuals Inc. in Windsor, Ontario. His paper was entitled "Distributions and the CGRM" published on *FundMonitor.com* on November 17, 1999. Also see Stephen L. Nesbitt, "Buy High, Sell Low: Timing Errors in Mutual Fund Allocations," *Journal of Portfolio Management*, Fall, 1995, pp. 57-60.

3) This finding based on work commissioned for this book and done by Norman Rothery, Ph.D. of *www.stingyinvestor.com* using data provided by FundMonitor and Fundata.

4) Duff Young, CEO of FundMonitor.com Corp. reported this finding in the *Globe and Mail*, May 9, 1998. It is available at *www.fundmonitor.com* under articles sorted by date.

5) Michael Thorfinnson and Jason Kiss, "The Overlooked Piranha," *Canadian Investment Review*, Fall, 1996, pp. 17-21.

6) Average index fund from PALTrak to July 31, 2002 as per Morningstar Canada. The median Canadian equity index fund MER from *www.globefund.com* as of July 31, 2002.

7) As per *www.globefund.com* as of August 31, 2002. The fund universe was selected out of all funds existing for the ten-year period with returns greater than -60%. The index return numbers provided by TD Newcrest who regularly backrun S&P/TSX return figures and capped indices—both of which didn't exist over the ten-year period.

8) Federal government regulations allowed foreign content limitations in RRSP accounts to increase by 2% every year from 10% in 1989 to 18% of book value in 1993. In 1999 the foreign content limit was increased to 20%, in 2000 to 25% and in 2001 to 30%. Mutual funds, to be fully RRSP eligible, must not exceed the foreign content limit threshold and almost all take advantage of it to boost their returns.

9) As per Norman Rothery based on Fundata information.

10) Ted Cadsby, *The Power of Index Funds*, Revised Edition, (Toronto: Stoddart Publishing Co., Limited), 2001, p.113. Emphasis is Mr. Cadsby's.

11) A capitalization weighted index is one whose constituents are weighted according to the total market value of their outstanding shares. These indices will move in keeping with the price changes of the underlying stocks. The Dow Jones Industrial Average is a price weighted index. Higher priced stocks have a greater percentage impact on the index than lower priced stocks. Dow historical information from Dow Jones Web

site, *www.dowjones.com*.

12) The 8% fund failure rate is from John Bogle, the founder of Vanguard Funds, in a TV interview August 2002. The 9% historical Canadian failure rate is from proprietary work done by Norman Rothery and Henry Lee using the *Globe and Mail* archives from 1978-1992. Also see John Waggoner, "Mutual Funds Vanishing at Record rate: Failed Concepts, Bad Sellers Lead to Liquidations, Mergers," *www.usatoday.com*, viewed September 9, 2002.

Chapter Three
Index Products: Which One is Best for You?

If you're now convinced that indexing is the most sensible approach to prudent investing, what, then, is the best way to index?

Hulking institutional accounts can simply replicate the index by buying everything in the index and in the right proportions. Done. The rest of us have to rely on index products, of which there are many, though it's easy to narrow down the field pretty quickly. A number of index-linked products require a degree of sophistication few of us desire to cultivate—like index futures and index-linked equity notes. On the opposite end of the spectrum, index-linked GICs are just barely an index product at all. For most investors, index mutual funds and ETFs are the most accessible and practical way to index. I'd like to say unequivocally that ETFs are always the best choice, but, in fact, like most things, it depends on your circumstances. It depends most critically on how much money you want to give over to passive investments, and on the product features that are most important to you.

If you've already made up your mind that indexing is the way to go, this chapter will help you decide what index products are best for you. We'll compare index mutual funds to ETFs and touch on index-linked GICs and index futures.

Any index product should trigger the following questions:

- Does it track the index you need?
- How closely does it track that index? (What's its tracking error?)
- How much are the management fees and other costs?
- Are there tax implications?
- Is it easy to sell?
- What is the minimum investment?

- How are dividends handled?
- How do redemptions/sales affect the product?
- Is it efficient to invest and withdraw small dollar amounts?
- Is it best for short-term or long-term positions?
- Is it restricted in an RRSP?

It's important to know the answers to these questions because buying an inappropriate product can cost you in returns, taxes and aggravation. By the end of this chapter you should have the information you need to understand most of the index products available today.

Index Mutual Funds vs. ETFs

In Chapter One we discussed the differences between actively managed mutual funds and ETFs. Much of that discussion doesn't apply to a comparison of ETFs and index mutual funds because index mutual funds are passively managed. Where an active manager is buying and selling positions in the fund regularly in order to boost returns, a passive manager simply positions a portfolio to replicate the movement of a target index. Passive funds experience a lot less buying and selling, and when trades do occur they are not for the purpose of making gains or preventing losses, they are made to better track the index. This difference in management approach makes index funds considerably different from their actively managed confréres, and more comparable to ETFs but with some notable differences.

Index Tracking

An index mutual fund, like an ETF, is designed to track a target index. The best performing index product is one that most closely tracks its index. Any deviation either above or below the index return is a tracking error. Of course, nothing will perfectly track a target index. Indices are abstract constructs. They don't live and breathe in the real world where trading costs add up. It's important to realize that an index is calculated, but not actually implemented, by the index sponsor. That means an index and its returns are blissfully unaffected by trading costs or price run-ups when its securities are changed. Index mutual funds and ETFs are, however, real things with real costs. Take for example the addition of Fluor Corp. to the S&P 500 Index in late December 2000. The stock went up $4 on the day from indexers scrambling to buy the stock in order to match the completely theoretical S&P 500.[1] That's some real-world pressure at work.

Index managers aren't exactly as idle as the Maytag repairman.

Tracking Methods

Replication

There are three different ways to track an index and both index funds and ETFs take advantage of all of them. The most straightforward tracking method is to completely copy the index by buying all the securities in proportion to their weighting in the index. This is called, obviously enough, "replication."

Optimization

Instead of replicating an index, a fund could buy a representative sampling of the index's securities. This is known as "sampling" or "optimizing." Managers resort to this because of restrictions on portfolio concentrations and foreign ownership, or as a way of coping with thinly traded stocks on some indices. Markets in which many listed securities lack liquidity create a problem for those trying to manage a replicated index in real time. Managers try to avoid this problem by carefully selecting liquid securities representative of the market they are trying to track without actually owning everything in the index. It's never perfect, which is one reason why developing country index products have greater tracking errors than similar products in more efficient markets. Optimizing can also result from an attempt to save fund costs. The fund manager is betting that leaving out minor securities won't much affect tracking but will definitely reduce transaction costs.

Derivatives

Finally, a fund itself can buy other index products like derivatives or ETFs. Fully RRSP eligible foreign index funds, for instance, typically buy forward contracts or futures on their target indices and put the lion's share of the portfolio into staid Canadian T-bills (which is how they get to be fully RRSP eligible despite giving full foreign exposure). This is known as a "derivatives indexing strategy."

Not all tracking strategies work equally well. Portfolios that do not perfectly reproduce their index have a bigger chance of running afoul of the index returns than replicated funds. Indexing strategy, then, plays a part in tracking error.

Concentration Limits

Securities regulation also impacts tracking. Mutual fund regulators stay up at night worrying about excessive concentration in mutual fund portfolios since diversification is one of the biggest benefits of mutual fund investing. Conventional mutual funds (that is non-index mutual funds) may not purchase a security if, after the purchase, the fund would have more than 10% of its net assets (at current market value) invested in the securities of any one issuer. Regulators relaxed this restriction for index funds first by capping them at 25%, and then as of May 2001, eliminating the concentration restriction altogether. This serves index funds well because any portfolio restriction always has the risk of throwing off tracking, though it can permit undesirable concentration.

ETFs in Canada have no regulatory restrictions on concentration, but that doesn't mean that all Canadian ETFs have no concentration caps. In fact, BGI Canada's sector funds have a 25% cap on the weight of any single security which reflects the cap set by the rules of the underlying indices themselves.

U.S.-based ETFs are not so lucky. They're restricted by law from holding a position in any single issuer worth more than 25% of the ETF's assets. Other restrictions apply as well. Securities that have a weighting of 5% or more within the fund cannot collectively add up to more than 50% of the fund's assets. Sector ETFs can run up against this restriction easily. Take, for example, iShares Dow Jones U.S. Energy Sector Index Fund whose index had a 38% weighting in ExxonMobil in February 2001. The fund had to optimize its positions by buying other oil and gas producers with a high market correlation to Exxon's stock.[2] It's not perfect, but it's the best that can be done.

Cash Flow

Cash flow is another reason index tracking can derail. The more cash in an index portfolio, the less well that fund will track its index. That's called "cash drag" and in a down market it can buffer the fund from a precipitous market crash. In a rising market cash holds the fund back from the market highs. Index mutual funds can be particularly hobbled by cash flow effects. Mutual funds take in and give out cash on a daily basis. A large rush of money into or out of a fund can create a pile of cash not tied to the index—always a risky situation.

ETFs don't have a similar cash flow problem. The reason is quite simple. ETFs don't have any cash (except what comes from dividends). ETFs don't redeem their units for cash, nor do they take in cash from new unit sales the way mutual funds do. Instead, what's called an "authorized participant" or in Canada, an "underwriter," uses their own capital to put together the stocks needed to constitute a creation unit. This basket of stocks is turned into an ETF unit in advance of market demand so there are always new ETF units available, and no cash standing idly by.

Dividends

Stocks within an ETF portfolio do sometimes spit out dividends so ETFs are not entirely without cash drag. Some ETFs can reinvest the dividends into the portfolio immediately upon receiving the dividend, while others must segregate the cash for quarterly distribution. Which method is used depends on the structure of the ETF, and, unfortunately, there are different structures. We'll talk more about those differences in Chapter Seven when we look at Canadian and U.S. ETF structures. For now it's enough to know that ETFs which can reinvest dividend cash have better tracking than those that have to coddle the cash separately. Even with today's low dividend rates, how they are reinvested can make a difference. In 2001, i6os, for instance, had $3.9 billion in assets and received $78 million in dividends. That's 2% of the fund's assets—hardly insignificant.

Index mutual funds get dividends, too, just like ETFs, but index funds can immediately reinvest the dividends in the fund when the dividends are received.

So, dividend cash is less of a tracking problem for index mutual funds than for ETFs.

Index Adjustments

The difference between index funds and ETFs is highlighted when there is a large addition to the index. Both index funds and ETFs sell the stock leaving the index (triggering gains, if any), and both buy the stock entering the index. But if the purchase is more than the sale, the index fund sells more of the other stocks in the index, thereby triggering more gains. In contrast, the ETF issues more units to the underwriters to finance the additional purchases. The ETF does not need to sell as much stock and so ends up triggering fewer gains. This isn't significant all the time, but big index changes will make the difference show.

Management Expense Ratio

With all the noted impediments to tracking, you may wonder how any product manages to keep hold of an index. It's not as easy as it may look and we've not even come to the most major and inescapable tracking impediment of all—the management expense ratio. The MER pulls on an index strategy like an undertow. Even if a manager could perfectly manage cash flow, avoid concentration restrictions and fully replicate the target index, the fund will still fall short of the index's return exactly by the amount of the fund's MER. There are some mitigating circumstances, though, that may find an index fund occasionally squeaking out a better performance than its index. Sometimes fund managers can make (or lose) a little money relative to the index when trading the index changes. And sometimes cash flow comes to their rescue.

To see how well an index fund has tracked its index, go to *www. globefund.com*, select a specific index fund or all index funds generally and in "charts" you can compare their performance one by one to their respective index. You can do the same for all of BGI Canada's ETF offerings. At printing TD Asset Management's ETFs were not listed on *Globefund.com*. BGI's U.S. site, *www.ishares.com*, also allows you to compare iShares to their respective indices, as does BGI's Canadian site, *www.iunits.com*. The American Stock Exchange is said to be working on a similar project for all its listed ETFs. The closer the fund's returns are to its target index return (after costs), the better the indexing strategy is working (unless it is an "enhanced" fund which we'll discuss below).

In general, ETFs have better tracking records than index mutual funds mainly because the new kid on the block has moved in with a lot less baggage; namely, much smaller MERs. MERs on U.S.-based ETFs range from 0.09% to 0.99%.[3] Canadian MERs run from a rock bottom 0.17% to 0.55%. Contrast that with 0.95% for the median index fund in Canada and you can see why less onerous MERs mean ETFs can more closely track their indices. This is not just an academic observation either.

Look at how a good Canadian equity index fund with a long track record has tracked its target index.

TSE 300 vs. Index Fund (fig. 18)

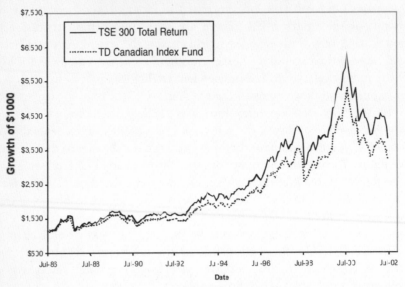

The longer an index mutual fund tracks an index, the more its performance will diverge from that index because of the cumulative effects of a relatively large MER.
Note: The TD Canadian Index Fund has an MER of 0.85%.

Source: www.stingyinvestor.com

Compare the tracking of a good index mutual fund as we've just seen, to a good ETF. TIPs 35, the predecessor to the i60, tracked the Toronto 35 Index. There are four lines in the graph below, but if you see only three, that's because TIPs and the Toronto 35 Index are so close they are indistinguishable. That's why we've superimposed diamonds on a solid line to show the marvellous symmetry of TIPs tracking. Not coincidentally, TIPs had an expense ratio of 0.04%. To see how other Canadian ETFs have tracked their indices, refer to the appendix and look at the fact sheets on each Canadian ETF. A tracking graph is included for each.

TIPs vs. Toronto 35 Index (fig. 19)

- Toronto 35 Index Total Return
- TIPs 35
- Toronto 35 Index Total Return - $500
- TIPs 35 - $600

TIPs 35 tracked the Toronto 35 Total Return Index so well, its line and the index line are indistinguishable.

Source: www.stingyinvestor.com

How do all these causes for tracking error add up?

According to a Salomon Smith Barney ETF research report February 2001, "In most cases tracking error is extremely small, many times no greater than the management fee." The average weekly return differential from its index for SPDRs in 2000 was 0.0016%. The iShares S&P 500 Index Fund from its introduction in May to the end of 2000 was 0.0013%. Optimized ETFs don't do quite as well. The iShares Dow Jones Energy Sector Index Fund for 2000 had an average weekly return differential of 0.037%. Still, you're unlikely to lose any sleep over those tracking errors.

Enhanced Indexing

Enhanced index mutual funds (there are as yet no enhanced ETFs) try to second-guess the market by overweighting certain securities within the index in the hope of enhancing returns. If it works, the fund will beat the market. If it doesn't, it will underperform the market by more than other index funds. It's almost a contradiction to the idea of indexing, but hope springs eternal in the hearts of some fund managers. National Bank's American Index Plus Fund is a good example of an enhanced fund. In August 2002 it had about 72% in SPDRs, the remainder in individual stocks. In three years to the end of August it did -10.77% compared to the S&P 500 composite index return of -9.08%. The difference in returns would be even more alarming if you included the decline in the value of the Canadian dollar during that period, something that would have only helped the fund. At an MER of 2%, this fund was no bargain. Enhanced funds should be treated with appropriate skepticism.

Not all enhancing strategies use subjective stock selection to boost index returns. A quantitative, rules-based leveraging strategy has been worked out by ProFund Advisors, a Maryland-based mutual funds company. ProFund has applied to the U.S. Securities and Exchange Commission for approval to launch a series of ETFs that use leveraging and/or shorting strategies to enhance returns. This is an interesting development in the world of ETFs and is being seen as the first small step toward actively managed ETFs. There is, however, no subjectivity involved in the leveraging process and because the methodology is entirely rules-based and mechanical, it is not an active ETF. It will be, if and when it is approved, a fascinating series of enhanced ETFs.

Management Expense Ratios

Because of their enormous impact on tracking, MERs deserve a little bit more examination. From an investor's standpoint, management fees are a necessary evil: funds cost money to run and the manager has to get paid. The companies that record the securities and their transactions must get paid, too, and so on down the costly line. These administrative costs come out of the fund and are calculated as a ratio of expenses to assets, hence the name, "management expense ratio" (MER). The MERs on index mutual funds in Canada range from 0.30% for one of TDs index e-funds to an eye-popping 4.9% for a fully RRSP eligible guaranteed (segregated) Japanese equity index fund. Most non-segregated retail index mutual funds have MERs around 0.9% and most are usually under 1%.[4]

These MERs may sound like a bargain when you contrast them to actively managed funds, but they're still bloated compared to the MERs on ETFs. This is one important aspect in which ETFs shine. MERs on ETFs in Canada range from a slender 0.17% to 0.55%.

Management fees represent money slipping from your account into the pockets of fund managers. There's nothing wrong with that if you have a fond relative in the fund business, but most of us would prefer to keep our gains to ourselves. The longer management fees and ancillary fund expenses erode your investment, the more damage they do. On the face of it, 1% either way doesn't seem too much to be paying for management, but you'd hardly be blamed for being resentful once you see how harmful it is to your long-term returns. Saving even 1% in management fees increases your returns by an astounding amount over the long haul. Saving 1% over 15 years will mean a 16% improvement in total returns. Thanks to the miracle of compounding, that shoots to 22% after 20 years, 25% in 30 years and an astounding 49% in 40 years.[5]

Obviously, the bigger the MER, the less well the fund will track its market. In the indexing world, you get what you *don't* pay for. The more you pay in management fees and expenses, the less you get in returns. Period. Always scrutinize MERs. The lower the MER, the more money you make. All other things being equal, select an index product with the lowest MER.

Expenses

You might think the MER gives the full cost of running the fund. It doesn't, and to my mind, regulators have abetted the mutual fund industry in this misleading practice. In fact, the MER doesn't tell the whole story. Trading costs, the commissions the fund must pay to brokerage houses for transacting trades, aren't included in any MER calculation. This means your actual costs of holding a fund are always going to be higher than the posted MER, and adversely affect the fund's net return. The more active the manager, the more the costs pile up. Trading costs have been known in extreme cases to be double the fund's MER.[6] Gratefully, an index product normally has so little buying and selling that the trading costs are usually miniscule in comparison to the size of the portfolio. In Canada, neither BGI nor TD pay any stock trading commissions for their ETFs because of favourable brokerage arrangements, but it wouldn't be unreasonable to expect some small trading commission costs with ETFs if the current favourable arrangements changed.

Taxes and How Redemptions Affect the Fund

Index mutual funds and ETFs are tax efficient because they are passive investments. With so little selling going on inside a passive portfolio, few realized capital gains are generated. That's good because index funds and ETFs, all mutual funds in fact, distribute their capital gains at least annually to unitholders who then must pay tax on those gains. Bottom line— the longer you put off paying tax on capital gains, the better.

There's another good tax feature of index mutual funds and ETFs. The distributions from Canadian ETFs and Canadian-index mutual funds retain their tax character. This means dividends from Canadian corporations are eligible for the dividend tax credit, and capital gains retain their tax-advantaged status. Canada Customs and Revenue Agency is not so favourably disposed, however, to dividends or capital gains from U.S.-based ETFs. All their distributions are dinged as income, but more on this and other tax-related matters in a later chapter.

But even in a tax-lean passive environment, ETFs have an advantage over index mutual funds. ETFs have something of a buffer from the onslaught of redemptions from retail investors. A redemption run on an index fund could force the manager to sell profitable positions in order to raise the cash to pay out the redemptions. This could impose capital gains tax liability on the remaining fund investors. In contrast, retail ETF investors, sell their units for cash on the open market which has no direct implications for the underlying fund.

ETFs can be redeemed for their underlying shares, but only institutional accounts would own a large enough position to form a redemption unit. Even for institutional accounts, selling an ETF is cheaper and easier than redeeming it. However, when a redemption does occur and the fund surrenders the underlying securities in exchange for its own units, Canadian tax rules view this as a deemed disposition, a sale of sorts, which triggers capital gains reckoning. (Tax rules are different in the U.S. and a redemption there does not result in a deemed disposition.) Canadian ETFs, then, do not entirely escape the redemption tax problems of index mutual funds. In 2001, a large number of i60 units were redeemed for a total value of $1.1 billion. That's fairly significant and is partly responsible for the fund paying out 41¢ per unit in capital gains in 2001. Although fund level redemptions aren't usually common, they happen in weighty amounts of 50,000 units and more.

You can surmise from looking at the difference between ETF capital gains distributions and index funds distributions just how much redeeming is going on because the capital gains from the underlying portfolio readjustments will be fairly similar (if the underlying indices are the same). However, a comparison of capital gains distributions in 2001 for some popular index funds and the i60 isn't a hands down win for the i60. Its 41¢ capital gain distribution in 2001 represented 0.92% of the i60's unit value. A few Canadian index mutual funds didn't distribute any capital gains at all that year, though the S&P/TSX Composite index funds at CIBC, Royal Bank, and TD Asset Management all had capital gains distributions in 2001—one of them around 2.2% of the unit value.

To get a true sense of tax efficiency you have to compare the distribution histories over a longer period and unfortunately with most index funds popping onto the scene in 1998 or later, there isn't much of a history to report right now. Don't look to 2002 to help settle the question either because it will be an unusual year in that the TSE 300 Index renamed itself the S&P/TSX Composite Index and with that went a reduction in the number of companies included in the index. That, of course, meant index products pegged to this index needed to sell their positions in the companies no longer included in the index. (As many as 75 companies may eventually be dropped so the index changes are being done in three-month intervals.)

In the U.S., fund level redemptions don't trigger any kind of capital gains liability, so U.S. ETFs have minute capital gains distributions. From 1993 to the end of 2001, SPDRs distributed 16¢ a share of capital gains in total. From 1998 to the end of 2001, DIAMONDS distributed no capital gains at all. (Historical distribution information for all U.S. ETFs is available on *www.amex.com*.) As a species, ETFs are just about the most tax efficient pooled investment you can get.

Is it Easy to Sell?

The ability to buy and sell an investment at a competitive price, its "liquidity," should be a big consideration in any investment decision. All mutual funds score high on ease of buying and selling but it's a little surprising that the mutual fund industry has grown so hugely successful with a product whose price cannot be determined when it is bought or sold. Investors buy and sell mutual funds without ever knowing beforehand at what price those trades are going to be executed. Imagine buying a car or a house, or doing your grocery shopping like that?

This strange arrangement stems from the way mutual funds are priced. At the end of each trading day a mutual fund company tallies up the value of all the fund's constituents, establishes a net asset value (NAV) and transacts all the buy and sell orders which have come in that day at that NAV. The pricing process is completely controlled by the mutual fund company without any market scrutiny because, remember, the actual portfolio holdings are not known on a daily basis. All this might sound rather sinister and prone to abuse, but in fact the mutual fund industry has a sterling record of fair dealings and has earned the trust of investors. Mutual funds have great liquidity because the mutual fund companies themselves buy and sell the units and are committed to ensuring the liquidity of their product and the integrity of their pricing. Nevertheless, this arrangement is in contrast to ETFs whose prices are posted in real time and subject to the scrutiny of the market as a whole.

Index mutual funds in Canada are almost exclusively no-load funds which means they can be bought or sold without commission. To discourage short-term trading, however, many fund companies impose a minimum holding period or charge a short-term trading fee. Altamira, for instance, charges a 2% penalty on many funds held less than 90 days. CIBC, the bank with the widest selection of index funds, does the same.

There is no such restriction on ETFs. If anything, the more ETFs trade, the better. The more trading, the better the apparent liquidity.

ETFs are as easy to buy and sell as a large and frequently traded stock, because that's what they are. ETFs such as SPDRs, DIAMONDS and Qubes are regularly among the most heavily traded securities on AMEX. In fact, ETFs account for half of AMEX's total trading volume.[7] In Canada the i60s were the fifth most actively traded security on the TSX in 2000 and the seventh in 2001. They have enormous liquidity. Even U.S. ETFs that have low trading volumes are perfectly liquid as long as their underlying securities are liquid.

As with all stocks, you have to have a brokerage account and pay brokerage commissions on an ETF transaction. This runs $29 at TD Waterhouse, $58 for a round trip buy and sell. Commission costs are trending down, too. At least one other discount brokerage charges $25. You don't have trading commission expenses with an index mutual fund but trading commissions are a small, fixed, non-recurring cost that are quickly surpassed by a pricey MER. And if you do your ETF trading within a fee-based account, you may escape commission charges completely.

The virtue of stock trading is that it brings with it complete price transparency and prompt, if not nearly instant, order execution. All the normal stock trading mechanisms are available for ETF transactions, too. In the U.S. you can short sell ETFs without waiting for an uptick. You can also buy ETFs on margin, trade them with stop loss or limit orders, and when available, even write options on them.

Prompt execution is more valuable than you might suspect. Remember that mutual funds are transacted only at the end of day after market close. The U.S. market as measured by the S&P 500 fluctuates on average 1.5% a day which translates into a possible 1.5% average loss each time you have to wait a trading day to execute your order. NASDAQ's number is 2.2% while the TSX's daily fluctuation is a more reassuring 1%. Those numbers represent the expected average risk you are taking each time you buy or sell an equity mutual fund.[8]

The Minimum Investment

Mutual funds have become hugely popular in good part because they require a small minimum investment. You can buy a mutual fund for as little as $500 at one shot or for $25 a month with no fees or penalties. Many people invest regularly with a fund company by arranging a monthly pre-authorized payment plan, otherwise known as a PAC. Mutual funds make it easy to withdraw large or small amounts from mutual fund positions regularly or on demand. There are no trading fees imposed, and with no-load funds there are no redemption fees unless you trigger a short-term trading penalty. It's also easy to automatically reinvest your dividends. Since almost all index mutual funds are no-loads, an index mutual fund invest-ment is singularly flexible in letting you into the game with small bits of money.

ETFs, on the other hand, are generally bought in board lots of 100 units (shares). It is equally easy to buy less than 100 shares of an ETF, but the minimum trading commission still applies. If you intend to actively trade your ETFs it's most cost effective to stick to board lots. For practical pur-poses, the minimum investment in an ETF can be relatively steep. One hundred shares of i60s in the fall of 2002 would run you about $3,400. One hundred SPDRs would set you back more than CDN $12,000, and a number of popular ETFs like DIAMONDS and MidCap SPDRs regularly trade around US$75 per share. The cheapest Canadian ETF in fall 2002 was the iUnits S&P/TSX Canadian Information Technology ETF trading around $2.80 For the most part, buying an ETF board lot will cost a whole lot more than the minimum $500 for a mutual fund purchase.

Any addition or withdrawal from an ETF position requires a buy or sell order and an associated trading commission. This makes reinvesting the quarterly dividends from equity ETFs impractical and a bit of a nuisance. (Canadian bond ETFs distribute their interest income semi-annually.) One brokerage in Canada, RBC Investments, has a dividend re-investment plan for i60s, as does Canadian ShareOwners whose service allows reinvest-ments and PACs on all iUnits. Perhaps with increased investor demand more dividend reinvestment services will become available. Until then you can stash those dividend cheques into a money market fund or treat them like birthday money from a kind aunt, taxable as they are. In 2001, i60s gave its unitholders $0.728 in cash for every unit.[9] With a board lot that's a generous aunt.

Short-term or Long-term Plays?

The mutual fund industry has gotten blue in the face advising clients that mutual funds are long-term investments. Not many investors seem to buy into that when they buy their funds because the average holding peri-od for fund investors keeps declining and is now around 2.5 to 2.9 years.[10] But investor behaviour aside, the longer you hold a mutual fund, the longer the MER compounds to corrode your returns. For the long term, there's no question the index product with the lowest MER is preferable.

For one or two years and an investment of around $10,000 or less, an index mutual fund is probably your better bet, says Steve Geist, Senior Vice President with TD Asset Management. The calculation goes something like this:

Over the short-term there may not always be a cost advantage to an

ETF over an index mutual fund, but in the longer-term the cost efficiency of an ETF shines, and the comparison with a conventional (load) mutual fund is unequivocal.

Cost Comparison: ETFs vs. Index Fund

Investment	$6,000		$10,000		$10,000	
Horizon	2 Years		1 Year		2 Years	
	ETF	Index Fund	ETF	Index Fund	ETF	Index Fund
Commission (in and out)	$58	$0	$58	$0	$58	$0
MER Cost	$42	$96	$35	$80	$70	$160
Total Cost	$100	$96	$93	$80	$128	$160

Assumes ETF MER of 0.35% and index fund MER of 0.8%, trading commission at $29.

RRSP Eligibility

Another attraction of index mutual funds is the selection they offer of fully RRSP eligible foreign indices. This allows investors to build a diversified indexing strategy completely within their RRSPs without having to compromise on foreign exposure due to foreign content restrictions. These index mutual funds are usually distinguished from their counterparts by "RRSP" in their name, like CIBC's International Index RRSP which is linked to the MSCI EAFE Index.

So far there are only two ETFs linked to foreign indices that are fully RRSP eligible. These track the S&P 500 index (iUnits S&P 500 Index RSP Fund) and the MSCI EAFE Index (iUnits MSCI International Equity Index RSP Fund).

Choice of Indices

Currently, Canadian ETFs fall short on the selection of fully RRSP eligible funds, but mutual funds can't match the extraordinarily broad range of indices ETFs track. You can find an ETF for just about any index you can think of. The breadth of U.S. ETF offerings makes it easy to gain exposure to just about any geographical area, economic sector, market segment, country or major investment style. This diversity proves very useful in portfolio construction, as we'll see when we put together some model portfolios.

Paradoxically, with 188 index mutual funds at last count, Canadians still don't have a huge selection of foreign indices to select from—and that's with all the major banks, insurance companies, and no-load fund companies falling over themselves to bring you an index product. It's not hard to find a S&P/TSX Composite fund or one using the S&P 500, NASDAQ, the

Dow, MSCI EAFE and the Wilshire 5000. But the huge selection of style and capitalization indices available in the U.S., like the Russell value/growth indices, and the large, mid and small cap indices, have not spilled over into the Canadian mutual fund industry. This can be a problem for those wishing to use index mutual funds to add, for instance, a small cap index to their overall index strategy, or a value index to capture the growth of a whole investment style.

Frustrated Canadian investors can only press their faces to the glass and look longingly at the tantalizing selection of low cost index funds sponsored by Vanguard Group, the second largest mutual fund company in the U.S. Canadians are prohibited from buying U.S. mutual funds, but the whole universe of 133 U.S. ETFs and HOLDRS (and counting) is open to us.

Where the Smart Money Goes

Canada got its first index mutual fund for the retail investor two years after the Vanguard Group gave all Americans their first shot at index investing in 1976. National Trust's TSE 300 Index Fund was launched in 1978.[11] Twenty-four years later index funds finally seem to have come into their own. Their ranks have swelled from 5 funds in 1996 with a hardly noticeable $618 million to over 188 funds duking it out in 2002 with $13.5 billion in assets.[12]

In the past few years, however, index mutual funds have seen an uncomfortable decline in assets as investors have yanked their money out in fear of uncertain markets. They've gone from $16.6 billion in December 2000 to $13.5 billion in August 2002. ETFs have not gone unscathed either. Canada's biggest ETF, the i60, went from $5.9 billion to $3.3 billion in the same period. Fair-weather index investors will almost certainly miss the best part of the inevitable market rebound as do most mutual fund investors who cannot help themselves from chasing last year's winners. Index mutual funds are, unfortunately, well suited to those who have little commitment to the indexing philosophy. The same might prove true of ETFs but at least the behaviour of one investor doesn't affect the tax liability of the next investor.

Index-Linked GICs

Index-linked GICs are designed for those taking their first timid steps towards indexing. These products are offered by banks and credit unions to appeal to regular GIC investors who are disappointed with low interest rates but who aren't ready to take the plunge into index mutual funds. The

GIC's principal is fully guaranteed but its return is linked to the performance of an index or set of indices. This sounds like an easy enough concept but its implementation can be complicated.

Let's look at TD Bank's index-linked offering as an example. They have three index-linked GICs, one linked to the S&P/TSX 60 Index, one to the S&P 500, and one based on an assortment of global indices. Each GIC comes in three-or five-year maturities. The returns are calculated by subtracting the closing value of the index at maturity from the value of the index when the GIC was purchased. (Technically, most index-linked GICs use the index values a day or two after purchase and a day or two before maturity.) You'd be excused for thinking if the index goes up 40% over three years, then your GIC would show a similar 40% return for that period. However, it doesn't work that way.

All index-linked GICs have either a cap or a participation rate that affects your gains. In TD's case the three-year GICs are capped at a 20-25% return depending on what index is involved. Capping limits how much you can earn on your GIC. A 25% cap means that your GIC will not earn more than 25% over the maturity of the GIC no matter how well the index does over that period. CIBC offers two index-linked GICs. They have no cap but they do have a participation rate of 55% or 65% which means that the investor gets only 55-65% of the index's gain over the investment period. CIBC's Market Mix GIC has a small guaranteed interest component.

A few years back these products used to be horrifically complicated because the growth on the index would be averaged and each institution it seemed had their own way of doing that average. Some averaged the index's movement monthly from the first month; others averaged only the last twelve months or the last six months, or maybe did the averaging only quarterly in the last year to maturity. As the period of averaging increases, the index's gains will always decrease so averaging in a generally up market is disadvantageous. Remember, too, that the participation rate and the cap were both based on this average. Royal Bank averages the monthly level of the index over the last year of the term. Some credit unions also average, but thankfully averaging is getting less common with index-linked GICs and the product is becoming far more straightforward.

Index-linked GICs are fully RRSP eligible—even the ones linked to foreign indices—and they can be bought in $500 to $1000 minimums. Your principal is fully guaranteed, and if you hit the market at the right time you can make considerably more than the ordinary GIC interest rate. Of course, you can also make nothing if markets are miserable and there are no dividend payments. You're also locked into these things until they mature. You cannot cash in these GICs (except for death and hardship) and all the gains are taxed as interest income at your highest marginal tax rate.

Moshe Milevsky, a finance professor at York University and author *of Money Logic: Financial Strategies for the Smart Investor*, says that the insurance on a five-year GIC (in the form of a principal guarantee) probably isn't worth putting up with the cap. Markets tend to go up especially over five years so he'd buy a three-year product on the most volatile market he could find and that way get the biggest advantage from the product's insurance.

He doesn't like averaging and always looks for the highest cap available, but fundamentally he'd rather buy an ETF with a put option. A "put" is a contract that allows you to sell the index at a prearranged price some time in the future. That automatically limits your downside risk while giving you full scope to soar with the index. Not exactly a simple strategy you can buy at the bank, but for folks with $10,000 or more to invest in index-linked GICs, it is a logical approach—though perhaps a big psychological stretch for habitual GIC investors.

Futures

Instead of buying your target index through a mutual fund or an ETF, you can get the same benefit by buying a futures contract on your index of choice. It takes some sophistication, serious assets and a special trading account, but for those determined to squeeze the last nickel out of their investment costs, it shouldn't be overlooked.

A futures contract is a legal obligation to buy or sell a specific commodity or financial instrument at a specific price at a specific time in the future. These contracts are traded on a futures exchange which sets all the terms of the contract except for the price. Each day the accounts of the two parties to the contract—the one who must sell and the other who must buy—are marked to market. That means the exchange tallies up the (symmetrical) loss or gain on both sides. When one party makes money, the other party loses exactly the same amount.

Marking to market is one of the things that distinguishes futures from options. An option gives you the right but not the obligation to buy or sell at a fixed price in the future. You can exercise an option or let it expire, and there is no daily marking of profits and loses. (Options are asymmetrical.)

Suppose you figure the S&P 500 is going to go up in the next few months. (Future contracts can go out as far as a year but one-month contracts are the most heavily traded.) You can buy one contract (expiring on the third Thursday in your target month) for 250 times the current value of the index. On September 24, 2002 the S&P 500 was at 833. One December contract would cost 250 x $833 = U.S.$208,250. Before you faint, know that you will have to come up with only a fraction of that amount to buy the future. One of the big attractions of futures is that they can be done on margin. On this futures contract RBC Investments required only about US$20,000 in a futures margin account to cover the December contract purchase. So for 10% or less of the contract price down, you execute your trade and watch your account daily for profits—or margin calls if you're losing money. You pay commission only when you get out of the contract. In RBC's case, that commission is US$90. A discount broker might charge as little as US$35.

Few investors like dealing with the intimidating capital requirements of full blown futures contracts, so the Chicago Mercantile Exchange has come up with something more retail user friendly—"E-mini futures." E-mini contracts are one-fifth the size of a conventional futures contract but with similar features of their larger counterparts, including being bought on margin. The E-minis come in monthly and quarterly contracts and are available on the S&P 500, the NASDAQ 100, S&P Midcap 400 and the Russell 2000. Options on the E-mini S&P 500 are also offered. (To learn more about these inventive Mini Me's, see *www.cme.com*.)

In Canada, futures and options trade on the Montréal Exchange. Canadian futures contracts exist on the S&P/TSX 60 Index and on four S&P/TSX sector indices: Information Technology, Financials, Energy and Gold. There is also an option on the i60 ETF itself. Options are planned for the sector ETFs.

What Index?

The most commonly used equity financial futures contracts in Canada are contracts on the S&P/TSX 60 Index. On U.S. exchanges the most popular are futures contracts on the S&P 500, NASDAQ 100, the Dow Jones Industrial Average Index, the Russell 2000, S&P MidCap 400 and the Fortune e-50 Index. For the more ambitious, other contracts can be arranged but the selection of indices is no where near as great as that offered by ETFs. There are only 18 indices available with standard futures contracts, and there's virtually no representation for sector indices.[13]

Tracking and Management Fees

Futures track an index as smoothly as the Montréal Métro hugs its rails from day-to-day, though intraday, the contracts can anticipate the market and trade rich or cheap. Marking to market generally means your contract's value will go up and down in daily synch with the index and in exact proportion, too. There are no management fees and transaction costs are limited to the small brokerage commission for the contract. Since you sell or reverse contracts before they mature, little of your money is consumed by the actual cost of the contracts which further improves your tracking. And don't forget that these contracts are done on margin. You get enormous exposure to a market index with very little of your own money tied up.

You do have to foot money to open a futures/margin account which requires some capitalization, but the nice thing is that T-bills are acceptable. You're not even losing money on the money tied up to support the margin account.

Taxes

Profits from futures contracts are taxed fully as income. You cannot elect to have them treated as on capital account (see Chapter Six.) Losses from futures contracts are fully deductible from income. You cannot hold futures in your RRSP.

Short-term or Long-term Plays?

A study by an analyst at UBS Warburg in New York concluded that futures are a cheaper way to get short-term exposure to financial markets but that long-term ETFs are better. That analyst believed the "roll costs" of contracts over time had more of an effect on costs than the MER on SPDRs. The analyst further pointed out that the minimum investment for futures trading was much higher than 100 shares of an ETF, and that ETFs are often linked to sectors where no futures contracts are available.

It's a matter of debate it seems. One other analyst, Jon Maier, doesn't agree. He thinks ETFs are always cheaper, short or long-term, when you take into account mispricing risk and market impact of the futures contract itself. Maier's Salomon Smith Barney report on exchange traded funds released in February 2001 calculates all costs of an ETF purchase at 23.16 basis points (0.23%). An identical calculation for a three-month futures contract would cost 60.14 basis points (0.60%) by his calculation and the longer the hold, the better ETFs look, according to Maier. He reports that the biggest advantage with futures is the ease with which they can be leveraged. ETFs can be margined but you can borrow only up to 50% of their value (70% if they're optionable). Futures will let you get away with margining up to 90% of the contracts' value.[14]

Leverage, of course, is a sharp double-edged sword. Most investors would rather not. Hillary Clinton is said to have made a tidy sum on cattle futures. Maybe by the time she's running for president there will be a livestock ETF. Until then it's likely most of us will content ourselves with relatively simple ETFs and leave futures to those who don't mind margin calls.

Index mutual funds, ETFs, or futures—you decide which product best suits your situation, how much money you want to give over to passive investing, and for how long. The longer the holding period, the more you should favour ETFs for their parsimonious MERs. As you'll see in the next chapter, there's a wealth of investment strategies suited for ETFs some of which would not be possible to replicate with index funds because the index selection is not as broad as the buffet offered by ETFs. And of course, index funds are hard pressed to come anywhere close to matching ETFs in rock bottom cover charge.

You might be surprised to discover that the American pioneer and outspoken advocate for low cost index investing has kind words to say about ETFs, without actually liking them.

ETFs or Index Mutual Funds?
An interview with John Bogle

John Bogle is founder of the Vanguard Group, the largest index mutual fund company in the world and the second largest mutual fund company in the U.S. He's an active advocate of low cost mutual funds, but not a great fan of ETFs despite the fact that Vanguard is the first U.S. mutual fund company to come out with an ETF, the VIPERs series. Mr. Bogle is retired from the day-to-day management of Vanguard.

As you read this keep in mind that Mr. Bogle is speaking from a U.S. perspective where the difference in annual costs between his hugely popular index funds and ETFs is quite small. The MER on Vanguard's S&P index fund is 0.18% (0.12% for a large minimum investment) vs. the S&P 500 ETF, the SPDR, with an MER of 0.12%. In Canada the disparity between index fund MERs and comparable ETFs can be much wider.*

John Bogle: ETFs are a truly great product badly used. There's no reason not to use an ETF for long-term holdings. I'd call it a flip of the coin for long-term investors. That says they're a very, very good product because the index fund is the killer app[lication]. There's no way to improve on it for the market as a whole. It gives you virtually 100% of the market's return and in the long run probably 1% of all managers can give you 100% of the market's returns over fifty years and that's just not very good odds. Why would somebody take a 1% chance when they're guaranteed to get the market's return in an index fund?

Now what is the reality with ETFs? The turnover rate of all stocks in the U.S. is about 100% a year. SPDRs is 1800%. The average holding is 12 days. That's a misuse of a big aggregated index. Turnover for Qubes is 3500% a year. It's a speculative medium [in which] shares are held for 2.2 days on average. It's a great way to trade the NASDAQ, but why would anybody in their right mind think they can make any money trading the NASDAQ? Trading is a loser's game.

I contrast it with a great Purdey shotgun. It's a perfect instrument for hunting and for suicide. I think many more investors are using these ETFs to commit financial suicide than they are to hunt for long-term returns. Anything that persuades people to trade more is against their best long-term investing interest.

We came out with VIPERs because we want to be competitive

in the marketplace. If everybody else is doing it we want to do it too. There are some potential tax advantages for our existing shareholders [because] we can move very low cost stocks into the VIPER class without a tax impact to the fund. [VIPERs will also be helpful in] getting traders now in our funds out of our funds into the trading shares.

I'm not madly in love with it. People have argued that we should not let people trade our funds: slap 'em down. We've tried to be fairly good at that. [We allow] one round trip every six months—very tough trading restrictions. Maybe we could do that a little bit better but in any event we've elected to go the other way. It may not be a decision I would have made but it's not a decision that's unrespectable.

An ETF is an index fund. If you buy and hold it for your investment lifetime of 50 years, it's completely indifferent as to whether you've owned a mutual fund or an ETF if it's a broad index. It's a distinction without a difference. What matters is how these funds get used. The evidence is overpowering that they're both marketed to traders and used by traders. All market mutual funds are boredom personified. ETFs are excitement personified. It's like sailing: hours of complete boredom punctuated by moments of sheer terror.

The ETF is great with the right long-term perspective because they keep costs and taxes low and those are crucial things. And that's good, but if they're used for trading, they're just another stock, maybe a little less risky one because of their diversification.

June 19, 2001

*The lowest cost Canadian index ETF is the i60 with an MER of 0.17%. Contrast that with the lowest cost publicly available Canadian equity index fund, TD's Canadian index e-fund, with an MER at 0.30% covering the S&P/TSX Composite Index. TD's comparable ETF has an MER of 0.25%. S&P/TSX 60 index mutual funds start at a low of 0.51% for Altamira's Precision Canadian Index compared to the 0.17% of the i60. (MERs from www.globefund.com as of August 31, 2002)

A Note about HOLDRS

Somewhere between a whole index and a hand-picked portfolio of your own making lies HOLDRS (pronounced "holders".) HOLDRS are exchange-traded baskets of securities, each typically containing 20 different stocks related by industry sector. These elect stocks remain in the portfolio unchanged for the life of the trust unless corporate events cause changes to the stock itself like reconstitution, delisting, etc.

HOLDRS stands for "**HOL**ding Company **D**epositary **R**eceipts" and despite that intimidating handle they're really the proletarian version of ETFs. For the cost of a stock trade and few other expenses, you can buy an instant portfolio with a very focused sector concentration. HOLDRS cover specialized sectors like business to business Internet companies, Internet architecture firms, and more diversified, established sectors like telecommunications, utilities and pharmaceuticals.

HOLDRS is a signature product designed and offered by Merrill Lynch & Co., Inc. in the U.S. and Canada. They've been popular. First introduced in 1999, there are now 17 HOLDRS trading on AMEX with US$3.6 billion in assets.[2] That is down from a high of $5 billion in 2000 in part due to Merrill Lynch's unfortunate habit of launching these highly specialized Internet and technology plays close to the market peak. Many early HOLDRS investors saw their high tech portfolios plummet—some by as much as 95%. Dismal timing aside, these products have a number of attractive features—and a few worrisome drawbacks.

On the attractive side, HOLDRS have no MER or any other ongoing fees or costs apart from a small annual trustee fee ($2 to $8 per 100 shares of HOLDRS) that is paid out of dividends and other distributions. If the portfolio doesn't generate enough income to pay the trustee fee—not a far-fetched scenario when dealing with Internet companies—the trustee fee is waived to the extent it can't be paid from distributions.

Because they do not have to comply with the concentration limits that apply to mutual funds and ETFs (in the U.S.), your HOLDRS portfolio will never be forced to sell a winning stock. This will spare you the sting of unwanted capital gains and the disadvantage of a smaller holding in a good investment. With HOLDRS, as with an individual stock holding, you can ride a winner as long as it runs and you decide when to sell it and trigger your gains.

HOLDRS also bring that wonderful creation/redemption process pioneered by ETFs into the clutches of ordinary retail investors. You can easily redeem HOLDRS for all its underlying securities. This gives you the freedom to sell the shares you don't want on the open market and keep the rest. The trustee charges a $10 fee per round lot of 100 HOLDRS shares for this service. Less likely but also possible, you can create 100 HOLDRS by surrendering the requisite number of shares of the underlying portfolio to the trustee who, for $10, will issue you HOLDRS in exchange. ETFs like SPDRs and i60s permit this creation/redemption only with huge share volumes of 50,000 or more which means, in practice, that only institutional investors and arbitrageurs can take advantage of that feature.

HOLDRS are bought, sold, created and redeemed in multiples of 100 shares and only in lots of 100. (ETFs, you'll remember, do come in odd lots.) Of course, because you can't buy anything less than a round lot of 100 HOLDRS, the proletariat buying these keepers had better have enough money for 100 shares. In September 2002 that would have meant forking over as much as US$10,600 for Regional Bank HOLDRS, or as little as $153 for the beat up Internet Infrastructure HOLDRS.

In addition to their accessible redemption feature, HOLDRS are retail friendly in another way. You get the voting rights associated with all the underlying shares. This is in contrast to other baskets of securities such as mutual funds and ETFs. With mutual funds, the beneficial owners do not get voting rights to the underlying securities. ETFs give voting rights only to those investors who hold a creation/redemption unit—typically about 50,000 shares or units of the ETF. The vast majority of retail ETF investors, then, would not have voting rights on the underlying securities. Social investors, eager to influence corporate behaviour through their voting rights will appreciate the voting feature of HOLDRS—and the flexibility to divest themselves of companies within the portfolio that don't make the ethical cut.

Along with these voting rights you'd better get yourself a bigger mail box because you receive all the investor relations mailings from the 20 or so underlying companies. The two non-sector HOLDRS, "Market 2000" and "Europe 2001," have around 50 companies in each of their baskets. If you take pity on your mail carrier's back and your recycling box, you can elect to receive most of these corporate mailings electronically.

Cheaper to hold and more flexible than ETFs, HOLDRS as a structure have a lot going for them. The actual execution, however, could use some work. With just a few exceptions, HOLDRS' portfolios are highly sector specific. As such they expose you to a lot more risk than a broad market index or even a sector mutual fund with a greater number of holdings. The risk hasn't been academic either.

As of early September 2002, not one U.S.-based HOLDRS' return from inception was in positive territory. Returns ranged from -10% for Regional Bank HOLDRS to more than -95% for B2B HOLDRS. Broadband and

Telebras were not much better at -90% and -82% respectively. As a group, their losses have been astounding.

The one winner has been the Canadian-based CP HOLDRS.[15] The CP HOLDRS was designed around the spin-offs of Canadian Pacific Railway and was launched in 2001. It landed on the market at C$50 and as of September 2002 it was chugging right along at around $65 a share.

The U.S. prospectus for HOLDRS lists an interesting risk factor that has proved more problematic than most would have expected. Under "Temporary price increases in the underlying securities," the prospectus says, "Purchasing activity in the secondary market associated with acquiring the underlying securities for deposit into the trust may affect the market price of the deposited shares." In other words, gathering up the shares to build a HOLDRS could inflate the price of the individual securities. Merrill Lynch was the subject of a class action suit by investors in the B2B Internet HOLDRS who claimed securities were put into the HOLDRS at inflated prices possibly due to some sort of manipulation at their IPO stage.[16] (Allegations have not been proven in court.) On March 14, 2000, the B2B Internet HOLDRS traded at US$108. By April 3, 2001 they were at $4.26. On September 13, 2002, they were languishing at $1.80.

There's another fundamental problem with HOLDRS. The portfolio is a snapshot in time. What goes in at the beginning stays in unchanged unless there's a spin-off, merger, consolidation or other corporate event that would cause any of the underlying securities to be withdrawn from AMEX. Until late 2000, all such events would be treated as though you owned the securities individually. You would receive directly the new share reissues, the buyouts, etc. and they would not be reflected in the fund. This means the number of holdings in the fund could shrink and the corresponding concentration of the remaining stocks would increase. Gradually your investment would become less diversified. An amendment to the rules governing HOLDRS now permits them to retain stocks resulting from those stock rending corporate events, but this doesn't entirely ameliorate the structural problem.

Suppose a private biotech company discovers a cure for cancer. They go public, and their stock immediately rockets skyward. A biotech HOLDRS put together before that company went public would miss out entirely on the biggest biotech shooting star in history. An index continually refreshes its holdings to keep up with market activity, so any index-based product like an ETF will not miss out on the next Viagra. The static portfolio construction will haunt any HOLDRS but especially those in a rapid growth sector—the very sectors these products have chosen to exploit.

Even leaving aside this problem, market appreciation and losses will, over time, change the balance of the HOLDRS underlying securities relative to each other. The longer you keep a HOLDRS, the more risky and less representative the portfolio may become.

Internet HOLDRS is a good example of the danger. This HOLDRS was launched with AOL at 19.6% of the original portfolio. Time Warner swallowed AOL which resulted in AOL Time Warner Inc. stock taking up 47% of the portfolio at a point when only 20% of Time Warner's revenue was coming from Internet-related businesses.

Lest you worry that the absence of an ongoing management fee will make HOLDRS a fleeting product, take heart. Merrill Lynch has not turned altruistic. HOLDRS finance themselves by charging a 2% underwriting fee at the initial offering (for 10,000 HOLDRS or more the underwriting fee is 1%), a charge that is paid only once and does not spill over into the secondary market.

Before grasping a HOLDRS for your own take a good look at the costs. Although a 2% underwriting fee may not seem unreasonable, keep in mind that the upside potential of a HOLDRS initial public offering (IPO) is not like the promise of a new stock IPO. HOLDRS are baskets of securities that have already had their own public debut. Just repackaging them into a HOLDRS and launching that as an IPO doesn't automatically create any new upside potential. You may find an underwriting fee palatable for a stock IPO with great expectations, but where's the similar excitement with a HOLDRS IPO? Also scrutinize that annual trustee fee. Should the price of 100 HOLDRS fall dramatically, you could be paying more money in trustee fees than the MER on an ETF. All U.S.-based HOLDRS trade on AMEX and all have options associated with them. (For more information on HOLDRS go to *www.holdrs.com*, an extensive site with prospecti. Also see the Appendix.)

Notes

1) Salomon Smith Barney research report on exchange traded funds, Feb. 6, 2001, p.16.

2) Ibid.

3) The former country share "WEBS", now the iShares MSCI series, carry MERs of 0.84% for developed markets and 0.99% for emerging markets; otherwise, U.S. ETF MERs tend to be 0.60% or less.

4) As of August 31, 2002, *www.globefund.com*, index fund universe. Note that segregated funds guarantee investors' capital which is one reason segregated funds have higher MERs than other funds.

5) This point is made graphically at *www.bylo.org* in an article entitled "Performance of Indexed vs. Actively Managed Portfolios" (CARs for the 15 years ending December 31, 2000), March 14, 2001. The article compares the returns of median mutual funds to median index funds over 15 years and calculates how profoundly the MER differential affects long-term returns. Also see *www.osc.gov.on.ca* for an MER impact calculator, and Norman Rothery, "Active Funds vs. Indexing," viewed September 28, 2002, *www.ndir.com/SI/articles/mutual.vs.tips.html*.

6) Donna Green, "Ask MoneySense" October 2000, for a more detailed discussion of the MER calculation and what it leaves out.

7) Scott Woolley, "SPDR Versus S&P Index 500," *Forbes.com*, July 8, 2002.

8) Fifty-two week standard deviations from Phillip Witter, CFA, CIM, Product Analyst, BGI Canada.

9) Capital gains are paid in units, not cash. Total distributions for the i60 per unit were $1.13.

10) The author was not able to find Canadian data on holding periods but there's no reason to think the Canadian holding period is that much different from that in the U.S. Two and a half year U.S. holding information from John Bogle, President of Bogle Financial Markets Research Center, founder and past chairman of The Vanguard Group, "Mutual Fund Directors: The Dog that Didn't Bark," Jan. 29, 2001 speech. Available on *www.vanguard.com/bogle_site/january282001.html* Also see Gavin Quill, "Investors Behaving Badly: An Analysis of Investor Trading Patterns in Mutual Funds," *Journal of Financial Planning*, November, 2001, article 11, *www.journalfp.net/jfp1101-art11.cfm*. This article states the 2.9 year holding period and the 5.5 year holding period in 1997.

11) Eric Kirzner, "Passive Investors' Choices Expand," *Globe and Mail*, May 2, 2001.

12) Index fund count and assets from Investor Economics, "Index Funds

Report: Quarterly Review," Fall 2000 for historical information, Summer 2002 for current statistics as of June 2002.

13) Kevin McNally, "ETFs versus Futures," Salomon Smith Barney research report, February 11, 2002, p. 4.

14) Salomon Smith Barney research report on exchange traded funds, Feb. 6, 2001, p.18, and UBS Warburg report by Jon Maier, March 13, 2001.

15) CP HOLDRS (HCH) trade on the TSX and the New York Stock Exchange. HCH options trade on the AMEX.

16) For more information on the HOLDRS suit see *www.holdrs.com/holdrs/main/index.asp?Action=QuoteH&symb=BHH* for press releases about the class action. Allegations have not been proven in court.

Part Two

Making ETFs Work for You

Chapter Four

Investment Strategies Using ETFs

Staking your money on one index among the countless out there seems to require either strong opinions or impressive self-confidence. Of the 120 plus ETFs available in North America, where do you begin? Well, in truth, the choices get narrowed down remarkably quickly because you want to establish two main goals in your overall portfolio: prudent diversification and intelligent asset allocation.

When investment gurus contemplate portfolios, they chant "diversification." Diversification lowers the blood pressure just as surely as yoga meditation, and is the uncomplicated essence of good portfolio management.

Part of good diversification is asset allocation. You've likely heard more times than you care to remember that asset allocation is responsible for 93.6% of your portfolio returns. That is possibly the most widely quoted false statistic in personal finance. The study, done by Gary Brinson in 1986, actually says, "Data from 91 large U.S. pension plans indicate that investment policy dominates investment strategy (market timing and security selection), explaining on average 93.6% of the variation in total plan return."[1]   In other words, asset allocation explained, on average, 93.6% of the variation in the portfolios studied. Variation, or variance, is a measure of the risk of an asset or an entire portfolio. So what the study is actually saying is that asset allocation is the predominant factor in controlling the riskiness of the portfolio. Perhaps not the profound conclusion of the misquotes, but an important observation anyway. Evening the peaks and valleys of your returns will give you a better opportunity to put compounding to good long-term benefit. Compounding works more quickly on consistent gains rather than an equivalent return spread over years of losses and gold strikes.

Because the Brinson study has been wildly misunderstood, it has been revisited a number of times. A more recent paper looks at this study, adds more empirical evidence, and wrings a more meaningful conclusion from it all. Roger G. Ibbotson and Paul D. Kaplan, in their article, "Does Asset Allocation Policy Explain 40, 90, or 100 Percent of Performance?" say:

> In summary, the impact of asset allocation on returns depends on an individual's investing style. For the long-term, passive investor, the asset allocation decision is by far the most important. For the short-term investor who trades more frequently, invests in individual securities, and practices market timing, asset allocation has less of an impact on returns. The impact of asset allocation on performance is directly correlated with investment style.[2]

So if you're going to be a buy-and-hold investor, your asset allocation should be your foremost consideration, and the key to an effective asset allocation is diversification.

Diversification means not putting all your eggs in one basket—not buying one stock when you can buy a number of different stocks to hedge your risk. Ditto for bonds and any other investment vehicle. Asset allocation is simply the process of extending the principle of diversification across asset classes. Holding 12 different stocks may mean you're diversified across equities (if you've selected stocks from different industries), but you're still exposed to the vagaries of the stock market without the backstop of bonds, cash, real estate, precious metals, etc.

Mutual funds made diversification and asset allocation easy. There's a mutual fund for any asset class you can think of and because of the large sums mutual funds pool, they can offer instant and broad diversification to anyone with $25 a month. It's a wonderful thing.

But by now you know ETFs are a cheaper way to accomplish diversification and quality asset allocation. So, if you want to take a bite out of your investment costs and have more flexibility with your investments, here are some easy-to-emulate portfolio construction models and investment strategies using ETFs to help you build a solidly diversified portfolio with readily amendable asset allocation guidelines and excellent tax efficiency. There's enough information here to start you on the road to do-it-yourself freedom.

For those who prefer to work with an advisor, this chapter will give you a good understanding of the strategies your advisor will have at his or her disposal so that your investment portfolio will not be held back just in the interests of keeping it simple. Advisors can add value when they're free to use every tool in the arsenal to build your wealth. You'll notice, too, that there's still a role in these strategies for actively managed mutual funds for those asset classes not yet covered by ETFs, or for those sectors where you might believe active management can still exploit some inefficiencies.

Keep in mind that ETFs can be bought or sold only inside a brokerage account. If you don't already have a brokerage account, it may seem like an unwelcome complication, but once set up, the flexibility and convenience it provides make it hard to ever want to do without it. A brokerage account is useful because you can hold just about everything but the junk in your basement in it. This means you can consolidate all your investments in one account if you like—with the exception of bank GICs which can't be transferred to another institution. You can easily open an account at no charge with a full-service broker or an on-line discount broker.

Time to put meditation aside and put ETFs to their practical use.

Core and Satellite

Core and Satellite is a popular portfolio construction method especially for the equity portion of a portfolio. This method starts by allocating the largest chunk of money to the least risky equity holding; namely, a broad-based equity ETF. Surrounding that core like electrons are smaller investments in industry sectors, management style, market capitalization and individual stock selection. This method is also known by the trademarked name, "Core and Explore," propounded by Charles Schwab in the U.S. The core of the portfolio is passively managed, but the exploratory parts can be either passively or actively managed. An important consideration for the electrons is their maneuverability. They're the ones you may wish to use to dart in and out in anticipation of changing market conditions or hold longer term as a secular play. They're the ones the money manager is counting on to boost returns above the index benchmark.

As the savvy investor knows, the asset allocation sets the return expectations. A good allocation finds a balance between what the investor needs to earn on his portfolio and his risk tolerance. Schwab is far from unique in stressing the critical importance of a good, client specific asset allocation as the foundation for portfolio management. Even mutual fund companies have had fairly sophisticated, proprietary asset allocation programs for years. Mackenzie Financial Corp.'s STAR program is one example. Schwab, however, is notable for the way it implements these allocations.

Core/Satellite Equity Allocation Strategy (fig. 20)

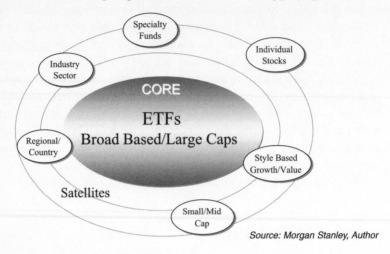

Source: Morgan Stanley, Author

The Asset Allocation Decision

After a client's initial asset allocation is determined, Schwab's approach is often to recommend that client's put half of each asset class in a passive vehicle—usually an ETF—to form the base of stability. Then the other half of each asset class is actively managed by selecting individual stocks or by over-weighting sectors with sector ETFs. This approach works especially well with a sector like technology in which individual stocks can be risky. A diversified portfolio with a broad selection of technology companies mitigates the business risk of individual stocks while still giving the chance to capture the potential of the whole sector. This Core and Explore™ approach provides lots of room for tactical portfolio changes letting managers and advisors overweight sectors without throwing off the structural asset allocation.

The Fixed Income Component

For fixed income, Schwab frequently recommends putting 50% in a portfolio of government bonds with staggered maturities (known as "laddering.") That portfolio remains constant and is held passively while the other half of the fixed income side is more actively managed with corporate bonds, income trusts and preferred shares. This strategy gives the flexibility to trade bonds in anticipation of interest rate changes, and to add to returns by trading based on changes in credit quality—the two major ways active bond fund managers make money.

It is also possible to "Core" the fixed income portion of your portfolio with ETFs. A proper combination of BGI Canada's iG5 and iG10 funds achieves ongoing exposure to a set portion of the yield curve with Government of Canada bonds. This leaves room to "Explore" with actively managed corporate or high yield bond mutual funds. There are also eight fixed income ETFs in the U.S., one of which is a corporate bond fund. Additional fixed income ETF offerings are expected on both sides of the border and with them, added flexibility for the fixed income side of your holdings.

You may not realize it, but there are more benefits to bond ETFs than may immediately appear. Individual investors like you and me have to buy bonds through brokerages who hold them in inventory. Although there is no commission charge on a bond purchase, there is an invisible charge taken by the house on the sale of a bond that is factored into the yield your bond delivers. A bond that might cost $900 per $1,000 face value will be sold to you for the purposes of example at $910 per $1,000. That extra $10 over wholesale cost is the brokerage's built-in (and most often undisclosed) commission.

Until recently, you and I were not privy to the wholesale cost of bonds. Investors had no accurate way to tell how large a cut the bond desk was taking on a bond transaction because the bond market prices were veiled from us. With the advent of on-line bond trading information services in 2000 through the introduction of E-Bond Inc., that has changed. However, for those of us not familiar with the on-line bond services now in Canada, the best you can get is a feel for current interest rate levels from looking at the yields of other bonds of a similar nature—if you can get current quotes of those bonds—and use this to judge the fairness of the yield on your particular bond purchase. That's about as close as you can come to figuring out whether you got a good price on your purchase.

With bond ETFs, all you have to worry about is the brokerage commission to buy the fund and the annual MER. You can bet the ETF is getting a better yield on their Government of Canada bonds than you would be able to get simply because of the size of their purchase. You can also bet that a $29 commission is a lot less than the money you lose in yield on an individual bond purchase. The real question is if the 0.25% MER is also less than the yield hit you'd take on an individual bond buy. It is definitely way less than the MER on a conventional bond fund which can easily run you 0.59% for an index bond fund to 1.93% for the AGF Canadian Bond Fund—which is hardly the most costly bond fund either.

Building Blocks

Similar to the Core and Satellite approach is the Building Blocks method of portfolio construction. In this model, decreasing amounts of money are allocated to increasingly risky equity groups. The base of the pyramid starts with a very broad-based passive investment such as TD Asset Management's S&P/TSX Composite ETF or iShares Russell 3000. Then, in decreasing weight might come a value and/or a growth ETF or mutual fund, then perhaps a mid cap ETF, followed by a sector ETF say in healthcare, and then finally the smallest block of all—individual stocks.

Equity Building Blocks (fig. 21)

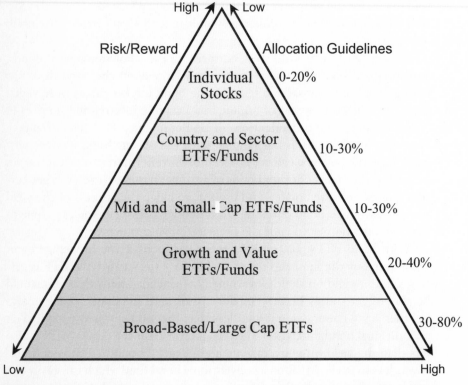

One of the many beauties of this approach is that your portfolio's return will probably stay fairly close to the return of its main holding. The approach also gives a disciplined framework so you shrink your exposure as the riskiness of the investment increases. It's a big temptation to make sizable bets on hot industries. The Core and Satellite and the Building Block strategies let you have some exposure to a favoured sector, style or stock, but in moderation and with due consideration for their inherent risk.

Naturally, not every possibility needs to be included in portfolios following this general core approach. Likely you'll find it enough to tilt your passive core with a favoured sector or a promising stock, but if you're game to try all the flavours, the good news is that Canadians can use domestic ETFs for just about every block in the pyramid. There are Canadian ETFs for broad equity indices, a Mid Cap ETF, a value and a growth ETF and four industry sector ETFs. And of course, for a U.S. equity component there is a wealth of selection with U.S.-based ETFs in increasingly sophisticated combinations of style and capitalization.

For the foreign content of RRSP portfolios, you're free to take 30% of your blocks and invest in U.S. ETFs that are counterparts to your Canadian position, though this may be impractical if your portfolio is not large and the 30% means buying less than a board lot of an ETF. You could also invest the growth and value portion of the pyramid in international mutual funds with those style biases, and to top up to 30%, swing in a U.S. sector ETF or a mutual fund specific to a U.S. or global sector. (See Core and Satellite components below for more ideas.) There are a limitless number of ways to utilize this strategy.

Want more exposure than the 30% foreign content allows? Consider the two fully RRSP eligible ETFs on foreign indices: iUnits S&P500 Index RSP Fund and iUnits MSCI International Equity Index RSP Fund.

Core Components: Broad Market/Large Cap Base (fig. 22)

Equity Exposure	ETFs		
	Type	100% RRSP Eligible	Foreign Content
CANADA	Broad	TTF, TCF	-
	Large Cap	XIU, XIC	-
UNITED STATES	Broad	-	IYY, IWV, VTI
	Large Cap	XSP	IVV, SPY, IWB, DIA
INTERNATIONAL	Broad	XIN	EFA

Step 1: Select one ETF from each desired **exposure** (one from broad OR one from large cap) and weight appropriately.

Fixed Income Exposure	ETFs		
	Credit (Maturity Term)	100% RRSP Eligible	Foreign Content
CANADA	Government (5 yr, 10 yr)	XGV, XGX	-
UNITED STATES	Government (short, mid, long)	-	SHY, IEF, TLT
	Corporate (mid)	-	LQD

Step 2: For fixed income allocations, select appropriate ETFs to match **credit** and **term** exposure.

Satellite/Tilt Components

Strategy	Exposure		100% RRSP Eligible	Foreign Content
STYLE/CAP	Growth Value		TAG TAV	IWZ IWW
	Mid Cap		XMD	IJH, MDY, IWR,
	Small Cap		-	IJR, IWM
INDUSTRY SECTOR	Energy		XEG	XLE, IYE, OIH, IXC,
	Financials		XFN	XLF, IYF, IYG, RKH, IXG,
	Healthcare	Broad: Biotech:	-	XLV, IYH, PPH, IXJ BBH, IBB
	Technology	Broad: Telecom:	XIT	IYW, IGM, MTK, XLK, IXN, IYZ, TTH, WMH
	Specialty	Real Estate: Gold:	XRE XGD	IYR, ICF, RWR -
COUNTRY/REGIONAL	Europe	Broad:	-	IEV, EZU, EKH
	Asia Pacific (Japan, Asia Ex-Japan)		-	EWJ, EPP
	Emerging Markets[9] (Latin America, South Korea, Taiwan)		-	ILF, EWY, EWT

[9] BGI and Vanguard are each expected to launch an emerging markets fund.

Step 3: Layer on to the core, one ETF for each desired exposure to strategically **tilt** the portfolio.

Sample ETF Portfolios

Building traditional portfolios is as easy as snapping Lego pieces together when you combine the Core and Satellite/Tilt components together to suit your needs. The following four portfolios showcase just how flexible ETFs are in helping you achieve your investment objectives. The number of possible portfolios is endless, limited only by your imagination. There is a suitability section at the bottom of each portfolio to help you consider the fit with your overall investment plan. Treat these sample portfolios as starting points that you can adjust based upon personal circumstances and investment objectives.

Don't hesitate to make portfolio substitutions based on personal preferences or current holdings. Almost all of the ETFs have a near twin or two, making them quite interchangeable. This also makes them quite useful for tax loss harvesting, a strategy we'll delve into in Chapter Six. In addition, switches may be made with virtually any active investment vehicle. For example, you may prefer a fixed income ladder of strip coupons inside your RRSP for some or all of your fixed income component. You will probably want to hold onto actively managed mutual funds that are performing well or that still have a punitive DSC penalty attached to a redemption. Individual stock selection, in certain sectors, may help round out a unique Core and Explore portfolio.

Sample RSP Portfolio (fig. 23)

ETF	Symbol	Sector/Market	% of Portfolio	MER
Fixed Income				
iG5 Bond	XGV	Cdn Fixed Income	15%	0.25%
iG10 Bond	XGX	Cdn Fixed Income	15%	0.25%
iShares 7-10 Yr. Treasury	IEF	U.S. Fixed Income	10%	0.15%
Equity				
TD S&P/TSX Capped Composite	TCF	Cdn Equity	20%	0.25%
Total Market Vipers	VTI	U.S. Equity	20%	0.15%
iUnits MSCI International	XIN	Int'l Equity	20%	0.35%
		TOTAL	100%	0.24%

Asset Allocation

Fixed Income 40%

Equity 60%

Geographic Breakdown

Canada 50%

U.S. 30%

International 20%

Suitability

Account Type:	RRSP
Asset Mix:	Balanced
Investment Strategy:	Buy and Hold, Periodic Rebalancing
Risk Tolerance:	Low to Moderate
Portfolio Content:	Complete Portfolio

ETFs "With Options"* Portfolio (fig. 24)

ETF	Symbol	Sector/Market	% of Portfolio	MER
Canada				
iUnits S&P/TSX 60 Index	XIU	Cdn LargeCap	20%	0.17%
United States				
DIAMOND Trust Series I	DIA	U.S. LargeCap	30%	0.18%
iShares MidCap 400	IJH	U.S. MidCap	10%	0.20%
iShares Russell 2000	IWM	U.S. SmallCap	10%	0.20%
International				
iShares MSCI EAFE	EFA	Int'l Equity	30%	0.35%
* All these ETFs have listed options.		TOTAL	100%	0.21%

Capitalization Breakdown   **Geographic Breakdown**

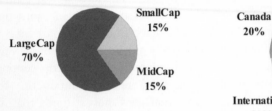

LargeCap 70%
SmallCap 15%
MidCap 15%

Canada 20%
U.S. 50%
International 30%

Suitability

Account Type:	Open
Asset Mix:	All Equity
Investment Strategy:	Hedging with Covered Call Writing/Put Buying Available
Risk Tolerance:	Low to Moderate
Portfolio Content:	Complete Equity or Core

Value Tilt Portfolio

(fig. 25)

ETF	Symbol	Sector/Market	% of Portfolio	MER
Canada				
iUnits S&P/TSX 60 Index	XIU	Large Cap	15%	0.17%
TD Select Canadian Value	TAV	Cdn Value	10%	0.55%
United States				
iShares S&P 500	IVV	Large Cap	20%	0.09%
iShares S&P 500/BARRA Value	IVE	Large Cap Value	10%	0.18%
iShares S&P MidCap 400	IJH	MidCap	15%	0.20%
iShares S&P 400/BARRA Value	IJJ	MidCap Value	5%	0.25%
iShares S&P 600/BARRA Growth	IJT	SmallCap Growth	5%	0.25%
iShares S&P 600/BARRA Value	IJS	SmallCap Value	5%	0.25%
International				
iShares MSCI EAFE*	EFA	International	15%	0.25%
* Int'l style ETFs not available		TOTAL	100%	0.18%

Style Allocation

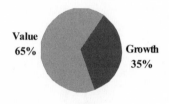

Value 65%

Growth 35%

Geographic Breakdown

Canada 25%

U.S. 60%

International 15%

Suitability

Account Type: Open
Asset Mix: All Equity
Investment Strategy: Value Style Bias
Risk Tolerance: Moderate
Portfolio Content: Equity Core

ETF	Symbol	Sector/Market	% of Portfolio	MER
Canada				
iUnits S&P/TSX Cdn. Gold	XGD	Canadian Gold	5%	0.55%
U.S.				
iShares S&P MidCap	IJH	U.S. MidCap	10%	0.20%
iShares S&P SmallCap	IJR	U.S. SmallCap	10%	0.20%
iShares DJ U.S. Real Estate	IYR	U.S. Real Estate	5%	0.60%
Global/International				
iShares S&P Global 100	IOO	Global Large Cap	25%	0.40%
iShares MSCI EAFE	EFA	International	20%	0.35%
iShares S&P Global Energy	IXC	Global Energy	5%	0.65%
iShares S&P Global Financials	IXG	Global Financials	5%	0.65%
iShares S&P Global Healthcare	IXJ	Global Healthcare	5%	0.65%
iShares S&P Global Technology	IXN	Global Technology	5%	0.65%
iShares S&P Global Telecommunications	IXP	Global Telecom	5%	0.65%
		TOTAL	100%	0.43%

Sector Breakdown   **Geographic Breakdown**

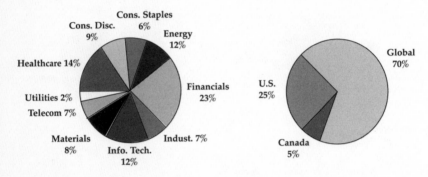

Note: Real Estate and Gold are sub-sectors of financials and materials respectively.

Suitability

Account Type:	Open
Asset Mix:	All Equity
Investment Strategy:	Global, Focused on Expected Growth Sectors
Risk Tolerance:	High
Portfolio Content:	Equity Explore

The Building Block method and the Core and Satellite approach anchors your portfolio in a passive index while giving you quite a bit of room to do some tactical maneuvering with a portion of your portfolio. You can adjust from value to growth when the economy starts heating up, or back to value as a more defensive play. You can tilt from sector to sector as you anticipate action, and you can still enjoy your individual stock picks. It's hard to imagine an easier to maintain portfolio that'll let you have so much fun.

Working out how much you should allocate to core and how much to satellite does take some thought. As a rule of thumb, the more risk averse you are, the greater the percentage of your portfolio should be put in the core—even up to 100%. Your portfolio will then perform in line with the asset classes you've chosen. No better. No worse. It's a trade off. You've given up the possibility of outperforming the market for the promise of not underperforming it (except by the amount of the small MER).

At the other extreme would be the 100% satellite portfolio—the swing for the fences approach. But as in baseball, when you focus on the home runs, you all too often strike out. Most investors will find comfort in a core position ranging from 50% to 70% of their portfolio, with the conservative crowd approaching 100%. As always, your investment decisions have to be in line with your financial goals and risk tolerance.

Rebalancing

The success of any asset allocation investment strategy depends on disciplined rebalancing. Over time your carefully allotted percentages are going to come unstuck. Not all the assets will grow in proportion to one another. What started off as a 10% position may have grown to 20%, and your core may look a little gnawed in comparison. Rebalancing is the process of bringing your portfolio's asset classes back in line with an optimal allocation.

As anyone who has sold a winner to buy more losers knows, this takes intestinal fortitude. The big temptation is to continue to let winners run. That's when greed overtakes reason. It is always best to leave something for the next guy. By rebalancing you capture your gains and plow them into asset classes that have yet to make their move. You lose out a little on the high end but chances are you capture the full movement from off the bottom of the next hot asset class. Rebalancing at least once a year has a smoothing effect on returns, which increases the benefits of compounding.

Unfortunately, rebalancing an ETF portfolio comes with commission costs and probably a tax bill (outside a registered account). This means you have to decide how religiously you want to keep to your ideal asset allocation. Rebalancing to adjust for a 5% deviation isn't worth it in a small portfolio, but it could be in a large portfolio. These are judgments you have to make, perhaps in consultation with a financial advisor or accountant. Don't let the tax tail wag the investment dog. Rebalancing has to be done to get the full benefit of these strategies, an important part of which is their defensiveness.

Sector Rotation

Sector rotation is a fairly aggressive investment strategy that ETFs make easy to execute, but unfortunately, not any easier to get right. Sector rotation managers invest in industry sectors they believe are poised for significant advances. Strategies vary greatly but generally fall into two camps based upon the expected holding period. Intermediate sector rotation is usually measured in months and attempts to capture cyclical moves. Secular strategies are based on multi-year trends.

The aim is to buy into a sector when it is still out of favour and to sell when it has peaked. Trouble is, nobody has a reliable crystal ball. Analysts have spent lots of time tracking historical sector performance in hopes of discovering some pattern or predictability to the ascendant sectors. Let's just say it's still an art—one that many managers think they can exploit. Plenty of ordinary investors unknowingly do sector rotation when they buy and sell industry-specialized mutual funds such as Internet and technology, health sciences funds, precious metals and funds with a preponderance of financial stocks like AIC's Advantage Fund. Sectors go in and out of favour but with a little cunning and some luck, most everyone thinks they can pick the next hot sector. As the technology stock crash has shown, a big part of sector betting is knowing when to leave something for the next guy, or sit through a gut wrenching downturn. Exiting a sector before its decline can be as important as jumping onto it before its rise.

To give you some idea of how volatile sector investing can be, here's a chart courtesy of Morgan Stanley Equity Research on the historical performance of major sectors.

The second chart shows relative performance by style and capitalization categories.

Historical S&P/MSCI Sector Performance (fig.27)

	1990	1991	1992	1993	1994	1995	1996	1997	1998	1999	2000	2001	YTD
Best	Consum. Discret. 13.8%	Health 53.2%	Financial 24.1%	Info. Tech. 19.3%	Info. Tech. 20.3%	Health 58.2%	Info. Tech. 44.8%	Financial 49.0%	Info. Tech. 78.5%	Info. Tech. 79.7%	Utilities 57.1%	Consum. Discret. 2.0%	Consum. Staples 9.4%
	Consum. Staples 13.5%	Financial 48.9%	Consum. Discret. 18.4%	Industrial 17.7%	Health 13.5%	Financial 53.7%	Financial 35.5%	Health 42.3%	Telecom Services 53.1%	Materials 25.6%	Health 25.6%	Materials 1.0%	Materials 6.0%
	Energy 13.4%	Consum. Staples 42.7%	Telecom Services 16.7%	Telecom Services 15.8%	Consum. Staples 8.7%	Telecom Services 41.8%	Consum. Staples 26.6%	Telecom Services 41.1%	Health 43.5%	Consum. Discret. 24.8%	Financial 24.8%	Industrial -7.3%	Energy 1.5%
Performance	Industrial 12.7%	Consum. Discret. 36.6%	Materials 11.1%	Energy 15.7%	Materials 6.6%	Consum. Staples 40.2%	Energy 25.9%	Consum. Staples 34.4%	Consum. Discret. 41.2%	Industrial 19.8%	Consum. Staples 19.8%	Consum. Staples -8.3%	Financial -4.5%
	Health 11.1%	Industrial 32.4%	Industrial 10.1%	Materials 15.6%	Energy 3.6%	Info. Tech. 39.1%	Industrial 24.9%	Consum. Discret. 33.3%	Consum. Staples 15.5%	Telecom Services 18.9%	Energy 15.5%	Financial -10.7%	Consum. Discret. -9.6%
	Telecom Services 8.8%	Materials 26.4%	Utilities 6.8%	Consum. Discret. 14.7%	Industrial -2.6%	Industrial 38.8%	Health 21.6%	Info. Tech. 27.8%	Utilities 14.9%	Energy 18.2%	Industrial 4.9%	Energy -12.3%	Utilities -12.8%
	Financial 7.4%	Utilities 23.9%	Consum. Staples 6.1%	Utilities 13.5%	Financial -2.9%	Utilities 32.7%	Materials 15.4%	Industrial 27.0%	Industrial 11.5%	Financial 3.8%	Materials -14.4%	Health -12.4%	Industrial -15.4
	Info. Tech. 6.6%	Telecom Services 13.5%	Info. Tech. 2.4%	Financial 11.3%	Telecom Services -4.7%	Energy 31.0%	Consum. Discret. 13.6%	Energy 25.2%	Financial 11.4%	Utilities -9.3%	Consum. Discret. -20.0%	Telecom Services -13.7%	Health -16.9%
	Materials 6.4%	Info. Tech. 11.9%	Energy 1.9%	Consum. Staples -4.4%	Consum. Discret. -7.6%	Materials 20.8%	Utilities 5.7%	Utilities 24.8%	Energy 0.8%	Health -10.3%	Telecom Services -38.8%	Info. Tech. -25.9%	Info. Tech. -32.8%
Worst	Utilities 6.2%	Energy 6.9%	Health -15.2%	Health -6.7%	Utilities -11.6%	Consum. Discret. 20.3%	Telecom Services 0.2%	Materials 8.1%	Materials 6.6%	Consum. Staples -15.5%	Info. Tech. -40.6%	Utilities -32.5%	Telecom Services -34.7%

Source: Morgan Stanley

Year to date through June 21, 2002. Performance for all cited indices is calculated on a total return basis with dividends reinvested. Categories are based upon S&P 500 GICS Sectors.

Historical S&P/MSCI Style Performance (fig.28)

	1990	1991	1992	1993	1994	1995	1996	1997	1998	1999	2000	2001	YTD
Best	Growth -0.3%	Small Cap 46.1%	Small Cap 18.5%	Internat. 30.5%	Internat. 6.2%	Value 38.3%	Large Cap 23.2%	Value 38.3%	Growth 38.7%	Growth 33.2%	Mid Cap 8.2%	Small Cap 1.0%	Value -4.5%
	Large Cap -3.2%	Mid Cap 41.5%	Mid Cap 16.3%	Small Cap 18.9%	Growth 2.7%	Large Cap 37.5%	Growth 23.1%	Growth 37.2%	Large Cap 28.7%	Internat. 25.3%	Value 7.0%	Mid Cap -7.0%	Internat. -4.8%
	Value -8.1%	Growth 41.2%	Value 13.8%	Value 18.1%	Large Cap 1.4%	Growth 37.2%	Value 21.6%	Mid Cap 34.5%	Internat. 18.2%	Small Cap 21.3%	Small Cap -3.0%	Value -7.4%	Small Cap -5.1%
	Mid Cap -11.5%	Large Cap 30.6%	Large Cap 7.8%	Mid Cap 14.3%	Small Cap -1.8%	Mid Cap 34.5%	Mid Cap 19.0%	Large Cap 33.3%	Value 15.6%	Large Cap 21.0%	Large Cap -9.1%	Large Cap -13.0%	Mid Cap -5.3%
	Small Cap -19.5%	Value 24.6%	Growth 5.0%	Large Cap 10.1%	Value -2.0%	Small Cap 28.4%	Small Cap 16.5%	Small Cap 28.4%	Mid Cap 10.1%	Mid Cap 18.2%	Internat. -15.2%	Growth -20.9%	Large Cap -13.3%
Worst	Internat. -24.7%	Internat. 10.2%	Internat. -13.9%	Growth 2.9%	Mid Cap -2.1%	Internat. 9.4%	Internat. 4.4%	Internat. 0.2%	Small Cap -2.5%	Value 7.3%	Growth -22.4%	Internat. -22.6%	Growth -21.2%

Source: Morgan Stanley

Year to date through June 21, 2002. Performance for all cited indices is calculated on a total return basis with dividends reinvested. Indices used for categories include: MSCI EAFE for International, Russell 1000 Growth for Growth, S&P 500 for Large Cap, Russell 1000 Value for Value, Russell Midcap for Midcap, and Russell 2000 for Small cap.

The current crop of ETFs make sector investing easy. Not only that, but ETFs bring an efficiency to sector investing that is hard to emulate because of the broad index approach they take. Instead of relying on a manager to make good representative picks in the sector at hand, an ETF simply snaps up the sector index and is done with it. There's no active manager risk and you can be assured that you're going to be along for the ride, though because of concentration restrictions perhaps not always the entire ride.

There are five sector ETF offerings in Canada, all by BGI Canada Limited. These iUnits are in energy, information technology, gold, financials and REITS (real estate investment trusts). More sector ETFs are expected in the future. In the U.S., there's an astonishing 47 sector ETFs, including 15 sector HOLDRS out of 17 HOLDRS in total.[3]

These are the sectors currently represented by ETFs and HOLDRS in the U.S.:

iShares Dow Jones Sectors
Basic Materials
Consumer Cyclicals
Consumer Non-Cyclicals
Energy
Financials
Financial Services
Healthcare
Industrial
Real Estate
Technology
Telecommunications
Utilities

Select Sector SPDRs
Consumer Discretionary
Consumer Staples
Energy
Financial
Healthcare
Industrial
Materials
Technology
Utilities

HOLDRS
B2B Internet
Biotech
Broadband
Internet
Internet Architecture
Internet Infrastructure
Oil Services
Pharmaceutical
Regional Bank
Retail
Semiconductor
Software
Telecommunications
Utilities
Wireless

iShares Goldman Sachs Sectors
Natural Resources
Networking
Semiconductor
Software
Technology

streetTRACKS Sectors
Wilshire REIT Index
Morgan Stanley
 High-tech 35 Index
Morgan Stanley
 Internet Index
Fortune e-50 Index

Others
iShares NASDAQ Biotech
iShares Cohen
 and Steers Realty Majors

HOLDRS

HOLDRS are fixed baskets of securities that trade on a stock exchange. (To learn more about them, see the end of Chapter Three.) HOLDRS have no concentration limitations, but U.S.-based ETFs, including sector ETFs, must abide by some concentration rules: no more than 25% of a fund's assets can be invested in a single security, and the sum of all securities in the fund making up more than 5% of the fund cannot collectively exceed 50% of the fund's assets. This diversification requirement is most likely to impinge on sector ETFs because of their relatively narrow focus. There is no similar concentration restriction imposed by regulators on ETFs in Canada, but BGI Canada's iUnits sector ETFs have a 25% cap on the weighting of any one company in its Canadian sector funds—in keeping with the 25% cap the S&P folks have imposed on their own index. Such restrictions ensure a diversified portfolio but they can affect the tracking of an uncapped index—and will—when highly weighted companies become market favourites as Nortel Networks did in early 2000 when it took over more than a third of the TSE 300's weighting.

Some Sector Strategies

Jumping in and out of sectors is for the self-confident, active investor or an investor with an investment advisor of similar qualities, but if you get it right it can give you spectacular returns. One capital intensive way to play the sectors involves buying up all the Sector SPDRs in weights that you judge to be most opportune. Since all nine Sector SPDRs equals the entire S&P 500 Index, you would have large cap exposure with your own customized sector weightings. Not only that, but you are then free to trade the sectors individually. Ideally, you'd be selling the falling sectors and riding the winning sectors and using the tax loss on the non-performing sectors to offset the capital gains on the ascendant sectors. You can do this, too, with the iShares Dow Jones sector ETFs which together make up all of the Dow Jones U.S. Total Market Index.

For those whose investment stakes are not so large, there are more modest ways of sector investing. Analysts have found some basic sector rotation patterns to be fairly consistent across market cycles based on the reaction of sectors to interest rate movements.

Sector Rotation Strategy Model (fig. 29)

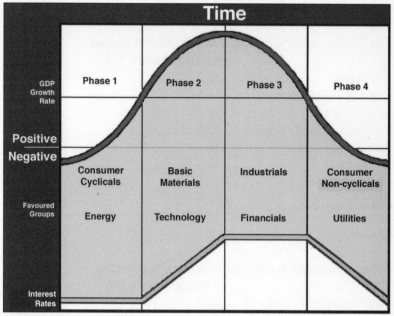

Reprinted with permission from *Technical Analysis of STOCKS & COMMODITIES™* magazine.
©1997 Technical Analysis, Inc., (800) 832-4642, *www.Traders.com*

Morgan Stanley have honed sector interest rate sensitivity to a fine point. They studied six business cycles to the end of 2000 and found that equity returns averaged 15.7% for the first six months following a second U.S. Federal Reserve interest rate cut, and 18.4% for the 12 months following the second rate cut. In an Equity Research Report called "Using ETFs to Capitalize on Sectors Favored for Recovery," the Morgan Stanley equity team says, "As soon as investors became convinced that the Fed was committed to promoting recovery, as evidenced by its second interest rate cut, aggressive sectors started to outperform defensive ones. After the second rate cut, investors began to focus on sectors that were positioned to benefit from economic and earnings recovery." [4]

Average S&P Sector Returns During Fed Easing Cycles Since 1981 (fig. 30)

Six-month period following the second Fed Easing

	Average Return (%)
Financials	19.0
Consumer Discretionary	18.5
Health Care	16.7
Information Technology	13.9
Consumer Staples	13.7
Industrials	13.0
Telecom Services	11.6
Materials	10.9
Energy	10.3
Utilities	8.5

12-month period following the second Fed easing

	Average Return (%)
Information Technology	20.9
Consumer Discretionary	19.9
Health Care	19.0
Financials	16.7
Industrials	16.5
Consumer Staples	15.7
Materials	13.8
Telecom Services	10.9
Energy	9.6
Utilities	6.7

Source: Morgan Stanley Equity Research, Jan. 20, 2001

Most sector rotation strategies are correlated to interest rate movements but there are any number of other economic factors that might serve a similar purpose with enough cleverness and research. Some sophisticated quantitative analysts are beginning to apply their trade to ETFs. This work makes ETFs all the more interesting to brokers and investors who want to employ ETFs in active trading strategies using sector and/or regional tilts. The fact that the target investments are diversified portfolios rather than individual stocks does mitigate risk, too.

Tantalizing? Here's how one investment company in Calgary weds fundamental analysis with ETF investments.

Fundamental Analysis and Sector ETFs

"We do an asset allocation approach to the investment process and we use twelve asset classes," explains Kevin Dehod, Vice President with McLean & Partners Wealth Management Ltd. "Each client has a different percentage in those asset classes depending on their risk tolerance."

Dehod says his company takes an active approach using individual sector ETFs.

They examine the companies within a sector ETF to find their current and projected price to earnings ratio (P/E) and the expected earnings growth of each individual company. They then blend the averages and if the sector as a whole is trading below its historical norms, that's a buy signal. "Before we buy an ETF, we look at the fundamental valuations first," he says. "Is it cheap historically? What's going on around the industry? These are the things we look at."

Dehod says that in the fall of 2001 his company overweighted consumer staples in the U.S. because they were concerned about an economic slowdown. "Our economic outlook caused us to go into very defensive, stable companies. Do you buy Gillette, Proctor & Gamble or Safeway? We decided to buy the consumer non-cyclical ETF. That was a smart decision because it hasn't done too badly relative to the market.

"That decision was based on a macro economic outlook, but we did our valuations as a check," he continues. "Consumer staples typically trade between 90% to 120% of the S&P 500 P/E. If they start to move toward 120%, we'll take a hard look at it."

Gold has been an even better play for the investment manager. "In Canada we wanted to take a fairly large position in gold in June 2001, but we didn't know what companies to buy because of hedging programs, international properties and so on. There's a lot of stuff going on in a gold company. But we knew the price to cash flow ratios in gold stocks were the lowest they'd been in about ten years. We also felt the U.S. dollar was overvalued and there's a strong correlation between a falling dollar and rising gold prices. We were also in a period of pretty close to negative short-term interest rates and gold tends to do well then, too." The company bought the BGI's iGold ETF, a portfolio of nine gold companies. "It worked like a charm," Dehod reports.

The company also tilts value and growth styles in the U.S. market especially in the midcap range. "About two years ago there was a huge divergence where growth stocks had way outperformed value stocks and growth's valuation metrics were much higher than the normal range. In that case you might want to tilt your portfolio towards more value then.

Being really aggressive, you could short the growth and go long the value."

Dehod uses broad based ETFs such as the iShares S&P Europe 350 Index Fund exposure and occasionally will venture into a country ETF. For Asia he prefers using an active manager. "You're better off going with a good stock picker on the ground over there," he feels.

To try Dehod's sector strategy yourself, you'll need access to similar number crunching. There are a number of companies who sell the kind of fundamental analysis required, like The Bank Credit Analyst in Montréal.

Here are two sample portfolios Dehod provided to give a snapshot look at his approach.

Growth Portfolio
McLean & Partners Wealth Management Ltd. (fig. 31)
www.mcleanpartners.com

Canadian Large Cap (25% Weighting)
iUnits S&P/TSX 60 Index Fund	10%
McLean & Partners Dividend Growth Stocks	90%
(Active Management)	

U.S. (19% Weighting)
McLean & Partners U.S. Dividend Growth Stocks	50%
(Active Management)	
iShares Dow Jones U.S. Healthcare	15%
iShares S&P/BARRA Growth	10%
Select Sector SPDR Financial	10%
iShares Dow Jones U.S. Utilities	10%
iShares Goldman Sachs Software	5%

Europe (19% Weighting)
Active Management	60%
iShares S&P Europe 350	20%
iShares MSCI U.K.	20%

Far East (9% Weighting)
Active Management	100%

REITs & Trusts (4% weighting)
Active Management	100%

High Yield Bonds (5% Weighting)
Active Management	100%

Market Alternative Equity (5% Weighting)
Hedge Funds	100%

Canadian Bonds (14% Weighting)
McLean & Partners Active Bond/Preferred Share Management	100%

Note: As of September 26, 2002

Balanced Portfolio
McLean & Partners Wealth Management Ltd. (fig. 32)
www.mcleanpartners.com

Canadian Large Cap (23% Weighting)
iUnits S&P/TSX 60 Index Fund	10%
McLean & Partners Dividend Growth Stocks	90%
(Active Management)	

U.S. (7% Weighting)
McLean & Partners U.S. Dividend Growth Stocks	50%
(Active Management)	
iShares Dow Jones U.S. Healthcare	15%
iShares S&P/BARRA Value	15%
iShares Dow Jones U.S. Consumer Non-Cylical	10%
iShares Dow Jones U.S. Utilities	10%

Europe (7% Weighting)
Active Management	50%
iShares S&P Europe 350	25%
iShares MSCI U.K.	25%

Far East (6% Weighting)
Active Management	100%

REITs & Trusts (3% weighting)
Active Management	100%

High Yield Bonds (3% Weighting)
Active Management	100%

Market Alternative Equity (5% Weighting)
Hedge Funds	100%

Canadian Bonds (46% Weighting)
McLean & Partners Active Bond/Prefered Share Management	100%

Note: As of September 26, 2002

Seasonality

Seasonality is a popular topic for quantitative analysts. Hidden among the barrage of market data, they look for and sometimes find odd regularities or associations. Perhaps the most well-known of these is the correlation between the U.S. markets and the presidential cycle. Usually the fourth year of an administration finds the market booming. Markets will continue going higher after the election of a new president and during his legislative honeymoon. Into the second year midterm markets start coughing with the worst of it around October. After that the cycle starts again and markets begin moving up.

Some commonly observed seasonal patterns with the S&P/TSX have lead to the saying "Buy when it snows. Sell when it goes." Buying the broad Canadian market at the end of November and selling at the end of March would have been profitable in 15 of the past 20 years, (reliability of 75%) The same pattern also existed with broadly based U.S. indices. Buying the S&P 500 at the end of November and selling at the end of March would have been profitable in 16 of the past 20 years (reliability of 80%).

Sectors also show seasonality. Selected sectors of the S&P/TSX Composite Index have been more profitable and reliable than other sectors during the end of November to the end of March period. Best performing sectors were Forest Products, Communications and Media, Conglomerates and Metals and Minerals.

There appears to be strong seasonal patterns in Canadian oil and gas stocks. "Buy when it's coldest. Sell when it's hottest." That advice means buying at the end of December and selling at the end of July. Had you done that for the past 16 years, you would have returned an average of 11% per period, 13 out of 16 years (reliability of 81%). If you'd done the opposite and bought at the end of July and sold at the end of December, you would have averaged a return of -1.8% per period during the past 15 years. Losses were recorded in 9 periods out of 15 (reliability of 60%).

Two Canadian investment advisors have formulated a simple calendar investing strategy. Brooke Thackray and Bruce Lindsay have done extensive technical work which shows, they say, that the best time to enter the market is October 28 and the best time to exit the market is May 5 (conservatively) or July 19 (aggressively). They say their method produced returns 50% higher than the TSE 300's return for the 15 years of the study. From the period historical data was available to them (1985-1999), they report that the TSE 300 returned 8.23% (without dividends) compared to their "Time In, Time Out" method with a 12.99% average return.[5] They've also had success beating the NASDAQ, S&P 500 and Dow Jones indices.

ETFs fit well with a timing strategy like this as they allow you to get full market exposure while also making it easy and inexpensive to enter and leave the market at precise times. And if Thackray and Lindsay haven't convinced you to step entirely out of the market, you could consider selling covered calls on your ETFs during periods of seasonal weakness.

While recognizing that equity markets, sectors and stocks do often have seasonal characteristics, investors should use a mix of technical, quantitative and fundamental analysis before buying any investment. But when you're ready to pounce on a perceived upswing, ETFs are ready and waiting to spring.

Regional Tilts, or Not

ETFs are also well situated for regional rotation or tilts. When you think Japan is about to emerge from its 12-year plus slumber, socking some money into iShares MSCI Japan might be for you. Foresee political unrest in Hong Kong? Short iShares MSCI Hong Kong. There are 21 country-specific ETFs (all iShares). If a single country is too narrow a bet for you, a clutch of geographically related country ETFs will serve, too. There's even an iShares EMU. Regional coverage is thin but growing. There is an ETF for the Asia-Pacific area without Japan, a Latin America ETF and new emerging markets ETFs expected out at the end of 2002.

For the more conservative, you might just want to get more general global exposure. Right now there are two ETFs and a HOLDRS that can give you that. SSgA's Global Titans has about 50 blue chip stocks from around the world. BGI's iShares S&P Global 100 holds 100 large global companies, and Merrill Lynch's Market 2000+ HOLDRs has 57 large stocks from an assortment of countries. But these products are all considered foreign content for RRSP purposes. Which brings us to an important point.

In your drive to get international exposure with ETFs, be careful to take note of RRSP eligibility. Don't hold BGI's new RRSP global ETFs outside of an RRSP account. They're designed to be 100% RRSP-eligible and as a result all the income from the iUnits S&P 500 Index RSP Fund and the iUnits MSCI International Equity RSP Fund is taxed as interest income and at your highest marginal rate. Non-registered accounts, as a result, should avoid them. (See the Appendix for new products under development.)

Global Sector Investing

Now that ETFs have made tactical sector and country investing devilishly easy, globalization may very well have diminished its usefulness. Take a deep breath. There's evidence that sector investing is most effectively done across global markets, at least in developed countries. Salomon Smith Barney research argues that globalization has meant many developed markets now move in close synchronization with each other, especially countries in the European Monetary Union. This change in correlations has led to a trend away from country-based investing in favour of global sector-based investing, at least in developed markets. In emerging markets, the country effect still seems strong.[6]

But take heart. There are now five global sector ETFs to the rescue. A series of five ETFs based on S&P's ten new global sector indices have been launched. They cover the energy, financial, healthcare, telecommunications and technology sectors globally. This gives investors a totally new way to structure their asset allocation. Europeans have already caught on to this as the number of sector ETFs listed in Europe has grown dramatically. This is a trend worth paying attention to. The only constant in the investment world is change.

Style Weighting

The investment management world is divided into two halves: value managers and growth managers. You might say they're arch rivals and seldom thrive together. During the technology frenzy in the late 1990s, growth investing completely eclipsed value. There were even headlines about famous value investors like Warren Buffett and John Templeton being icons of times long gone. Technology was to so profoundly change our productivity that price to earnings ratios no longer had any significance and these old guys just couldn't accept the world had changed around them. Companies without earnings were exploding with promise and their stock price rode along with the optimism. Then, POW! These companies exploded right in their investors' faces. And the bargain hunting value style of investment management reasserted its dominion in 2000.

In a pure textbook sense, growth and value are opposing money management styles. In the reality of the marketplace, only a minority of money managers are extremists. Most subscribe to an approach that includes both camps to some extent, so let's lay out the camps. Staunch growth managers look for companies with faster than average gains in earnings over a specified period, usually a few years. They don't take much notice of price to earnings, or price-to-book ratios. During the tech bubble, some growth managers didn't even hold out for actual earnings growth. A company with the likely prospect of above-average earnings growth was enough to ignite their buy buttons. Sometimes growth managers are really momentum investors in disguise, jumping on stocks whose price shows a lot of upward movement.

This would make pure value investors cringe in horror. These are the old-fashioned, bargain-minded folks who look for companies with good fundamentals but in an industry that's fallen out of favour. Value managers have to hold their noses to buy a stock with a price to earnings ratio over 20. Contrast that with all the growth managers who bought Nortel Networks when its P/E was over 100.

In some years, typically when the economy is contracting, value managers look smart. In other years, growth managers get the glory. For the entire period between 1994 and 1999 large cap growth stocks delivered much higher returns than large cap value stocks, but from 1994-1997 value stocks lead the pack for both mid and small caps.[7] From 2000 on, value once again seems in ascendance. The prudent mutual fund investor should have a mix of both investment styles. With ETFs you can go one better and actually trade on anticipation of broad investment style changes, or tactically weight your portfolio with a growth or value bias. You might, for instance, want to go heavy on growth at the beginning of an economic expansion, and then tilt your portfolio in favour of value as the expansion slows.

Here's a list of the 20 style-based ETFs:

Broad Market Growth
>iShares Russell 3000 Growth
>TD Select Canadian Growth

Broad Market Value
>iShares Russell 3000 Value
>TD Select Canadian Value

Large Cap Growth
>iShares S&P 500/BARRA Growth
>iShares Russell 1000 Growth
>streetTRACKS Dow Jones U.S. Large Cap Growth

Large Cap Value
>iShares S&P 500/BARRA Value
>iShares Russell 1000 Value
>streetTRACKS Dow Jones U.S. Large Cap Value

Mid Cap Growth
>iShares S&P MidCap/BARRA Growth
>iShares Russell Midcap Growth

Mid Cap Value
>iShares S&P MidCap/BARRA Value
>iShares Russell MidCap Value

Small Cap Growth
>iShares S&P SmallCap/BARRA Growth
>iShares Russell 2000 Growth
>streetTRACKS Dow Jones Small Cap Growth

Small Cap Value
>iShares S&P SmallCap/BARRA Value
>iShares Russell 2000 Value
>streetTRACKS Dow Jones Small Cap Value

These style ETFs are based on four different indices each of which defines "value" and "growth" in different ways. (See "Making Sense of the Indices" Appendix for more details.) Before you buy one, make sure you know just what kind of value or growth you're getting into. As of March 2002 there were 15 companies in the Dow Jones U.S. Large Cap Growth Index which were also in the S&P 500/BARRA Value Index, and 30 companies in both the Dow Jones U.S. Large Cap Value Index and the S&P 500/BARRA Growth Index.[8]

The Capitalization Curve

Market capitalization is a measure of a company's size—and size does matter. Large cap companies tend to move in tandem. Similar patterns are also seen with small and mid cap groupings. Smaller cap stocks have fewer research analysts following them and are subject to greater price swings. This makes them particularly ripe for a smart stock picker to exploit—though even at that, the majority fail to match their benchmark indices.

According to Morningstar (U.S.) research, from 1986-2001, 81% of large cap managers, 67% of mid cap managers and 56% of small cap managers underperformed their benchmarks after costs.[9] So no matter what part of the capitalization curve you want to pursue, indexing is still the best way to do it.

Analysts at Morgan Stanley believe mid and small cap stocks tend to do well during an economic recovery, especially when stock valuations are relatively low compared with large caps. Their research also leads them to conclude that mid caps "offer the best risk/reward ratios over long periods of time...while their performance is highly correlated with small caps."[10]

A savvy investor could shift from mid caps to large caps and back again as the relative valuations and general economic conditions change. Add a style dimension to that and you could hedge your bets a little with ETFs in mid cap growth and large cap value.

You can ignore the capitalization factor completely by investing in broad based ETFs like the Wilshire 5000, but you could get more octane out of your investments by making the right call on the capitalization curve.

Using Options with ETFs

Options may conjure complicated, obscure trading strategies that only Nobel prize winners can really understand. But in truth, there are some simple and conservative option strategies that can and should be used by more investors to minimize risk and increase returns. One of the great advantages of ETFs is that they can use all the same option strategies commonly used for single stock holdings as long as there are option contracts available on the ETF. So far, there are options on all the HOLDRS, all the Select Sector SPDRs, and many of the larger, more popular ETFs.

Here's a list of the ETFs with options and where the options trade. Currently the sole Canadian-based ETF option trades on the Montréal Exchange, but more are expected in the future.

ETFs and HOLDRS With Options (Fig. 33)

Trading Symbol	Exchange Traded Funds	Major Options Exchange
	Canadian Market	
	Large Cap	
XIU	iUnits S&P/TSX 60 Index Fund	MONTREAL
	U.S. Market	
	Broad Market	
IWV	iShares Russell 3000 Index Fund	AMEX, CBOE*
VTI	Total Stock Market VIPERs	AMEX

Trading Symbol	Exchange Traded Funds	Major Options Exchange
	Large Cap	
DIA	DIAMOND Trust Series 1	CBOE
IWB	iShares Russell 1000 Index Fund	AMEX
OEF	iShares S&P 100 Index Fund	CBOE
QQQ	NASDAQ-100 Index Tracking Stock	AMEX, CBOE
FFF	streetTRACKS Fortune 500 Index Fund	AMEX
	Mid Cap	
IWR	iShares Russell Midcap Index Fund	CBOE
IJH	iShares S&P MidCap 400 Index Fund	AMEX
MDY	Standard & Poors MidCap 400 Dep Rec	AMEX
	Small Cap	
IWM	iShares Russell 2000 Index Fund	AMEX
IJR	iShares S&P SmallCap 600 Index Fund	AMEX
	Broad Market Growth	
IWZ	iShares Russell 3000 Growth Index Fund	CBOE
	Broad Market Value	
IWW	iShares Russell 3000 Value Index Fund	CBOE
	Large Cap Growth	
IWF	iShares Russell 1000 Gr Idx Fund	AMEX
	Large Cap Value	
IWD	iShares Russell 1000 Val Idx Fund	AMEX
	Mid Cap Growth	
IWP	iShares Russell Midcap Growth Index Fund	CBOE
IJK	iShares S&P MidCap 400/BARRA Gr Idx Fund	AMEX
	Mid Cap Value	
IWS	iShares Russell Midcap Value Index Fund	CBOE
IJJ	iShares S&P MidCap 400/BARRA Val Idx Fund	AMEX

Trading Symbol	Exchange Traded Funds	Major Options Exchange
	Small Cap Growth	
IWO	iShares Russell 2000 Gr Index Fund	AMEX
IJT	iShares S&P SmallCap 600/BARRA Gr Idx Fund	AMEX
	Small Cap Value	
IWN	iShares Russell 2000 Val Index Fund	AMEX
IJS	iShares S&P SmallCap 600/BARRA Val Idx Fund	AMEX
	Consumer Staples	
XLP	Consumer Staples Select Sector SPDR Fund	AMEX
	Energy	
XLE	Energy Select Sector SPDR Fund	AMEX
IYE	iShares DJ US Energy Sector Index Fund	CBOE
	Financials	
XLF	Financial Select Sector SPDR Fund	AMEX
IYF	iShares DJ US Financial Sector Index Fund	AMEX
	Healthcare	
XLV	Health Care Select Sector SPDR Fund	AMEX
IBB	iShares NASDAQ Biotechnology Index Fund	AMEX, CBOE
IYH	iShares DJ US Healthcare Sector Index Fund	CBOE
	Industrials	
XLI	Industrial Select Sector SPDR Fund	AMEX
	Materials	
XLB	Materials Select Sector SPDR Fund	AMEX
	Technology-Broad Based	
IYW	iShares DJ US Technology Sector Index Fund	AMEX
IGM	iShares Goldman Sachs Tech Index Fund	CBOE
XLK	Technology Select Sector SPDR Fund	AMEX
	Technology-Internet	
FEF	streetTRACKS Fortune e-50 Index Tkg Stock	AMEX

Trading Symbol	Exchange Traded Funds	Major Options Exchange
	Technology-Other	
IGN	iShares Goldman Sachs Networking Index Fund	CBOE
IGW	iShares Goldman Sachs Semiconductor Index Fund	CBOE
IGV	iShares Goldman Sachs Software Index Fund	CBOE
	Telecommunications	
IYZ	iShares DJ US Telecom Sector Index Fund	AMEX
	Utilities	
IDU	iShares DJ US Utilities Sector Index Fund	CBOE
XLU	Utilities Select Sector SPDR Fund	AMEX
	Broad Based Global	
DGT	streetTRACKS DJ Global Titans Index Fund	CBOE
	Broad Based Regional	
EFA	iShares MSCI EAFE	CBOE

Trading Symbol	HOLDRS	Major Options Exchange
	Consumer Discretionary	
RTH	Retail HOLDRS	AMEX, CBOE
	Energy	
OIH	Oil Service HOLDRS	AMEX, CBOE
	Financials	
RKH	Regional Bank HOLDRS	AMEX, CBOE
	Healthcare	
BBH	Biotech HOLDRS	AMEX
PPH	Pharmaceutical HOLDRS	AMEX, CBOE
	Technology-Internet	
BHH	B2B Internet HOLDRS	CBOE
HHH	Internet HOLDRS	AMEX, CBOE
IAH	Internet Architecture HOLDRS	AMEX, CBOE
	Technology-Other	
BDH	Broadband HOLDRS	AMEX, CBOE
SMH	Semiconductor HOLDRS	AMEX, CBOE
SWH	Software HOLDRS	AMEX, CBOE
	Telecommunications	
TTH	Telecom HOLDRS	AMEX, CBOE
WMH	Wireless HOLDRS	AMEX, CBOE
	Utilities	
UTH	Utilities HOLDRS	AMEX, CBOE
	Broad Based Global	
MKH	Market 2000+ HOLDRS	AMEX
	Regional	
EKH	Europe 2001 HOLDRS	AMEX

AMEX = American Stock Exchange
CBOE = Chicago Board Options Exchange

Covered Call Writing

One of the most common and conservative option strategies is "covered call writing." Writing a call on a stock or ETF is simply selling a contract that gives the contract buyer the right, but not the obligation, to buy the asset at a specific price some time before the expiration of the contract. You have the obligation to sell that asset at the agreed price if the contract is exercised. A call is "covered" when you own the asset you are writing the option on. If you didn't own it already, that would be, in the street's vivid language, a naked call.

Suppose you own 200 i6o units at a current market price of $34 and you believe the market is going to stay fairly flat for the next three months. You could write two call options on your 200 units to sell them at $35 any time during the next three months. You'll receive a premium for the sale of the option, say $1.40 per share to equal $280 (200 x $1.40). As long as the market does not go above $35, (what's known as the strike price), you'll keep your units. If you end up having to sell your units, you've lost out on any appreciation of the units above $35, but you've pocketed the $280 premium. Options come in a wide variety of expiration dates. Conventional options can go as far out as nine months. Beyond that there are "LEAPS," or **L**ong-term **E**quity **A**ntici**P**ation **S**ecurities, that go out as far as three years and are available on many U.S. ETFs.

Put Options

If you want to protect the value of your ETF position you can buy a put option at a strike price of, say, $30. Buying a put gives you the right, but again, not the obligation, to sell the ETF at a certain price before the expiration of the contract. You have to pay the premium but in return you get a guaranteed price for your current holding. The option premium in this case is just like paying an insurance premium, because you are essentially insuring your ETF's value for the period of the contract. If the market value goes below $30 near the expiration of the contract, you could exercise the put and sell your ETF position for $30 per unit or sell the put and lower the effective cost of your ETF position.

Call Options

A call option gives you the right to buy a security at a specified price before the expiry of the contract. In exchange for paying a premium, you get the opportunity to capture future gains on an index without having to buy the index. You risk the option premium and that's all; whereas if you bought the ETF and it dropped in price you could be exposed to a much greater loss and you'd have a whole lot more money tied up.

As you can imagine, ETFs are suitable for all kinds of option strategies —limited only by imagination and the availability of options. If you're just starting with options, it's a good idea to enlist the help of an options licensed full-service broker who can help you direct your strategy, remind you of expirations and generally lead you through the process. In the next chapter we'll show you how one investment advisor uses covered calls to enhance his clients' returns.

Short Selling

ETFs can be sold short like any other stock. Short selling involves selling something you don't own in the anticipation that its price will go down. In order to do this your brokerage must borrow the stock which you must eventually return by buying on the open market. The short seller pays interest to the stock lender until the lender requires the shares returned or until the short seller voluntarily closes the position. To close the position, the short seller has to purchase the stock at the then current market price and return it to the lender. If the price has gone down, the short seller has made a profit by selling high and buying low. If, on the other hand, the stock has gone up in price, he's lost money by selling high and buying back even higher. Perhaps it sounds like Russian roulette, but short selling ETFs might be thought to be less risky than short selling individual stocks.

First of all, there's a huge bank of ETF shares available so you're unlikely to get something known as a "short squeeze" in which so many shares are loaned out that there are too few in circulation to comfortably buy back and close all the short positions. This causes the price of the shorted shares to go up and ruin the strategy.

Second, it is arguably easier to forecast general index trends than it is to predict the future value of an individual stock. Suppose you think the U.S. market is going to decline because of threats of war. You can short sell a SPDR or a DIAMOND. If you've made the right prediction, you get to buy back the ETF you previously borrowed (and sold) for a price lower than you sold it.

Most importantly, because of their diversified nature, ETFs are exempt from the uptick rule in the U.S. market. There, a short sale can occur only if the last sale was at a higher price than the sale before it (an uptick) or, if the last sale was flat, the previous sale to that must have been higher. ETFs can be shorted on the same price or on a downtick, which is a tremendous advantage in a falling market.

In Canada, no stock can be sold short into a declining market but there is no uptick rule. A short sale must be done at a price no less than the price of the last board lot trade in that stock. Even Canadian-based ETFs have to observe this rule.

You would want to short sell an ETF when you are confident the index is going to go down—or to hedge a long position in the same index, although buying a put option is a far less dangerous strategy to accomplish the same end.

Go with Caution

Many of these ETF strategies involve some sort of market timing. Tilts, rotations, style weightings; all these require a bet on the shape of things to come in the market. That's why John Bogle, the founder of Vanguard Group and arch advocate for index mutual funds, says that ETFs are like giving investors a loaded shotgun. ETFs are easy to trade; therein lies their beauty and their power to harm. Frequent trading most often results in poorer returns because the investment decisions are made in the heat of emotion and often disconnected from a long-term strategy. Market timing is a tool to be used in moderation, and is not recommended for novice investors who are best advised to hold a core broad index and perhaps, a small assortment of style/cap indices.

Technical Analysis and ETFs

Sophisticated investors with a penchant for technical analysis will welcome the ease ETFs bring to their strategic implementations.

The Sport of Kings (Who Cheat)

Technical analysis has been called the sport of kings (who cheat legally). By charting price movements and trading volume, technical analysts try to identify market trends as they emerge. Chip Anderson, the founder of *stockcharts.com*, likens it to betting on a horse-race after the race has started. You'll have an advantage by being able to put your money on an early leader, but you won't win every time because leaders don't always finish first. Charts don't predict the future but, says Anderson, they will help you improve your odds of picking the winning horse.[11]

Interpreting charts to drive investment decisions may sound a little akin to palmistry unless you believe two things. First you must believe that price and volume action reflect all factors that can affect the future price of a stock. Then you must also believe that the market is not random; and trends are significant. With that foundation, seeing heads and shoulders in graphs and playing tick-tack-toe in point and figure charts will be the stuff dreams are made of.

Those dreams likely include ETFs because they are singularly useful for those chartists who track broad market movements. For the price of a single trade, you can capture the movement of an entire market in the time it takes to place an order. The really confident investors can also short a market using ETFs.

Two excellent technical Web sites have sections dedicated to ETFs. One site, *http://decisionpoint.com* tracks U.S. ETFs daily in a report they cleverly call the "Spider Web Daily." That subscriber-only service issues technical buy and sells on all U.S. ETFs. Another subscriber-only service at *http://dorseywright.com* provides an ETF iShares sector manager that builds portfolios using relative strengths. Their Conservative Sector ETF Portfolio and the Aggressive Sector ETF Portfolio are updated weekly and display the number of ETF shares to buy for any given portfolio size.

Fixed Income Meets ETFs

ETFs are too good an idea to restrict to equities. The broad diversification and transparency ETFs bring to other asset classes is an even bigger advantage in the fixed income area. Given the large minimum investment of a bond purchase ($10,000 or more), it is hard for investors to get a well diversified fixed income portfolio with good exposure to many maturity periods. That's why so many resort to bond mutual funds, but the drawback with those, of course, are their relatively high MERs, not to mention the tax inefficiency of active management.

Fixed income ETFs give you up-to-the-minute pricings, instant transactions, modest management fees and the freedom to tactically manage your fixed income investments in a way not feasible before. You can select a narrow maturity range or buy all three Treasury ETFs for exposure to the full yield curve, and you can easily pop in and out as your interest rate forecasts change. Being able to buy 100 high quality corporate bonds of assorted maturities is also a huge convenience and cost savings. Professional bond managers have long used corporate bonds to boost returns in many conservative government bond portfolios and now you can do the same—only better—by mitigating your risk with buying a whole portfolio of corporate bonds in one fell swoop.

U.S. fixed income ETFs have different characteristics from their Canadian counterparts. Canadian fixed income ETFs hold only one bond at any one time; whereas U.S. ETFs hold a portfolio of bonds and that leads to a number of important differences.

U.S.-based Fixed Income ETFs

Index-based
There are currently eight fixed income ETFs in the U.S.:

Fund	Ticker
iShares Lehman 1-3 Year Treasury	SHY
iShares Lehman 7-10 Year Treasury	IEF
iShares Lehman 20+ Year Treasury	TLT
iShares GS $ InvesTop™ Corporate	LQD
Treasury 1 FITRS	TFT
Treasury 2 FITRS	TOU
Treasury 5 FITRS	TFI
Treasury 10 FITRS	TTE

All eight of these ETFs are pegged to bond indices. The Lehman Treasury Bond indices are distinguished by the maturity duration of the underlying bonds: one short-term, one mid-term and one long-term index. The GS $ InvesTop Corporate Bond Index contains 100 investment grade corporate bonds of assorted maturities. The FITRS (pronounced "fighters") track U.S. treasury indices provided by Ryan Labs. More information on these fixed income ETFs and their underlying indices can be found in Appendix B. MERs on all these funds are a slender 0.15%.

Just a Sampling
However, none of these ETFs actually hold all the bonds in their respective indices. BGI, who manages the iShares, uses an approach called "stratified sampling" to select the bonds they believe are most representative of the overall index. The index is broken down into groups of similar bonds, and only a few bonds in each group are purchased for the fund. This sampling keeps costs down while still enabling the fund to track the index closely.

Dividends
U.S. fixed income ETFs pay interest income monthly. (Canadian

investors are subject to withholding tax on these distributions.) Capital gains are paid annually in cash.

Canadian Fixed Income ETFs

Not Index-based

Canada currently has two fixed income ETFs:

iUnits Government of Canada 5-year Bond Fund   XGV
iUnits Government of Canada 10-year Bond Fund   XGX

Neither of these funds are pegged to an index. Each fund holds one Government of Canada bond at a time. About once a year the bond is sold to buy another government bond closer to the fund's target duration. These funds run on a 0.25% MER.

Dividends

Interest income is paid semi-annually in cash. Capital gains are paid annually in new shares that are subsequently consolidated. (See Chapter Seven for more information.)

Managing Your Fixed Income Component

Bonds are an important component of any well-diversified portfolio and that is not just a motherhood statement. In the past four years, bonds have had a low correlation to the S&P 500.[12] That means bonds have generally done well when stocks have suffered.

Interest Rate Anticipation

Bond prices fluctuate with interest rate movements and the correlation is exact. As interest rates rise, bond prices go down. When interest rates drop, bond prices go up. It is an inverse relationship. Generally, long-term bonds are affected more dramatically than short-term bonds by interest rate swings simply because of their longer duration. Bond managers tend to stay with shorter maturities when they anticipate interest rate hikes, and favour longer maturities during periods of falling interest rates. ETFs allow you to do the very same thing. You can take defensive positions or opportunistic ones with the swiftness and ease of a single transaction and the cost of one brokerage fee all the while knowing you are protected from individual credit risk by owning a diversified bond portfolio.

Credit Quality Plays

Professional bond managers often look to the corporate bond sector for undervalued bonds. The most attractive of these are bonds from solid companies in beat up industries. Because the whole industry is unattractive, the bonds of any company within that industry will have to pay a premium interest rate to attract purchasers. Bond managers figure the likelihood of a solid company defaulting on its bonds is low and are happy to scoop up the interest premium.

This is an extremely difficult strategy for an individual investor to emulate. The analysis of credit risk is something best left to professionals. However, there are times in the market when corporate bonds generally pay a much higher interest premium than the risk they represent. This frequently happens in times of market turmoil or when investors have a pessimistic outlook on future corporate earnings.

Buying a basket of good quality corporates, like those in the iShares corporate bond fund, will mitigate the individual credit risk and will give you a chance to pump up your returns. Being able to jump in and out of the corporate market with your assessment of risk makes this an especially attractive opportunity especially when you need only one trade to accomplish this.

Principal Risk

There is one drawback to fixed income ETFs, but it is a fault they share with bond funds. Bond portfolios do not mature. The value of the fund is solely determined by market prices for the underlying securities. If, on the other hand, you held an individual bond to maturity, fluctuations in its value would be irrelevant to your return. Barring defaults, you will get the interest rate at which you bought the bond regardless of where interest rates go at any time, and your principal is fixed. In a portfolio with no maturity, this certainty does not exist and it is possible to lose principal with a bond fund or ETF.

Extremely risk adverse investors are probably better off sticking with individual bonds if they can tolerate no capital loss.

The Easiest Portfolio of All

After you've waded through complicated portfolio strategies you might be ready to settle into the couch, put your feet up and be paralyzed by indecision. That's when you call an investment advisor or manfully resolve to do the easiest thing possible without abdicating your responsibility altogether—employ the Couch Potato Strategy. This is a strategy formulated by Scott Burns, a U.S. personal finance journalist in 1991. It has the virtue of being dog simple, drop dead easy and really cheap.

Simply put half your money in an S&P 500 index and the other in to a U.S. government bond fund and put on your slippers. Rebalance to 50-50 once a year and guess what? From 1973 to 1990, the strategy would have returned an average of 10.3%, outscoring 70% of managers in those 17 years.

The strategy continued to do well through the 1990s, according to Glenn Flanagan and Tim Whitehead, who adapted this approach for Canadians in an article for the June 1999 issue of *MoneySense* magazine. Their Canadianized version for RRSPs has a third in a Canadian bond index fund, a third in a TSE 300 index fund and the last third in a fully RRSP eligible S&P 500 index fund. Backtesting the portfolio (because there were no RRSP-eligible index funds around a few years back) the pair determined that the Canadian Couch Potato Portfolio returned an average 13.7% over the past 25 years: "Its performance easily outdistanced both the TSE 300's performance over that period (10.9%) as well as Canadian long-term bonds (11.8%)." You can check on the Canadian Couch Potato Portfolio's current returns at *www.moneysense.ca*. It continues to outpace the S&P/TSX Composite Index (with MER) on an annualized basis.

Of course, the costs of the portfolio would become positively miserly if instead of index funds you employed ETFs to do the heavy idling. There's an ETF for all three asset classes now, so you can afford a glass of wine while you're lounging on the couch.

Canadian Couch Potato ETF Portfolio (fig. 34)

Weighting	ETF	MER
15%	iG5 (XGV)	0.25%
15%	iG10 (XGX)	0.25%
25%	TD Comp or TD Capped (TTF/TCF)	0.25%
30%	iRussell 3000 (IWV)	0.20%
15%	iIntR (XIN)	0.35%
100%	Portfolio Totals	0.25%

At a 0.25% MER for an ETF Couch Potato Portfolio, this strategy is as cheap as it is easy.

Resources

Some helpful resources are waiting to be discovered on BGI's U.S. Web site, *www.ishares.com*. There's a customized portfolio tracker and a customized watch list service. You can find an ETF allocator and an index tracker to see how various industry groups are performing. Refer to a handy consolidated price and symbols sheet for iShares, determine the historical premium and discount for any iShares, and look at a tracking error chart for any index associated with an iShares.

Advisors have access to even more sophisticated on-line tools. There's an allocation calculator and an asset class illustrator for determining the historical risk/return of a hypothetical portfolio. Core and satellite advocates will love the hypothetical portfolio tool to help you design satellite approaches.

What the Expert Says:

An Interview with Paul Mazzilli, Executive Director at Morgan Stanley in New York, and Director of Exchange Traded Fund Research.

Donna Green: You've written a lot about using investment strategies using ETFs, especially the Core and Satellite approach.

Paul Mazzilli: *Yes, Core and Satellite sounds so simple but it took a long time to get there. Now it's even in the CFA manual for chartered financial analysts training. I had worked in a prior job with a group that worked with some of the big, smart pension plans in the U.S. We found that currently as much as 40% of major pension plans are indexed. That's the core. It's hard to beat the markets in general so why not have all your portfolio in something that looks just like the market at a very low cost, well-diversified way? That's the whole core strategy.*

DG: What should be the core?

PM*: We've written research reports on the different cores: S&P 500, Dow Jones, Russell 3000, Wilshire 5000. Interestingly, they all pretty much represent the broad market and move together. I'm not comfortable giving asset allocation ranges because everybody's situation is different. People should work with their financial advisor to figure that out.*

DG: And outside the core?

PM*: On top of the core you can have sector allocations, growth versus value allocations, large cap versus small cap, real estate, international. Traditionally these smart pension plans would do it through outside managers. Now you can do it with ETFs.*

Finally, on top of the pyramid there's individual stock selection. We're not saying you should index everything. As a matter of fact some of these very large pension plans with as much as a $100 billion in assets, have their own research analysts who probably focus on less than 150 stocks. And these are the most sophisticated plans in the world. They're saying, "We're going to minimize risk by having a core; we're going to add value by asset allocation decisions to different sectors or styles, international markets, and then we're going to really focus on stock picking where we can add value but we've reduced our risk because it's a small part of our portfolio." In that section if you can beat the market, your overall portfolio is going to beat the market, too. Individual investors can emulate this.

DG: Is there anything ETFs are especially good for?

PM: *Diversified asset allocation. Four fixed income ETFs are now available in the U.S. which allows a total ETF solution to asset allocation –U.S. equities, international equities and U.S. fixed income.*

People tend to forget about overall asset allocation, growth versus value, different sectors, bonds, foreign markets which all the academic studies show make for the efficient frontier. If you want to get into sectors you have no exposure to, you can do it through ETFs.

If you wake up and have the idea you want to go long financial stocks because you think the Fed cutting rates is good for financials, how do you do it? You can get an idea but it takes days to figure out which stocks in that sector to buy. You may buy two stocks and it turns out that one of them has an earnings disappointment. You may have made a great call on the sector but been exposed too much to one stock. With an ETF, you decide you want to go long financials, the minute the market opens you can be long that sector; and more importantly you are long that sector in a very diversified way so if one stock blows up but the sector does well, you are protected.

Fees are much lower on ETFs, too. The average U.S. ETF [MER] is about 30 basis points. The average conventional mutual funds is about 140 basis points and the average [MER] for a U.S. index fund tracking the S&P 500 is 68 basis points. The iShares S&P 500 is 9 basis points. They're much more tax efficient, too. Index funds in their own right are very tax efficient but what people don't realize is that other shareholder activity creates capital gains. We did a study that for the last nine years since SPDR existed it paid two very small capital gains distributions. The average open-end index fund has paid 2% per year in capital gains because of redemptions.

2000 was an extremely difficult market in the U.S. and yet there was a record $345 billion paid out in capital gains distributions and that came from portfolio turnover driven in part by redemptions. Some people had the misfortune of buying an Internet fund in March and finding it worth 75% less at year end but still got whacked with a capital gains distribution because throughout the year, the fund was shrinking and selling assets it bought at lower prices in previous years and realizing gains. A big part of gains went to fewer investors at the end. In some extreme cases you could have got 90¢ of gains on your $1 investment at year end. The only way [U.S.] ETFs create capital gains is through index reconstitution which would not happen to nearly this extent.

DG: Any advice to investors now?

PM: *You have to be careful with some sector ETFs, what's in them versus what you think you are getting. Some of them can be more concentrated in a few stocks than you might think, and may be less pure than you think, also. The technology SPDR, for instance, includes some telecom names.*

Right now many people have losses on their mutual funds. It may be a good time to capture those and go into an ETF.

And watch out for fees.

July 13, 2001

NOTES:

1) Gary P. Brinson, L. Randolph Hood and Gilbert L. Beebower, "Determinants of Portfolio Performance," *Financial Analysts Journal*, July/August 1986, pp. 39-44. See *http://publish.uwo.ca/~jnuttall/asset.html* for an outstanding discussion of how the Brinson study has been widely misconstrued.

2) Roger G. Ibbotson and Paul Kaplan, "Does Asset Allocation Policy Explain 40, 90 or 100 Percent of Performance?" printed in the Jan/Feb issue of the *Financial Analysts Journal*. On-line at *www.ibbotson.com/research/papers/Asset_Allocation_Performance/Does_Asset_Allocation_Expl*. Thanks to Dan Hallett for this reference.

3) Standard & Poor's reclassified its sector indices in keeping with the new "Global Industry Classification Standard (GICS)." In June 2002, S&P Select Sector SPDRs were realigned to reflect these new sector definitions. The Healthcare Select Sector SPDR replaced the former Consumer Services Select SPDR, and Consumer Discretionary Select Sector SPDR replaced Cyclical/Transportation. Basic Industries was renamed the Materials Select Sector SPDR.

4) Paul J. Mazzilli, Dodd F. Kittsley, James P. McGowan, "Using ETFs to Capitalize on Sectors Favored for Recovery," Morgan Stanley Equity Research North America, January 29, 2001, p. 4.

5) Brooke Thackray and Bruce Lindsay, *Time In, Time Out: Outsmarting the Market Using Calendar Investment Strategies,* (Oakville: Upwave Media Inc., 2000), pp. 100-101.

6) Salomon Smith Barney Equity Research Report, "The Global ETF Investor," May, 2001.

7) Paul J. Mazzilli, Dodd F. Kittsley, James P. McGowan, "Style Investing with ETFs: Growth and Value Plays," Morgan Stanley Equity Research North America, February 14, 2001, p.7.

8) Paul Mazzilli, et al, "ETF Quarterly: Index-linked Exchange Traded Funds," Morgan Stanley Equity Research, June 29, 2002.

9) As quoted by Paul Mazzilli and Lorraine Wang, "Exchange Traded Funds: Invest Down the Capitalization Curve with ETFs," Morgan Stanley Equity Research, May 28, 2002, p. 2.

10) Ibid., p. 1.

11) Chip Anderson, "Predicting Future Human Behaviour is Hard–Duh!" *stockcharts.com's* Market Summary, September 21, 2002.

12) Adam Gebler and Kristin Bradbury, "Fixed Income iShares: Simple, Cost-effective and Targeted Access to Bonds," Barclays Global Investors publication for advisors, Summer, 2002, p. 3. From August 1998 to April

2002 Treasuries had a -29.88% correlation with the S&P 500. From June 1992 to April 2002, that correlation was 4.92%.

Chapter Five

Using ETFs with an Advisor

In the crowded financial services industry, you are a valuable asset. Brokerages, financial planning firms, mutual fund companies, banks and insurance companies are struggling among the throngs to distinguish themselves in your eyes. They are all keenly aware that satisfying your needs efficiently is the key to their prosperity and ultimate survival. Part of the urgency motivating so much change in financial services is the growing commodification of basic financial services. Just as you're likely to buy gasoline based solely on price, so increasingly sophisticated investors are likely to shop for financial services with a sharp eye to fees. The Internet has empowered investors not just through the wealth of low cost choices available for stock trading, but mostly through the explosion in the breadth and depth of investment information available at the click of a mouse. Brokerage firms used to have something of a monopoly on respected analysts and technical specialists. Today, these same analysts are fighting for credibility, undermined in fact or in perception by their firms' corporate underwriting activity.

If you're like most, you'd like the help of a trusted and competent financial advisor to help you coordinate all your financial needs: investing, insurance, tax planning and estate planning. Trouble is, most of us feel we've got too little money to be of interest to any advisor with those kinds of skills, or we're afraid of paying too much for more promise than delivery in an industry notorious for its inherent conflicts of interest. We end up continuing to buy the mutual funds *du jour* through our familiar mutual fund salesperson or stockbroker and promise ourselves at some point to get thoroughly organized. In many cases that probably means deciding to completely revamp your portfolio yourself and sign up with an on-line discount broker. (You may even have bought this book in anticipation of doing just that.)

There's nothing wrong with such a do-it-yourself ambition but each year you put it off takes you another year further from your goals. It's also unnecessarily complicating your life, because the industry has grown sensitive to the worry about corrosive costs and the conflicts of interest between advice and commissions. The industry's response has been the development of a variety of "fee-based programs," sometimes known as "fee-for-service" programs.

Fee-based Programs Can Save You Money Over a Portfolio of Mutual Funds

Fee-based programs have become the fastest growing programs in the financial services industry and for good reason. For one flat fee, based on a percentage of your assets, you get asset allocation planning, investment advice, ongoing contact with an advisor whose interests are perfectly aligned with your own, and a consolidated statement, usually with on-line access.

Any firm competing for your investment dollars will have some type of fee-based program. The larger firms will likely offer an assortment of programs as do all the major brokerage firms. Minimum account size and fees vary with each program. The higher the minimum asset requirement, the lower the fees.

Happily, ETFs and fee-based advisors go together like a soup and sandwich. A fee-based advisor wants to justify his fee by saving you money over a mutual fund portfolio with an average MER of 2.5%, so he's motivated to get you the best products with the lowest costs. No conflict there, so investors are voting with their feet. For the year ended June 30, 2002, assets in all fee-based accounts were up 13.4%, which is more impressive than it may seem.[1] The bear market diminished assets already under administration, so a positive growth in assets means new assets were introduced to more than offset the losses.

Fee-based arrangements represent a different business model—a new way of structuring your relationship with a financial specialist. It's a relationship in which the costs are spelled out explicitly, unbundled from the investment products and left open to scrutiny—and, for larger accounts, negotiation. That's a big departure from the conventional arrangement with mutual funds.

"People don't have any idea how much they're paying in fees [with mutual funds]," observes John Hood, a fee-based investment counsellor running his own firm in Toronto. "I was looking at a portfolio referred to me that was full of mutual funds. The client was paying $50,000 a year in management fees, which was ridiculous."

That's not so extraordinary either. A $2 million portfolio with an average MER of 2.3% will cost $46,000 a year in management fees, $10,000 to $20,000 of which goes to the advisor as a trailer fee. A million dollar portfolio, something most of us aspire to upon retirement, costs $23,000[2] a year if fully invested in mutual funds with average MERs. Hood charges a flat 1% of assets for his services on $400,000 minimum accounts. On a $1 million account that's $10,000 in fees—a far cry from $23,000. Often you'll find fee-based advisors who vary their fee with increasing account size.

However, it's not a clear-cut savings of $13,000. Sometimes the investments themselves have costs. Bonds have commissions built into their prices and stocks have trading commissions. ETFs and low cost, no-load mutual funds have MERs, too. And as is the case with all mutual funds, the MER does not include the trading commissions on trades done within the fund. Always ask your advisor the total costs of your investments, including MERs and expenses over and above the MER. In a fee-based environment, you want to be sure you're in an arrangement that is genuinely better (and cheaper).

ETFs a Perfect Fit for Fee-based Programs

Because of this drive to keep fees competitive and total costs low, Hood uses ETFs extensively in his client portfolios. But not just because of their razor-thin costs. "ETFs allow me to compete [with the big firms] simply because of their performance. I know, particularly in the U.S., that I'm going to outperform 90% of the portfolio managers out there simply because I use an indexed based product on a long-term basis," he says.

"Another advantage of ETFs is that they clarify things," Hood notes. "Clients know roughly where they are just by knowing how the indexes are doing."

The simplicity has other strengths. "A lot of planners," continues Hood, "have a client meeting every year, get the $13,500 RRSP contribution and dribble it in bits and pieces into the latest hot funds. In ten years the client's going to have 40 funds. It's nuts. It's diversification cubed." These fund *du jour* folks can end up with an inefficient, high-cost portfolio that dramatically underperforms.

But then Hood has also seen advisors convert a mutual fund portfolio with 30 funds into a portfolio with 40 ETFs. "That doesn't make any sense either," he says.

To his mind, a $700,000 portfolio can comfortably employ about 15 ETFs. More than that and he thinks the portfolio is either over diversified or has lost its focus.

Hood uses ETFs heavily on the equity side of his portfolios. For fixed income he uses bonds and a covered call writing strategy. "I buy stocks that pay a dividend and sell long-term options against them. That lets me significantly boost the yield on the income portfolio," he says. He calls his method "index, hedge, and grab the cash." So between ETFs and his blue chip covered call writing strategy on the fixed income side, he says he's able to effectively compete with big brokerage houses and their research facilities.

Hood is far from alone in understanding the advantages of ETFs in fee-based programs. Keith Matthews is another fee-based investment advisor with a passion for ETFs. Matthews is Vice President, Sales and Marketing, and a fee-based advisor with PWL Capital Inc. in Montréal. PWL Capital uses ETFs widely in the equity components of their client portfolios.

"For 0.75% to 1.5%, we will build you the best portfolio possible. I am now going to go out into the universe of all possible products for the best after-fee portfolio. When we look at the thousands of different mutual funds out there—dealing with management drift, management change, I get surprises. They're not tax efficient. I can't control the inflows or the outflows of cash into the portfolios that impact my client. When you look at all these different aspects, you can't ignore the power of exchange traded funds.

"Studies show clients are better off working with investment advisors. The no-load mutual funds have given better rates of return than load mutual funds on paper, but the actual returns captured by clients has been much higher in load portfolios. Having an advisor pays dividends in the long-term world. Staying the course, fee for discipline, for long-term asset rebalancing, these have been proven to be of tremendous value to clients.

"A fee-based manager is trying to maximize your after-tax return. It's all about after-tax. Over 10-years, managing in a buy and hold environment, making slight modifications, using ETFs and a variety of other securities, you will get a better after-tax return relative to the other alternatives available out there. Period," Matthews says unequivocally.

PWL Capital uses individual government and corporate bonds, real estate investment trusts (REITs), a mix of large, mid, small cap ETFs and some sector exposure through ETFs. They use ETFs extensively for Canadian, U.S. and European exposure. For European equities they use iShares S&P Europe 350 Fund and Dow Jones Global Titans, an ETF that holds 50 of the world's biggest blue chip global companies. As for other regions and asset classes, the firm considers them too volatile for their high-end clients. PWL's minimum account size is $500,000.

Noting that ETFs are pure asset pools, unlike equity mutual funds that will hold cash and foreign equities, Matthews says, "ETFs empower investment advisors to do very exact asset allocation. There's nothing passive in that. Handing the investment decision off to a fund manager is really being passive. Where's the accountability in that?"

Passion for the fee-based approach runs deep in many advisors who have set themselves apart in this way. Matthews is a case in point. "Fee-based is about how I can best grow your portfolio over 10 years—after costs, after taxes—not how can I generate the most amount of commissions from you."

A Cost Survey Of Different Fee-based Arrangements

As a consumer you do have to be cautious about the kind of program you choose with a fee-based advisor because fee-based doesn't always mean rock-bottom pricing. There's an assortment of programs and arrangements a fee-based advisor can recommend and some are more expensive than a portfolio of conventional mutual funds.

Generally the most expensive fee-based accounts are a kind of wrap program that pools investors' assets in some way—either with mutual funds or with proprietary pooled funds. Wraps are accounts that provide ongoing monitoring and asset allocation rebalancing for a fee based on a percentage of invested assets. Typically, they are sold by one party but managed by another. This distinguishes them from fee-based investment counsellors like Hood and Matthews who actually execute the investment decisions themselves. Pooled wrap programs are offered by mutual fund companies, brokerages, banks and trust companies.

Mutual Fund Wraps

Wrap programs can use an assortment of retail mutual funds as a sort of fund-of-funds approach. Called "mutual fund wraps," they generally have the highest fees. You pay a fee for a consolidated allocation service as well as the standard MER on the underlying funds. Examples of these programs include Mackenzie's STAR program and CIBC's Choice Funds among others. These programs have low minimum investments from $2,500 to $5000.

Pooled Wraps

Wrap programs can also use proprietary in-house mutual funds known as "pools." These pools usually have lower MERs than conventional load funds, but the programs themselves also impose a service fee. Minimum account sizes range from $10,000 to $100,000. AGF Harmony, CI Insight,[3] and Frank Russell Canada's Sovereign programs (distributed by RBC Investments, TD Waterhouse and ScotiaMcLeod) are examples of pooled wraps. A balanced portfolio in these three programs could run from 1.61% to 3.13%. Other programs of the same ilk can run to an astonishing 3.60%.[4]

Segregated Wraps

A third kind of wrap program offered by a brokerage is a "segregated wrap." These programs use an investment manager or a number of different managers who invest your money directly in individual securities. They can be customized to take into account your current holdings, but have high minimum investments, from $250,000 to $1,000,000. Fees are quite variable from company to company and often negotiable to some extent. Typically, a company might give the advisor a 25 basis point bargaining window, half of which comes from the advisors' remuneration, but anything greater than a 25 basis point discount on fees usually comes completely out of the advisor's cut. Program fees range from as much as 2% to as low as 0.40% for a $2,000,000 portfolio mostly in fixed income. Most, but not all, of these accounts come with a fixed number of free trades per year.

Are Wraps Cheaper?

In mutual fund and pooled programs, transaction charges are typically over and above the program fee and the MER of the funds. Despite their costs, pooled programs are often touted by investment advisors as being tax efficient. The investment service fee on non-registered accounts (only) is tax deductible, and some pooled funds calculate and assign the capital gains tax liability of each investor as they exit the pool so that the remaining investors don't get stuck paying the tax for the clever investor who bailed out before a distribution. However, these features don't come anywhere near compensating for the cost of the programs themselves. Except for accounts with large minimums, in almost all cases you'd get off a lot cheaper by simply holding load mutual funds and getting your advisor to do an annual rebalancing to an asset allocation you determined together.

"...[A] hybrid approach that uses regular mutual funds and other low-cost products (i.e. exchange traded funds, bonds, etc.) can provide investors with a very well-diversified, tax-efficient, and low-cost portfolio and provide ample compensation for your advisor," says Dan Hallett, Senior Investment Analyst with Windsor, Ontario-based Sterling Mutuals Inc. in his study of pooled wrap programs in an article in *Canadian MoneySaver*.[5] His conclusion: stay away from these wrap programs and find a better way.

The better way is to work with an advisor to find the best and lowest cost investments around. That mandate becomes less complicated when it is in the context of a transparent fee-based relationship.

Fee-based without Wraps

Just as you have to be careful of institutional fee-based programs, so do you have to exercise some discrimination with the portfolios of fee-based advisors. Not all portfolios are equal—especially when it comes to costs. Two advisors may both charge 1% in fees, but their portfolios could end up being significantly different in total costs after the embedded costs on the recommended investments are taken into account.

A fee-based advisor has the same tools at his or her disposal that any other advisor does, but has the freedom of choosing even those that don't pay a commission. The most cost-effective portfolio would be composed of individual bonds, stocks and ETFs in an account with an unlimited number of free trades. The least cost-efficient portfolio would be one entirely of load funds with a fee on top, which believe it or not, is still available in the marketplace.

Somewhere in the middle is a fee-based account holding zero per cent commission front-end load funds, but watch out for this. Front-end equity funds generally pay 1% a year in trailers to the advisor, which is discreetly charged to you through a plump MER. Fee-based advisors should be making their money on your fee, not on your embedded costs. Sometimes, though, advisors can't find the right type of investment in a no-load fund or with an ETF and must resort to a front-end fund at zero commission. Your advisor may want, for instance, an actively managed fund for emerging markets or Latin America. There's nothing wrong with this so long as you understand the advisor is, in effect, double-dipping—getting a fee and if not a commission, then a trailer fee funded through the higher MER you are paying on that fund. In these cases, scrutinize the asset allocation carefully. Plenty of advisors believe you don't need exotic asset classes and that they add only volatility.

To better accommodate fee-based advisors, fund companies have come out with different classes of funds that are essentially no-load with reduced MERs. These funds have no DSC penalties because they don't pay the advisor a commission on the sale of the fund, and they sport lower MERs.

"F" class units ("F" stands for "fee-based") have stripped the commission and trailer costs out of the MER leaving only the fund company's cost of running the fund. Another reduced MER class is called "I" class, standing for "institutional." "I" class units have MERs slightly higher than F units because they still pay an advisor a small trailer fee. They are designed for clients with high minimum investments. Mackenzie Financial Corp.'s I class, for instance, is exclusively for those with $500,000 invested in Mackenzie funds—and possibly in the context of a fee-based arrangement with an advisor.

But again, exercise caution. These reduced MER classes are not all the same. "The vast majority of clients don't know that I class units pay the advisor more than is disclosed up front in the fee-based arrangement," observes John De Goey, a financial advisor with Assante Capital Management Ltd.'s office in Toronto. "Clients don't ask about trailers or read the fine print. The net effect is that the client thinks 1% is fair, and the advisor thinks 1.25% is fair so they both feel they've struck a good bargain but it's likely the client won't understand just what the advisor is being paid. How much is fair compensation is open for debate but the disclosure of this compensation is not debatable. It should be absolutely transparent."

The Ontario Securities Commission (OSC) seems to agree. Under their "Fair Dealing Model," the OSC has proposed increased disclosure on trailer fees. Whether or not that comes to pass, the moral is to be sure you know exactly what and how your advisor is being compensated. Fee-based accounts can hold more within them for your advisor than you might think.

How One Advisor Uses ETFs with His Clients

ETFs and F Class Funds

De Goey uses an assortment of relationship models with his own clients but he prefers the fee-based approach he has designed. As he likes to put it, he sells parts and service separately. His approach has broad-based ETFs at its core with F class mutual funds added for some active management in sectors he believes are less efficient.

Here are two sample portfolios De Goey might recommend for his clients:

Aggressive RRSP:	(70% passive, 30% active) (80% equity, 20% fixed income)	**(fig. 35)**
Fixed Income:	C.I. Signature High Income	5%
	C.I. World Bond	5%
	iUnits Gov't of Cda 5 Year	10%
Canadian Equity:	iUnits S&P/TSX 60 Capped	20%
U.S. Equity:	iUnits S&P 500 RSP	20%
International Equity:	C.I. Emerging Markets	5%
	C.I. Signature Global Small Companies	5%
	iUnits MSCI International Equity RSP	20%
Alternative (Hedge):	Mackenzie Alternative Strategies	10%
	Total	100%

Conservative, Non-RRSP:	(65% passive, 35% active) (50% fixed income, 50% equity)	
Fixed Income:	C.I. Signature High Income	10%
	C.I. World Bond	10%
	iUnits Gov't of Cda 5 Year	20%
	TD Real Return Bond	10%
Canadian Equity:	TD Select Canadian Value ETF	15%
U.S. Equity:	TD U.S. Index	15%
International Equity:	iShares EAFE	15%
Tangibles:	NCE Petrofund	5%
	Total	100%

De Goey has a tiered fee structure, or as he calls it, a marginal fee rate. He charges 1.4% on assets under $250,000; 0.7% on assets between $250,000 and $2 million, and 0.35% on anything over $2 million. This is his fee before GST. It does not include transaction costs (which at Assante is $85 per stock or bond trade) nor does it include MERs on the investments. You may not think taking the MERs into account adds much but watch what it does to the all-in costs. Here are the total costs to De Goey's clients as he calculates them.

Fee Schedule (fig. 36)

Asset Level Approach/ Mix	<$250,000	$500,000	$1,500,000
Typical Wrap Account	2.9-3.4%	1.6-3.1%	1.5-2.7%
Traditional Mutual Funds*	2.40%	2.40%	2.40%
Customized** 30% passive	2.50%	2.15%	1.80%
Customized 50% passive	2.30%	1.95%	1.60%
Customized 70% passive	2.10%	1.75%	1.40%
Customized 90% passive	1.90%	1.55%	1.20%

* Assumes an all equity portfolio.
** Costs for all customized portfolios assume 1.4% MER on F class mutual funds and 0.4% MER on ETFs.

A 50% passive portfolio of $250,000 would have an all-in cost of 2.3%, not all that different from the average MER for a Canadian equity fund, but as De Goey sees it, he is offering his clients better tax efficiency, tax deductibility of fees on non-registered accounts and a personalized investment policy statement. And as assets climb, total costs diminish. A $500,000 portfolio would pay only 1.95% in annual costs.

Due to technical reasons beyond his control, De Goey could not, for a time, offer his clients F class funds. This highlights another issue you should be on the lookout for. Firms, by their organization and licensing and by their back office systems, limit the product universe available to their representatives. Furthermore, plenty of financial planners can't sell bonds, individual stocks or ETFs because they're not licensed to do so. These financial products require a securities license. Mutual fund salespeople are required to have nothing more than a mutual funds license which does not equip them to sell or even administer individual securities, including ETFs. These advisors are restricted to mutual funds because they have not undertaken to obtain a securities license or because their firm has not structured itself so as to be permitted by regulators to hold securities licenses on behalf of employees—a necessary condition of having securities licensed personnel.

If you hire a fee-based advisor, first make sure the firm is able to transact securities like stocks, bonds and ETFs, and that the advisor herself is securities licensed. Paying a fee to someone to simply select mutual funds is a little like golfing with one arm tied behind your back—it's not terribly effective. Then make sure your advisor has no other restrictions in acting on your mandate: "Build me the best possible portfolio." Too many times the actual portfolio falls short of the ideal because of avoidable practical obstacles. Don't tolerate the obstacles. Find a firm and an advisor who can give you the universe—of investment products anyway. Why limit your range of investment possibilities and your chance at better returns?

For an investor, the draw to fee-based is the independence of the advice. As a fee-based investor, you pay a flat fee based on the size of your account; as a result, the advisor should be free to recommend the best investments for your situation without heed to how well the product will help their monthly commission numbers.

ETFolios

Unlike John De Goey, not all advisors have access to ETFs for their clients. Many advisors are licensed to sell mutual funds only and cannot recommend securities or even oversee a portfolio containing securities. Guardian Capital Advisors Inc. has opened a door to ETFs for mutual fund licensed advisors by introducing their ETFolios program.

ETFolios is a service that gives investors ETF portfolios customized to their individual risk tolerance and investment objectives, with automatic rebalancing. The innovation in this is that these cutting edge portfolios are designed to be accessed by the mutual fund advisor. No longer do clients of mutual funds licensed advisors have to be excluded from the benefits of ETFs.

The program has a $50,000 minimum with a minimum 1% management fee. Add to that an average MER of about 0.25% for the ETFs themselves and the advisor's 0.50% to 1% optional trailer fee, and you're all-in costs are no more than 2.25%. On taxable accounts, these fees are tax deductible which brings the after-tax cost on a taxable account down to 1.55% for the top tax rate in Ontario. The service is also designed to capture tax losses where applicable.

According to Sri Iyer, Manager, Portfolio Engineering at Guardian, individual ETFs "morph into something with different risk and return characteristics when assembled in a portfolio." He should know. The ETFolios team has run 10-year back-testing on many of their portfolios for a perspective on their risk/return profile.

Iyer also notes that ETFolios is "a core method to transition advisors' books from a commission to a fee-based practice."

Why Advisors Have an Interest in Going Fee-Based

This may surprise you, but advisors have a powerful motivation to be transitioning to fee-based arrangements. For one thing, a fee-based advisory practice is worth about twice what a traditional transactional business can fetch on the resale market.[6] When advisors retire or change careers, they typically sell their "book of business" to another advisor for some multiple of annual revenue. Fee-based practices attract a high price because their income stream is more steady and reliable, and the business is easier to transfer into another's care.

Fee-based arrangements also attract higher net worth clients and permit the advisor to position himself as a money coach or consultant rather than a salesman. All in all, your advisor has got plenty of incentive to give you the most efficient portfolio possible, for a fee.

Something more subtle is at play, too. A fee-based business, if done wisely, can give brokers and advisors a freedom from their companies that they've never had before.

Dean Alexander, CFA, is an independent portfolio manager in Vancouver, managing over $250 million in assets. He uses ETFs for his U.S. and international exposure, of which he's a big fan. "I think they're one of the best investment ideas I've seen come along in the 32 years I've been in the business," he says. Alexander believes they are superior to actively managed large cap mutual funds particularly in U.S. and international markets. "The larger cap market is very efficient," he says, "and it's difficult for an active manager to beat the returns that can be earned on a well-constructed ETF." He believes investors looking for better returns from active management are best to focus on small caps where managers can uncover good companies before they become widely followed.

"Any broker must question why they are putting their clients into the typical mutual fund with high fees and back end charges," Alexander continues. "By using mutual funds the broker restricts the clients' options and is giving control of the client to somebody else," he says. "A broker would be much better off charging a 1% fee and using an ETF portfolio. It is better for the client and it is better for the broker. The broker retains control of the client and the clients get the benefits of mutual funds at a fraction of their cost.

"You can run a very viable business on 1%," he asserts, and he should know. He's been doing it for 12 years. (His fees are 1% or less.) Alexander breaks down the math by assuming most veteran brokers control on average about $50 to $100 million in assets. One per cent of $100 million is a cool million. Even after the company takes its share, Alexander says, "If he can't have a comfortable life on that income, there's something wrong.

"The smart brokers," he continues, "are going to start building portfolios with ETFs and charging 1%." If the broker's company decides to change the rules of the game, the broker is free to walk with his clients, who are tied to no other product than the broker's skill. The broker can then set up his own firm or transfer to a more welcoming company. "To the competent, ethical people in the business, ETFs give the brokers the opportunity to get out of the midst of big institutions."

So you see, your advisor does have many reasons for transitioning to a fee-based arrangement, and even better reasons for using ETFs to do so.

What's a Fair Fee?

Just how much that fee should be is up to you to decide. For accounts under $100,000 the best strategy is almost certainly to do it yourself with a simple Core and Satellite strategy or the Couch Potato Portfolio (see Chapter Four.) For accounts from $100,000 to $250,000, a 1% fee is getting off easy as most fee-based advisors reserve the magical 1% charge for larger portfolios. After $250,000 you're in a good position to negotiate the fee—especially with the fixed income portion of your portfolio.

Remember, your advisor has as much interest in adopting a fee-based arrangement as you have. You can't get what you don't ask for, so bargain hard for the best deal you can get. Your advisor will appreciate that bargaining because in the end, if you're both satisfied with the arrangement, you'll be a loyal client and she'll have a steadier cash flow. Then again, recognize you'll be writing a cheque every quarter or authorizing a monthly automatic debit to your investment or chequing account to pay these investment advisory fees. But don't kid yourself. Lower transparent investment costs are certainly in your best interest. Higher hidden charges, while being out of sight and out of mind, are detrimental to your portfolio's long-term returns and to your ultimate security.

John Bogle is a pioneer of low-cost investing in the U.S. He founded the Vanguard Group, the largest index mutual fund company in the world and has spent most of his life urging the investment industry to "give investors a fair shake" with reasonable fees. In an interview for this book he shared his insights about fee-based advisors. Although his is a no-load company, he believes in the value of advisors for most people, with a caveat to the costs. "People have to think very carefully about how much that fee ought to be," he says. "I don't think 1% is unreasonable for $50,000. But when you get up to very large amounts, 1% is a huge amount. Get out a compound interest table. Take a look at the difference between 10% and 9% over an investment lifetime of 50 years. Just that little 1%: the difference is staggering. A dollar at 10% is going to be worth $117 in 50 years. A dollar at 9% is going to be worth $74. If you want to put $10,000 around that it's $1,170,000 vs. $740,000 to the investor at a 1% difference. That's $430,000 to the croupier. Think of that. A third of the return is taken by the croupiers. The investor puts up 100% of the capital and takes 100% of the risk to get two-thirds of the returns. People have to focus on the long-term and the impact of costs.

"Advisors should do their fishing in a low-cost pond," Bogle continues. "Of all the strategies that absolutely works—that's it. You can take any comparison of any mutual fund you've ever seen in your life and cut it any way you want. If you compare the high cost quartile with the low cost quartile over any reasonable period of time, the low cost quartile wins. That's as close to a certainty as you get in this world."

Of course, Mr. Bogle is not a big fan of ETFs because he believes they encourage too much trading and a short-term perspective. But that's an argument for another day.

To my mind, anything that gives investors lower costs and greater flexibility is a good thing, and there's nothing preventing ETF investors from holding on to them indefinitely.

If anything, it's cheaper to hold an ETF long-term than it is to hold an index mutual fund long-term.

Why Your Financial Advisor Might Not Recommend ETFs:
An Interview with Duff Young

Duff Young is CEO of *FundMonitor.com*, a Toronto-based provider of research and portfolio analytics for financial advisors.

(He gave this interview in 2001 before any products using ETFs were available for sale by advisors with a mutual fund license. What Young says does not take into consideration the one core product incorporating ETFs that has since become available to mutual fund licensed advisors, Guardian Capital Advisor's ETFolios service. With the exception of this product, however, advisors with mutual fund licenses still cannot access ETFs for their clients and Young's remarks remain pithy and insightful.)

Donna Green: Not all financial advisors can deal with ETFs, isn't that right?

Duff Young*: Sometimes there are challenges to working with a financial advisor if you are an ETF fan. Specifically I'm talking about financial advisors who are licensed only to sell mutual funds. I believe in financial advice and do not sell my research to do-it-yourselfers or discount brokers. My clients are financial advisors. That said, I think that many advisors have to change precisely because of ETFs and the very compelling nature of what they offer. I'm telling advisors every day to either upgrade their license or move to a firm that can offer a full range of securities. They don't want to become stock jockeys and I don't want to push them away from their strength in financial planning. I'll tell you candidly that I do notice that the fully licensed guys aren't necessarily the cat's meow either. Too often you see financial advisors now becoming stock jockeys. Let's be serious, brokers are not investment managers. Very often clients are jumping out of the pot of mutual fund MERs into the fire of a heavily traded individual stock portfolio.*

DG*:* Should an investor wanting ETFs just seek out a broker?

DY*: A broker doesn't spend 100% of his time picking stocks, so he is fundamentally less well-equipped than a mutual fund manager. A broker has to deal with clients all day long, to sell and sooth, and coax and report to clients. I would venture to say that whereas an investment manager spends 80% of his time picking stocks, a stockbroker couldn't spend 20%.*

The middle ground, the Promised Land, is somebody who does financial planning and can get you ETFs. That is the perfect place to be and it is a still small but increasingly common minority. You can find this type of person who is an expert at financial planning but capable of selling securities at the fee-based shops, of course, and people like this are at all the brokerage firms. Probably a good 15 to 20% of their population fit this description beautifully and a similar proportion of mutual-fund-only dealers are inclined to use the services of jitney brokerage arrangements to facilitate individual securities trades on behalf of their clients. This is a wonderful trend that I vigorously encourage even though it is not without its administrative headaches. I suspect we will not get the regulatory "OK," to allow financial planners the privilege of recommending ETFs, but it is deserved.

It is illegal for a mutual-funds-only licensed advisor to actually do anything that is in furtherance of a trade in securities. A financial planner has to be very careful. Sadly you can't ask your planner whether an ETF is right for you because technically he can't answer. That's a big issue dealing with a financial advisor.

In reality, a good financial planner who is not fully licensed does a tongue-in-cheek kind of recommendation: "Well, yes, I certainly like the U.S. market today. I certainly like passive investing for a certain part of your portfolio, Mr. Johnson. And CIBC and a few other firms do have some decent index funds but they are expensive. Now there are cheaper alternatives available. Hmm, what do you think of that?" Playing the "nudge, nudge, wink, wink" game is an important reality for most investors in dealing with a financial planner today.

Your guy isn't a bad guy but you can't ask him about ETFs so expect an honest answer. Number one he can't really answer— it's illegal. Number two, he's got some biases, although that may be changing because he might be biased towards fee-based soon, and technology is probably going to encourage that.

DG: How does an investor play the "nudge, nudge, wink, wink" game?

DY: "Do you think it's important to be really cheap in passive investing?" [Client]

"Yes." [Advisor]

"Do you know of any lower cost index funds than the one you are recommending?"

"Yes."

"Is the SPDR a cheaper index fund?"

"Yes."

"Would you be angry with me if I were to put 30% of my portfolio's core holding in SPDRs?"

"No."

"Are you making a formal recommendation?"

"No."

I'm saddened by these regulatory limitations. A lot of advisors are very good people who would be happy to play the "nudge, nudge, wink, wink" game.

DG: Will financial advisors embrace ETFs?

DY: *I think financial advisors should use ETFs because they make so little of the 2.3% MER [on mutual funds] anyway. There's no new net growth in money coming in [in mutual fund sales]. So there's no deferred sales charges coming to these guys. They are living only on trailer fees. Trailers are only 50 basis points on 2.3%. A financial planner would be far better off to charge you 60 basis points and get you a bunch of iUnits. You'd only pay 80 basis points, he's making 20% more money, and your costs would fall by 65%. Those are the mathematics of unbundling.*

Soon there will be a better backbone in place that will allow fee-based planners to monitor and charge on assets at various institutions, and that will fuel demand for ETFs because planners will be able to recommend, monitor and access fees based on ETFs that reside elsewhere. If we mean financial planners who aren't fully licensed, then we have to change "recommend" to the "nudge, nudge, wink, wink" game.

DG: Will ETFs change the marketplace?

DY: *Paradoxically, instead of making the rest of the marketplace more cost competitive, the arrival of this new cheap competitor is going to make the rest of the marketplace more wild. In order to justify its fees, which will not change, active managers are going to have to start swinging for the fences a little bit more. Far too many of them have been closet indexers all along. Ironically, I expect average MERs are going to skyrocket because the market is going to polarize. ETFs will grab the cheapskates' business and in a search for balancing a portfolio with really active stuff, I think hedge funds are going to take off. They are expensive, but worth it, and appropriate in a balanced portfolio when complemented with ETFs.*

July 11, 2001

Notes:

1) Earl Bederman, "Getting to the Fee-based Future Before it Gets to You: Opportunities and Challenges in the Wealth Market," a presentation at the Investment Funds Institute of Canada's 16th Annual Conference, September 18, 2002, 17th slide.

2) A $23,000 management fee cost on a $1 million portfolio assumes an 80% equity, 20% fixed income asset allocation with some above average MER equity funds like international specialty funds offsetting lower MER fixed income funds to average 2.3%.

3) CI Insight also offers an F class option.

4) Information on fees and minimum account sizes from a proprietary report, "July 2002 Pooled Wrap Update," by Dan Hallett, CFA, Senior Investment Analyst at Sterling Mutuals Inc. in Windsor, Ontario. The report surveyed only wrap programs that use mutual funds or pool funds. Segregated wrap programs usually have higher minimum account size requirements and lower fees.

5) Dan Hallett, "Pooled Wrap Programs: The Asset Management Maze," in *Canadian MoneySaver Magazine*, February 2001 and March 2001. This is an insightful and well-researched two-part article about pooled wrap programs.

6) "2002 Practice Transitions Report: Practice Value and Data Survey for Buyers and Sellers of Financial Services Firms," by FPtransitions, *www.FPtransitions.com*, viewed September 19, 2002, p. 64. Thanks to Mark Yamada at Guardian Capital Advisors Inc. for this reference.

Chapter Six

Taxes: Implications and Strategies

An RRSP is a Canadian tax haven. Your retirement investments are as good as sunning themselves on a beach in the Cayman Islands while they're nestled in an RRSP account, but your investments outside an RRSP are battling the harshest Canadian element of all—taxes. Outside of a tax sheltered account, taxes are the biggest expense most investors confront— bigger than commissions *and* management fees. This chapter will take you through the tax considerations of ETFs, both domestic and U.S.-based, and explore some tax strategies using ETFs. For the purposes of this discussion, we'll assume your investments are taking the full brunt of Canada Customs and Revenue Agency (CCRA), formerly Revenue Canada, outside a tax sheltered account and held on capital account.[1]

Taxation of Canadian-Based ETFs

From a personal tax point of view, made-in-Canada ETFs are just like Canadian mutual funds. At the end of the tax year you get a T-3 detailing the nature and amount of income from your ETF. There will generally be some dividend income and some capital gains and possibly some interest and foreign income—just like a conventional mutual fund. (Mutual funds that are structured as corporations instead of trusts generate T-5s rather than T-3s.)

Just as with mutual funds, the income an ETF receives may come from capital gains on security trades, dividends from holdings and interest. This income flows out of the fund to unitholders in the form of distributions that are taxable. It's hardly obvious, but having taxable distributions is actually an advantage because distributions minimize the total tax paid overall. This is why mutual funds and ETFs make distributions. Income kept within a fund is taxed at the highest tax rate. Passing the investment income to unitholders allows that income to be taxed at personal marginal tax rates which may be lower than what the fund would otherwise have had to pay. That's why less total tax is paid when the fund's income is distributed to unitholders rather than being retained within the fund.

And again, like mutual funds, the tax character of a Canadian ETF's distributed income is retained when it is passed to unitholders. A Canadian dividend stays a dividend and a capital gain stays a capital gain, giving unitholders the advantage of the dividend tax credit and the 50% break on capital gains.

In absolute terms, ETFs generally distribute far less income than most actively managed mutual funds. As we discussed in Chapter One, because ETFs do so little buying and selling within the fund, ETFs are remarkably good about keeping their gains to themselves and not troubling investors with large distributions. Even the i60s noteworthy capital gains distribution in 2000, by ETF standards a relatively large 3.1% of net asset value (NAV), compares favourably to many actively managed funds. In 2001, the i60 capital gains distribution was just 0.92% of its NAV.

Timing of Distributions and Tax Records

Most equity ETFs distribute income quarterly and capital gains annually at the end of the year. A small number of U.S. ETFs, including fixed income iShares, distribute income monthly. Bond iUnits, Canada's fixed income ETFs, pay income semi-annually and capital gains annually. For Canadian ETFs, all distributions are paid out in cash except for capital gains distributions. These are paid out at the end of the year in additional units of the ETF. U.S. ETFs pay all distributions in cash.

Canadian distributions are recorded by the brokerage that holds your ETFs. Further, it's the brokerage that issues the annual T-3 slips, not the ETF sponsor company. For those used to getting their tax slips from mutual fund companies, this is a bit of a departure and according to Steve Rive, General Manager for BGI Canada Limited, is a source of confusion to some ETF investors. Brokerages are responsible for issuing the tax slips for their clients' ETF distributions; whereas, mutual fund companies issue T-3 and T-5 slips for their unitholders.

Taxation of U.S.-Based ETFs

Owning an American ETF is just like owning a U.S. stock. The income generated by the ETF is treated as ordinary income for Canadian tax purposes, just as is a U.S. stock dividend. Capital gains treatment applies on the sale of the ETF as it does on the sale of any stock.

U.S.-based ETFs are classified under U.S. tax rules as Regulated Investment Companies, or RICs for short. Distributions of dividends to Canadian residents from RICs are subject to a 15% withholding tax unless the distributions are being paid to a deferred income plan such as an RRSP or pension plan. A tax treaty between Canada and the U.S. exempts retirement accounts from withholding tax on RIC dividend distributions. As a result, U.S. ETFs held within an RRSP or RRIF receive their distributions free of withholding tax. Held outside of a tax deferred plan, U.S. ETF dividend distributions are subject to withholding tax. And remember, U.S. ETF dividend income is not eligible for the dividend tax credit which is reserved only for the dividends of Canadian corporations.

Distributions of capital gains from RICs don't incur withholding tax, but the bad news is that the capital gains portion of the distribution doesn't retain its character for Canadian tax purposes. You may not, however, be required to include all of the distribution from a U.S. ETF in your income under a new Canadian tax rule, but people in the tax field believe that the new rule is so complicated that taking advantage of it is vastly impractical. (For those who really want to know how it works, follow the footnote.)[2]

Janice Russell, Tax Partner and leader of the Canadian Investment Management Tax Practice of PricewaterhouseCoopers LLP, notes, "Canadian holders of iShares may be fully taxable on iShares distributions but will be eligible for a foreign tax credit in respect of withholding tax paid." The same applies to any U.S.-based ETF, not just iShares. In other words, you won't be taxed twice on your U.S. ETF income. The foreign tax credit will apply to the money withheld by the U.S. government. Due to the practical difficulties in applying the Canadian tax rule, your Canadian tax bill may very likely be calculated on every penny of U.S.-based ETF income without dividend tax credits or an advantageous 50% inclusion rate for capital gains.

A Tax Advantage

From a tax perspective, you might think that it makes no difference whether you hold a Canadian mutual fund that owns a U.S. ETF, or you hold the ETF directly yourself. Either way, the dividends are subject to the 15% withholding tax (in non-tax-deferred accounts). Apart from being more cost-effective to hold the ETF directly and thereby avoid the mutual fund's MER charge, it is also more tax efficient to hold the ETF directly.

The difference is in how CCRA allows the foreign tax to be recouped. Canadian mutual fund unitholders get a foreign tax credit on the withholding tax their mutual fund paid. On the other hand, Canadian ETF owners have the choice of declaring a foreign tax credit or an outright tax deduction. This is an advantage because tax credits can be used only against taxes owing. A deduction lowers your taxable income and is more serviceable than a tax credit.

Adjusted Cost Base for ETFs

Distributions always bring to the wary investor's mind the Adjusted Cost Base calculation (ACB). The ACB of an investment is its average cost including acquisition costs (trading commissions) and reinvested distributions. You need the ACB to figure out the capital gains on an investment because it's the sale price minus the ACB that determines the capital gain (or loss). Fortunately, there are no special considerations in calculating the adjusted cost base of ETFs. It's pretty straightforward.

ACB = (total purchases + acquisition costs + reinvested distributions - return of capital) ÷ units purchased

Monthly and quarterly ETF distributions are paid out in cash (unless your brokerage has an arrangement to reinvest them) but the end-of-year capital gains distribution gets reinvested (Canadian ETFs). That capital gain distribution becomes part of your ACB so keep track of all the distributions you receive by keeping the T-3 slips issued from your brokerage. Your T-3 slip will also record any distribution that is considered a return of capital. (I'll explain how that can happen in Chapter Seven.) A return of capital is not taxed but it is included in your investment's total cost which is why it has to be subtracted from your adjusted cost base. Your trading commissions to buy the ETF units are also included in the ACB.

Controlling your Capital Gains

Apart from the capital gains embedded in a distribution, you can trigger a capital gain yourself by selling an ETF you own. Be it Canadian or U.S., you do get to avail yourself of the 50% capital gains inclusion rate when you make a profit on the sale of your ETF. That means that you are subject to tax at your marginal tax rate on only 50% of the realized gains.

The other 50% is tax free. So if you are looking to maximize your after-tax returns with U.S. investments, you would favour U.S. investments with few distributions and a good potential for capital gains upon the sale of the investment. That describes a number of U.S.-based ETFs.

SPDR, for instance, are famously tax efficient even for a Canadian investor. Since their inception in 1993, SPDR have distributed only 16¢ in fund-generated capital gains altogether. In 2000 and 2001 the MidCap SPDR distributed no capital gains at all. You can learn the distribution history of all the AMEX-listed ETFs at *www.amextrader.com*. Click on "data," under the ETF section, select an ETF and then click on "distribution history." Be careful, though. A long history of minimal distributions doesn't always mean history will repeat itself. In 2000 some European iShares paid out hefty distributions after years of minimal income. The iShares MSCI Germany, for instance, paid out $2.53 altogether on a share trading in the teens.

In the case of the MSCI Germany ETF, a change in the concentration limits in the underlying index was responsible for the large distribution. Concentration reductions and index reconstitutions are the most common reasons for large distributions in an ETF that normally runs without so much smoke. The best defense against surprise distributions is knowing what's in the underlying portfolio so you can be on the lookout for things that might pose a problem in the future.

If you're concerned that the Canadian taxation of a U.S.-based ETF will offset the ETF's fundamental tax efficiency, stick to the large and midcap U.S. funds. They generally have low turnover within their portfolios and correspondingly lower distributions. Those with taxable accounts should be cautious with style-based ETFs and the small caps as these regularly move companies in and out in keeping with the changes within the indices themselves, and thus throw out more distributions. For reasons explained below, U.S.-based ETFs are structurally more tax efficient than Canadian ETFs because they generate fewer capital gains; so, even if you have the *potential* to pay more tax on the distributions from a U.S.-based ETF, in most cases you're getting far fewer distributions than you would get with a Canadian mutual fund holding the same underlying assets.

In-Kind Redemptions at the Fund Level

At the personal tax level there's a considerable difference between the tax treatment of U.S. and Canadian-based ETFs. There's a big difference at the fund level, too, because of the way "in-kind redemptions" are taxed.

An in-kind redemption happens when those giant creation/redemption units of 50,000 ETF shares or so are exchanged for the underlying securities in the fund. In the U.S., in-kind redemptions are non-taxable. This means the transaction is not treated as a disposition under U.S. tax law, so U.S.-based ETFs don't incur a capital gains tax liability from in-kind redemptions.

It doesn't work this way in Canada. Here, an in-kind redemption is viewed as a disposition by the fund which results in the fund *and* the unitholder having a potential capital gains tax liability on the same gain. While a capital gains refund does exist at the fund level to address this potential double taxation of the capital gains, the mechanism does not work perfectly. An ETF can be liable to pay the capital gains tax resulting from a redemption or distribute the capital gains to unitholders for them to subsequently pay the tax. This difference in tax treatment makes U.S.-based ETFs more tax efficient than Canadian ETFs and less likely to distribute capital gains than Canadian ETFs.

However, Canadian ETFs may be able to designate capital gains to the redeemer in the future. Steve Rive says, "Under the new regime, which is effective now, but does not become mandatory until the 2003 tax year, the fund will be able to designate gains realized on the redemption to the redeeming unitholder. The redeemer will then be able to reduce their proceeds of sale by the amount of the distribution (to avoid double taxation)." The new rules are still under discussion, however, and further changes are still possible. It will take a track record of a few years to see if this new regime and any subsequent changes to it in fact makes Canadian ETFs as tax efficient as their U.S. counterparts.

Superficial Loss Rules

Canadian investors may have one small tax break over their American counterparts when it comes to ETFs.

Both countries want to prevent what's known in Canada as superficial losses—trades that trigger a loss simply to offset some previously incurred capital gains. One of the hallmarks of a superficial loss, to CCRA's mind anyway, is repurchasing the disposed investment within 30 days of having sold it.[3] This shows the purpose of the sale was to cash in on some tax losses—not to get rid of a dog. Suppose you sold SPDR for a loss but immediately bought an iShares S&P 500. Your underlying positions would be virtually identical. You simply sold one S&P 500 ETF and replaced it with another. In the U.S., most tax experts believe your capital loss would be disallowed.

In Canada, these kinds of tax loss switches between ETFs or index mutual funds were considered safe because you own different properties even though their constituents are the same (keeping in mind the provisions of the general anti-avoidance rule). However, in 2002 CCRA issued a technical interpretation that dealt with the issue of identical properties and tax losses. Jamie Golombek, Vice President, Tax and Estate Planning, with AIM Funds Management Inc. and head of the Investment Funds Institute of Canada's tax committee, says CCRA seems to be changing this understanding: "Say you own a TSX Composite index fund from institution A and you sell it for a loss, then [within 30 days] you buy a different index fund on the same index from institution B, or an ETF on the same index. CCRA is saying that's an identical property and the loss is denied."

Golombek goes on to say, "I think CCRA is wrong from a legal point of view because these are different legal entities. They can't be identical."

Until this gets straightened out, the most prudent thing is to switch between similar but not identical indices when doing tax loss selling. You could, for instance, sell a TSX Composite fund or ETF and replace it with a TSX Capped ETF. A broad U.S. ETF like the Wilshire 5000 could be replaced with a Russell 3000. A Canadian growth ETF could be replaced with a Canadian Mid Cap ETF. There's no end to creative matchmaking.

U.S. Estate Tax Considerations

U.S.-based ETFs are attractive investments for Canadians looking for U.S. index exposure, so it's important to understand the consequences to your estate if you should die with a significant position in U.S. investments.

Canadian residents who are not U.S. citizens are subject to U.S. estate tax on the value of their U.S. assets owned at death. U.S.-based ETFs are U.S. assets so they get included in the tally. Whereas Canada taxes only the increase in value of assets owned at death, the U.S. system taxes the entire value at death. If you're a Canadian resident who is not a U.S. citizen and your worldwide estate is less than US$1.2 million, there is nothing to worry about with respect to your U.S.-based ETFs. They won't be subject to U.S. estate tax. If, however, your worldwide estate is greater than US$1.2 million, your U.S.-based ETFs will be taxed. The good news is that your ETFs are eligible for an estate tax exemption equal to the greater of US$60,000 or the enhanced exemption provided under the Canada/U.S. treaty. Under this treaty, U.S. assets are eligible for an exemption equal to a standard exemption of US$1,000,000 (in 2002) multiplied by a formula that divides the U.S. assets by the value of the estate's worldwide assets. The standard (but prorated) exemption of $1,000,000 will go up to US$3.5 million by 2009.

The U.S has repealed the U.S. estate tax for 2010. It is fully expected this repeal will last for 2010 only and that thereafter some standard exemption amount will be reinstated. Keep in mind that Canada gives foreign tax credits for U.S. estate tax to minimize the chance of double taxation. In the best case, the investor pays the higher of the two taxes, but quite likely the payment is split between the U.S. and Canadian tax collector. As Russell prudently warns, "Canadian residents with large U.S. holdings, including ETFs, should consider obtaining estate planning advice to deal with the issue of U.S. estate taxes."

Foreign Reporting Requirements

The ever-vigilant CCRA doesn't want Canadians investing abroad without the knowledge of the government lest someone avoid paying their fair share of tax. Canadian residents who own specified foreign property that at any time of the year exceeds $100,000 in total value, must file a Foreign Income Verification Statement (T1135) with their personal income return. The "specified foreign property" includes shares of foreign corporations and interests in trusts, which includes ETFs. Foreign-based ETFs would have to be reported if your total specified foreign property is greater than CDN$100,000.

Tax Saving Strategies

Avoiding mutual fund distributions

At the end of a mutual fund's fiscal year, the fund distributes its income if it has any. Sometimes these distributions can be large and trigger a proportionately large tax liability. This is especially painful when your distributions are automatically reinvested in new units of the fund. You don't see any cash from the distribution but nevertheless have to pay CCRA to cover the tax liability. In a money-losing year, that adds insult to injury. There is a way to avoid this: sell the fund before the record date for the distribution and avoid the distribution altogether. However, this might trigger capital gains and unbalance your asset allocation. There's not much you can do about the capital gains, but you can keep your assets covered by buying an ETF that is comparable to your fund's holdings. This judicious mutual fund sale might save you some taxes if the tax on the fund distribution is greater than the tax on half your capital gain. Replacing the fund with a similar ETF will mitigate the asset allocation damage that selling a strategic mutual fund could have on your portfolio's overall balance. Just be careful not to walk into a distribution on the ETF side. Also watch out for changes in the distribution policy of some mutual funds. A call to the ETF sponsor for a distribution estimate would be a good idea.

Tax Swaps and Tax Loss Harvesting

Selling one security for tax purposes and immediately purchasing a similar investment is called a "tax swap." It is done not only to escape mutual fund distributions, but often with the intention of crystallizing a capital loss to offset a capital gain now or in the future. ·

Crystallizing a loss for tax purposes, otherwise known as "tax loss harvesting," is done because of the tax rules regulating the relationship between capital gains and capital losses. Capital losses can be claimed against capital gains to offset the tax liability arising from the gains. The rules allow you some choice as to when you apply your capital losses. You must first claim your loss in the year you triggered it, but then you can apply it to a gain claimed any previous year back to three years, or carry the capital losses forward indefinitely into the future.

Swaps allow investors to maintain or alter their market exposure and asset allocation when they take a loss. You could, for instance, dump a Canadian tech mutual fund and buy an iUnits S&P/TSX Canadian Information Technology ETF. You'd gain the tax loss on the mutual fund but still have similar technology exposure and no worries about the superficial loss rules. Swaps work well between mutual funds and ETFs, be they sector plays or broad indices. And with the growing number of ETFs, it's now even possible to swap between different ETFs in the same sector or asset class. This is an especially appropriate strategy if you feel your targeted market sector is bottoming.

You gain some tax management flexibility and, as your ETF is fully invested, you get to ride the sector's full upswing when it happens. And if you want to repurchase your original loser, ETFs can help you maintain asset exposure while you wait out the 30 day superficial loss rule. You can sell your original holding, declare a capital loss to offset some capital gain liability, and then buy a sector ETF in the industry you still want to cover. After 30 days you can sell the sector ETF and repurchase your original languishing investment. In this way, you will have avoided a superficial loss but still have kept your industry exposure. With any luck, you might also pick up your original stock at no more than you sold it for.

Equitizing Cash

Pension funds and other big institutional investors use ETFs widely for something called "equitizing cash." The name doesn't sound appealing, but the technique is popular. Equitizing cash simply involves taking cash and quickly turning it into equities—usually an extremely liquid, broad-based equity ETF. This enables managers to be in the market just in case one of those big up days hits—the kind of days pundits say make up only 1% of the time but account for half your returns. (Of course, you also have the risk of hitting a day everyone would rather forget.) For taxable accounts, this has the happy result of avoiding interest income, which is taxed heavily, in return for potential capital gains and dividend income.

Individual investors can also equitize their cash. ETFs provide a way to turn the interest income of cash into less punitively taxed income with little loss of liquidity and the benefit of market exposure, though with some added risk. Of course, this has to be done in the context of your entire portfolio because taxation shouldn't be the only investment consideration, though it's one that is too often neglected—it's only the after-tax return that pays for those trips to Hawaii.

With the introduction of fixed income ETFs, cash can now be easily "bondized," too.

Micromanaging Tax Liability in an Index

Broad indices like the S&P 500 and the Dow Jones Total Market are made up of a number of industry sectors. In the U.S., all these sectors are represented by ETFs so it's possible to own a whole index by buying all of its component sectors in the right proportions via ETFs. The nine select sector SPDRs, for instance, fully replicate the S&P 500. Naturally, your total costs will be higher using this strategy as you'll have higher MERs and incur many more commission charges, but the advantage is in being able to micromanage each sector's losses and gains. As one sector slumps you can sell it to use that loss to offset the surge in another sector.

You can even try to enhance your returns by custom weighting the various sectors rather than keeping them in sync with the broader index. If you already own a lot of technology or financial stocks, you might want to underweight those sectors. Got a hankering for consumer staples? Here's the chance to easily overweight that sector. It's not a strategy for a couch potato, that's for sure.[4] The ETF Allocator on *www.ishares.com* will certainly help with this strategy.

Taxation of Option Strategies

Option strategies can be taxed in two different ways depending on whether the options are treated for tax purposes on capital account or on income account. The general rule of thumb is that an option strategy is speculative and thereby on an income account and fully taxed. If, however, an option is used to hedge an investment you already own, this is not considered speculative and the option will be treated as on capital account.[5] The following discussion will assume you are using options on capital account. (You can refer back to Chapter Four for an explanation of the option strategies discussed below.)

Call Options

The purchaser of a "call option" has paid a premium for the opportunity to buy a security—like an ETF—at a certain price by a certain date in the future. Should the option expire without being exercised, the premium paid becomes a capital loss in the taxation year in which the option expires. If instead the option is exercised, the option premium is added to the cost base of the ETF. A call option holder has one other course of action open to her. She can sell the option on the secondary market before its expiry. The net gain or loss that results from that sale is a capital gain or loss in the year the option is sold.

The premium paid to the writer of a call option (the person who promises to sell a security at a certain price by a certain date in the future) is considered a capital gain. Should the option be exercised, though, the option premium is instead added to the proceeds of the security sale. That way it becomes part of either a capital gain or a capital loss.

Put Options

Someone who writes a "put option" promises to buy at a certain price up to some specified time in the future. Someone who buys a put is buying the right to sell at a certain price some time in the future. The premium paid to the writer of a put option is treated as a capital gain. If, however, the option is exercised, the premium is subtracted from the cost of buying the ETF units. This means the adjusted cost base of the ETF will be lower than it would be otherwise, leading to higher capital gains when those ETF units are sold.

If a put option expires unexercised, the buyer of that put can claim the premium he paid for it as a capital loss in the year the put expired. If he sells the put on the secondary market, the net gain or loss is taxed as a capital gain or loss in the year it is sold. Should the put be exercised, the premium paid to buy the put is deducted from the proceeds of the ETFs sold. This reduces the resulting capital gain, if there is one. Alternatively, it increases the capital loss.

When the writer of either a put or a call buys an offsetting option to protect his position, the cost of acquiring that offsetting position is treated as a capital loss.

Knowing how your option strategy will be taxed should be a factor in determining its viability as a strategy.

Short Selling

Short selling, the practice of selling shares you don't own, is speculative so the proceeds are generally taxed as on income account, which means the profits are fully taxed. However, taxpayers can make a 39(4) election with respect to their Canadian securities that will have the effect of treating all their Canadian stock transactions as on capital account. (Unfortunately, there is no similar election for options or foreign securities.) This is a once-in-a-lifetime declaration and there's no going back once you've made it. (This election is not available to traders and dealers.)

Taxes are a can of worms. Normally, the party loaning the shares has neither a loss nor a gain since the loan is *not* considered a disposition. However, when the tax rules with respect to short selling were devised, ETFs weren't even a twinkle in the TSX's eye. As a result, the securities lending tax rules don't apply to trust units. This is unfortunate because the party lending the ETF units to a short seller is thereby deemed to have disposed of them and should declare the capital gain or loss resulting from that deemed disposition. One can only hope the Department of Finance will see the unfairness of this and amend the rule.

Tax Efficient ETFs Ideal for Retirement Compensation Arrangements (RCAs)

"ETFs make absolutely excellent RCA investments," says Gordon Lang, President and Chief Actuary with Gordon B. Lang and Associates Inc. RCAs are supplemental pension arrangements for senior executives or successful entrepreneurs. They have unusual rules that require 50% of all contributions to be deposited with Ottawa in a "refundable tax account," or RTA for short. The other half of the contribution stays in the RCA in investments. All investment income in the RCA account, including realized capital gains, is subject to refundable tax. "Many large companies have all their RCA money invested in T-bills or other short-term assets which are exactly the worst kind of investments to have in one of these accounts," he says. Most RCA assets are held in the plan for a long time and over a

10 to 15-year span he says, "short-term assets are the lowest yielding asset group and the highest taxed."

"I've always looked at the twin objectives of RCA investing to minimize the amount of money in the refundable tax account and to maximize money in the RCA invested account," continues Lang. That would suggest RCA investments should favour assets that do not generate much taxable income or realized gains. A buy and hold style equity mutual fund fits that description as does an equity ETF, but Lang thinks the ETF is by far the preferred investment. "For fairly large amounts, the beauty of ETFs is that they are inexpensive to manage. The management fee is low and the cost of buying them isn't high. And you have a lot less rebalancing or selling of securities." Based upon research conducted by BGI Canada, U.S.-based ETFs can make a difference of up to 50 basis points in after-tax return within an RCA.

Few RCA managers, according to Lang, have thought through the implications of short-term fixed income vehicles. "The level of expertise in the RCA market is abysmal," he says. "Most of the liabilities are essentially with respect to final average salary pension plans. The risk there is salary inflation and the best way of meeting that risk is equities. Short-term investment returns bear very little relationship to long-term salary increases and to the liabilities associated with them."

The tax efficiency of ETFs makes them a good investment for you, too, with or without an RCA.

A Tax Expert Talks about Common Tax Mistakes

Jamie Golombek, Vice President, Tax and Estate Planning with AIM Funds Management Inc. generously provided this interview. I had the luxury of inserting my own comments after his.

Jamie Golombek: *A lot of people overlook constructive tax loss selling. In October and November, investors should look at their portfolio for tax losses, but don't sell an investment just for tax purposes. You should look for something that has not met your target and which you are planning to sell anyway. Think about selling it towards the end of the year instead of selling it a few months later so you can take those losses and apply them against other gains that year and in particular against any potential capital gains distributions from funds.*

This often comes up right at the end of the year but it's too late to do it at the end of December because you have to start worrying about cut off dates and settlement dates. We tell investors in October and November to sit down with their advisor, review their entire portfolio, and make a decision as to whether this is the right time to sell something that's under water.

Howard Atkinson: *It's best not to leave tax loss selling to the very end of the year for another reason, too. The November to April span is a seasonally strong period in the market so tax loss selling should generally be done in October.*

JG: *To help in tax planning, AIM provides financial advisors with a list of estimated distributions 4-6 weeks in advance of fund distributions. We even post them on our Web site so advisors can help their clients plan for them.*

HA: *That's a valuable service for investors and helps in their tax planning. ETF providers also generate capital gains distribution estimates well ahead of the distribution date. And for those who might want to manage their tax bill by trading around fund distributions, ETFs allow this more easily than mutual funds because the trades occur in real time with real time prices.*

If you are a conscientious asset allocator, the last thing you want to do is sell to avoid a distribution or for the tax loss and be without that asset exposure. Like Murphy's Law, that's the time the class will go up in value. In 2001, Nortel scooted up 90% from its low in September to its high in December. If you'd sold it for a tax loss, you'd have missed out on that bounce or had to buy it back 31 days later at a higher price. I suggest keeping asset class exposure in these cases so the iUnits S&P/TSX Canadian Information Technology Index Fund (XIT) would have been a good proxy. Of course, if an investment no longer fits your objectives then you don't need to replace it, but if you do replace it, do so right away because of seasonality considerations.

Switching into an ETF allows you to keep your asset class exposure without running afoul of the superficial loss rules provided you sit it out for 31 days and so long as the original security doesn't hold the same index as the ETF.

JG: A lot of people try to save money by doing their tax returns themselves. I don't think that's a bad idea so people can learn how taxes work. Nevertheless, it's a good idea every few years to pay an accountant to review your tax return. Unless you work in the area, you may be missing opportunities, simple things.

Suppose you've sold some stock this year and you have a lot of gains and you're also making large charitable donations. An accountant would say, 'Wait a minute, shouldn't we be donating stock to the charity? You'll save yourself half the capital gains tax.'

HA: That's a very good point. I believe accountants' fees are low as a percentage of what they can save you. You've only got three years to carry back capital losses and if you lose out on claiming them then, you've lost recouping capital gains tax paid in the past. (Losses can be carried forward indefinitely, however.)

JG: Investors are getting a big refund every year because of their RRSP contributions. An accountant would likely suggest you reduce your withholding tax from your paycheque instead.

HA: You get a reduction in tax withholdings when you show CCRA you are contributing the money to an RRSP. Unfortunately, ETFs aren't a good vehicle for periodic investments. For that, mutual funds are better.

JG: On seeing both a husband and wife's tax returns, an accountant might have a few suggestions, too. Suppose the wife is working full-time and the husband is at home looking after the kids. What a great opportunity for an income splitting spousal loan. These are very simple ideas that can be introduced with a review of investor's tax returns.

HA: I once heard an accountant say that for most investors the only thing you can do legally to mitigate taxes is to deduct, divide and defer. The three 'D's' he called them. Deduct the maximum allowable expenses, divide the income by income splitting as best you can, and defer paying taxes for as long as possible. One of the ways to defer tax is to avoid realizing your capital gains every year. ETFs are particularly good at letting you control your capital gains.

JG: *A lot of people are using the tax planning guise 'Oh, They'll Never Find Out,' when it comes to foreign holdings. That's not tax planning, that's tax evasion. And CCRA has innocent ways to find out. All Canadians have to report and pay tax on their worldwide income and the penalties are very severe if you don't.*

HA: *That's something investors holding U.S.-based ETFs may not be completely aware of. Canadians must report specified foreign assets with a total cost over CDN$100,000 at any time during the year. This includes shares of foreign corporations, including U.S.-based ETFs.*

September 24, 2002

Notes:

1) Being held on capital account as opposed to being on income account. It means that only 50% of capital gains would be taxed and 50% of losses would be deductible. When investments are held on income account there is no break for capital gains.

2) The new Canadian rules on capital gains distributions from RICs say an investor who receives a distribution from a U.S. trust will be taxed on the amount of the distribution that represents income of the trust as calculated under Canadian tax rules. Since U.S. ETFs are trusts, this might have you thinking you can ignore 50% of the capital gains income from a U.S.-based ETF trust. Problem is that as an investor you can't know how the ETF's capital gain was calculated in the first place, so you can't know positively how much of that distribution to include in your income. The two countries have different ways of calculating capital gains. The practical upshot of this is that ETF investors in Canada are not safe in assuming they can discount the U.S. capital gain by 50%. If you do and get questioned by CCRA, the burden of proof is on you and since there's no way to determine how the U.S. gain was arrived at, CCRA wins by default. Furthermore, this new rule doesn't apply to ETFs that are corporations in which case all the distributions are included fully in income anyway. (All the MSCI iShares series are structured as corporations.)

3) Superficial loss rules are a little more complicated than just the 30-day rule. Neither you, your spouse, your corporation nor other affiliated people can buy the asset, or an identical asset, within 30 days before or after your sale of it. This turns out to be a big problem for mutual funds who sell parts of their holdings at a loss, but because they still retain part of the (larger) position, cannot claim the capital loss.

4) Thanks to Paul Mazzilli, Executive Director and Director of Exchange Traded Funds Research at Morgan Stanley in New York, who wrote about this strategy in "ETF Strategy Guide," put out by Morgan Stanley Equity Research Department, July 2001.

5) For a full discussion of income versus capital accounts, see CCRA's Interpretation Bulletin IT479R. You can find this at *www. gov.ca*. Go to CCRA and search on "Transactions in Securities."

Part Three

Where ETFs Came From and
Where They Are Going

Chapter Seven

Lifting the Hood: How ETFs Work

Remember when Japanese cars suddenly made North American cars look like gas-sucking tanks? ETFs are revving up to do the same thing to the mutual fund industry—but don't anticipate a rollicking demolition derby yet because fund companies will respond with innovations of their own. To have the best chance of understanding future new fund products it's a good idea to know the inner workings of today's innovations. Here we'll lift the hood to look at some detailed issues affecting ETFs. They're not inherently complicated, but you do have to get close to the oil to understand their finer points. We'll show you how you can know you are getting a fair price for an ETF, how distributions are treated, how dividend payments and other sources of cash work inside an ETF, and the differences between American and Canadian ETFs. We'll also discuss what happens when an ETF is closed down, a circumstance that is scheduled to befall four funds in 2002. Finally, we'll explore the interesting but little-known hazards of index construction as it affects ETFs. For those not mechanically inclined, feel free to skip to the next chapter.

Are You Getting a Fair Price?

The value of an ETF unit is initially set as a fixed percentage of the underlying index. For i60 units it's one-tenth the S&P/TSX 60 index. (For iUnits sector funds it's one-quarter the index value; TD's Composite and Capped Composite ETFs are one-three-hundredth.) Thus, when the 60 index is at 355, an i60 should be around $35.50. Of course, that would be way too easy. Dividends and other sources of cash (which do not get reinvested) also have to be factored into the unit price.

BGI Canada's Web site says, "The trading price of an ETF is approximately equal to the trading value of the underlying securities held in the fund plus any undistributed net income." This is correct as far as it goes, but unless you know what that undistributed net income is, you can't calculate the net asset value (NAV) for yourself. And it's important that you know this otherwise you can't determine if you are buying an ETF at a fair price, which means one that is close to NAV. (The price of most ETFs track their respective NAVs well most of the time, but it's prudent to check.)

Undistributed net income is made up of the estimated cash amount per unit, and something known as a "distribution price adjustment." The estimated cash amount is a tally of dividends received by the fund but not yet declared as distributions. The distribution price adjustment reflects an amount per unit declared as distributions (and therefore deducted from the NAV) but not yet paid to unitholders. Usually the distribution price adjustment will be zero since there are just a few days every quarter between the declaration of distributions with ETFs and their payout to unitholders.

To figure out how much you should be paying for an ETF here's a formula you can use to get a close approximation:[1]

Current index value + estimated cash amount per unit + distribution price adjustment = NAV
    (divisor)

The divisor is the ETF's fraction of the index. In the i60's case, the divisor would be one-tenth. The numbers for the estimated cash amount and the distribution price adjustment per unit are less easy to come by. Only the fund administrators know that information, and even at that, the daily cash amount is an estimate done one day in advance. For iUnits, you can find these numbers on BGI Canada's Web site, *www.iunits.com* "daily fund values/baskets." BGI Canada, the sponsor of the iUnits, updates the NAV for all their Canadian ETFs daily on their site so you don't have to do the calculation yourself. TD Asset Management's site, *www.tdassetmanagement.com*, also gives a NAV value per unit as of the close of the previous day's market and how that changed from the last daily close. They also report an estimated cash amount and a distribution price adjustment.

Things are a lot easier in the U.S. for savvy ETF investors. AMEX, where almost all ETFs trade, broadcasts every scintilla of information you would ever want to know about an ETF through seven ticker symbols per ETF. To find these ticker symbols go to *www.amextrader.com,* "exchange traded funds," click on the desired ETF and then its spec sheet. (Note that AMEX is in the process of consolidating the information on AMEXtrader onto the AMEX site.)

These are the seven ticker symbols for S&P Depositary Receipts (SPDRs):

Ticker Symbols for SPDRs (fig. 37)

SPY	Trading Symbol	SPX	Underlying Index Trading Symbol
SXV	Intraday Value	SXV.SO	Shares Outstanding
SXV.NV	Net Asset Value	SXV.EU	Estimated Cash Amount
		SXV.TC	Total Cash Component

Source: www.amextrader.com

The market value for SPY is quoted in real time, and is the trading price for the SPDR shares. The "intraday value" is the estimated value of the underlying portfolio calculated every 15 seconds. With this and the estimated cash amount, it's easy to see how much of a premium or discount the market price represents. The "net asset value" (SXV.NV) is computed per share at the close of the market each day and includes the value of the underlying securities plus portfolio cash (accrued dividends) but minus accumulated expenses. The figure for "shares outstanding" (SXV.SO) is also as of the end of the previous day. The "estimated cash amount" (SXV.EU) is, as its name implies, an estimate for the current day based on the actual cash holdings in the fund at the close of the previous day.

Ticker Symbols for DIAMONDS (fig. 38)

DIA	Trading Symbol	INDU	Underlying Index Trading Symbol
DXV	Intraday Value	DXV.SO	Shares Outstanding
DXV.NV	Net Asset Value	DXV.EC	Estimated Cash Amount
		DXV.TC	Total Cash Component

Ticker Symbols for Qubes (fig. 39)

QQQ	Trading Symbol	IXNDX	Underlying Index Trading Symbol
QXV	Intraday Value	QXV.SO	Shares Outstanding
QXV.NV	Net Asset Value	QXV.EU	Estimated Cash Amount
		QXV.TC	Total Cash Amount Per Creation Unit

Source: www.amextrader.com

Having this information available by ticker symbol makes it easy and straightforward to get timely information about the financial underpinnings of an ETF.

You can find all seven ticker symbols associated with every ETF that trades on AMEX on *www.amextrader.com*.

Shockingly, many Canadian brokers don't have access to these ancillary

ETF ticker quotes because it is an election on their data service which costs money. Don't be surprised if even your full service fellow charging you $95 a trade doesn't get these tickers without going through the same steps as you.

The values for these ticker symbols are cranked out Monday through Friday around 4 p.m. in New York. As it happens, a number of ETFs trade until 4:15 p.m. New York time, but rather than getting a sharper price at the end of the trading day, the spread between bid and ask widens at the end of the day and at the beginning of the morning until the most recent numbers are digested. If you're going to buy an ETF, it's often best to avoid those periods.

Some ETFs Trade Later in the Day than Others

Many U.S.-based ETFs trade 15 minutes after the close of the regular market.

Here's a list of the ETFs that trade from 9:30 to 4:15 p.m. New York time.

• All broad-market ETFs
• iShares Sector Index Funds
• iShares International Index Funds
• streetTRACKS Dow Jones series

All others stop trading at 4:00 p.m. Eastern Standard Time.

The AMEX Web site (*www.amex.com*) is like the Wall Street Journal of ETFs with a huge wealth of information about all their listed ETFs. Their site also includes an ETF screen and a total return calculator. AMEX is clearly committed to ETFs because the trading volumes ETFs generate are AMEX's revenue lifeline.

The Toronto Stock Exchange understands the importance of ETFs as the i60s are one of the most actively traded shares on the exchange. The Canadian ETF universe now numbers 16 funds and the TSX's site (*www.tsx.com*) features a separate section on ETFs. That seems only fitting since the TSX was the sponsor for Canada's first exchange traded fund, TIPS. (After 10 years TIPS, which had by then become TIPs 35 and TIPs 100, merged with BGI Canada's i60 Fund in 2000.)

Liquidity

Liquidity is the ease with which an investment can be bought and sold without substantially affecting the market price of the investment. Trading volume is a good indication of liquidity. The more a stock trades, the more liquid it is. Typically, the more liquid an investment, the narrower the spread between the bid and ask price. ETFs with big assets are highly liquid—like the i6os, Qubes, DIAMONDS, SPDRs, the iShares S&P 500, most of the style and capitalization ETFs like the iShares Russell series, and the S&P Mid and Small Cap series. In general, broad market ETFs trade swiftly and frequently and are widely held.

Liquidity seems to be a concern with lightly traded ETFs such as iShares Goldman Sachs Natural Resources Index ETF, with an average daily trading volume of less than 25,000 shares. Some country iShares also have low volumes like the iShares MSCI Belgium ETF with $9 million in assets and only 10,000 shares traded on average a day.[2] Normally such thin trading volumes would pose a problem for an institution wanting, say, to move 10,000 or more shares. Spreads can widen in these circumstances but remember that ETF prices are ultimately tied to the value of the underlying securities. As long as these securities are liquid and the arbitrage mechanism is not impeded, the price of even a thinly traded ETF should stay fairly resonant with the NAV. Even if the ETF itself is not a model of liquidity, the liquidity of the underlying portfolio should prevent excessive price discrepancies. According to an ETF report put out by Goldman Sachs Derivative & Trading Research (June 29, 2001) "...the dollar volume of the trading activity in the underlying stocks is more significant in assessing liquidity than the dollar volume of the ETF."

How is Cash Handled?

You might wonder how cash can get so plentiful in an ETF portfolio. After all, isn't one of the reasons ETFs are superior to mutual funds is because they have so little cash? Well, yes, ETFs still have a lot less cash proportionally than most mutual funds because they don't have to deal with redemptions in cash or cash influxes waiting to be invested. ETFs strive to be investment rich but cash poor—and try as they may, they still have some pesky cash hanging around. And in order to make sense of an ETF's price, you must take this into account.

ETFs get cash from a few sources. First, their underlying stocks generate dividends. Most ETFs pay out their dividends quarterly and their capital gains annually, but between payouts, the dividend income must be mopped up somehow. Canadian equity ETFs don't reinvest the dividend income they receive into the underlying securities. Instead, they put that money into a separate account. That account generates interest income which helps to pay the fund's expenses. As a result, Canadian equity ETFs don't generally distribute interest income—only dividend income and capital gains which are taxed more lightly than interest income.

Cash can sometimes arise from the creation of new ETF units between dividend quarters. The creation of new ETF units requires three things: the basket of securities to make up the ETF; cash for dividends already received on those securities; and, cash equal to the value of any accrued dividends. The cash received in this process gives rise to a return of capital at a future distribution.

Cash within bond ETFs like the iG5 and iG10 is distributed semi-annually as interest income when it is received. On the other hand, interest income received by the fully RRSP eligible i500Rs is reinvested into the fund.

And because these ETFs are pretty streetwise critters, they also scarf a few dollars from lending their securities to short sellers. This was a source of income for TIPS when it was around and TIPS' exemption from the general prohibition for funds against lending securities was passed on to the i60's. In early 2001 regulators changed the rules to permit all mutual fund trusts to lend their securities. Now all Canadian ETFs, and mutual funds that are structured as trusts, can lend out their own securities and charge a fee for doing so.

Canadian vs. U.S. ETF Structure

The legal structure of investments may seem like a pretty arcane thing, but these legal differences can make a difference to your costs and ultimate returns. All ETFs in Canada now are structured as mutual fund trusts so they all must conform to the same rules and labour under the same restrictions. Their U.S. counterparts, however, come in a few legal varieties and this structure makes a difference in how they treat their dividend income, whether or not they can lend securities, and how they are permitted to track the index.

Exchange Traded Unit Investment Trusts

The oldest ETFs, SPDRs, DIAMONDS, Qubes and the S&P 400 Mid Cap SPDRs, are exchange traded unit investment trusts (UITs). With the

UIT structure, dividends and income are not reinvested, the underlying securities cannot be lent and the index must be replicated. Optimization is not permitted.

Exchange Traded Open-end Index Mutual Fund

Sector Select SPDRs, all iShares and streetTRACKS ETFs are exchange traded open-end index mutual funds. This more contemporary structure permits the funds to reinvest dividend income the moment it is received, and it gives the funds the flexibility to optimize their index strategy if they so desire. Lending securities is also permitted, so this is by far a more flexible structure for ETFs.

Both ETF structures distribute dividends and capital gains so for a U.S. resident, there is no tax treatment difference between the different legal structures. There's no difference in tax treatment between these structures for Canadian residents either; unfortunately, all U.S. ETF distributions are treated as ordinary income by Canadian tax collectors, unless you can provide a capital gains distribution breakdown acceptable to CCRA.

Exchange Traded Grantor Trust

This is a legal structure used by HOLDRS. HOLDRS are different from index-linked ETFs. Some might say that, strictly speaking, they're not ETFs at all, but because they are generally included in ETF discussions, we've included them here. Most HOLDRS initially contain 20 stocks that are never changed or rebalanced in any way. Investors receive the dividends directly and have voting rights. It is almost like owning the 20 stocks individually except that they can be traded easily as a group. HOLDRS do not lend securities, reinvest dividends or use derivatives. (See the end of Chapter Three for a more extensive discussion of HOLDRS).

Structure Comparison of ETFs (fig. 40)

Characteristics	Exchange Traded Mutual Fund Trust (U.S.)	Exchange Traded Unit Investment Trust (U.S.)	Exchange Traded Grantor Trust (U.S.)	Exchange Traded Mutual Fund Trust (Cdn.)
Dividends	reinvested until quarterly distribution	not reinvested	paid directly when received	not reinvested
Index strategy	may optimize	replication only	cap-weighted basket	may optimize
Loan securities	yes	no	no	yes
Derivatives	may use	may not use	may not use	may use
Funds	iShares, streetTRACKS, Sector SPDRs	SPDRs, 400 SPDRs, DIAMONDS, Qubes	HOLDRS	iUnits, TD ETFs

Source: Morgan Stanley Equity Research for U.S. ETFs, author for Canadian ETFs

The Canadian ETF structure

ETFs in Canada are structured as mutual fund trusts. A trust preserves the tax characteristics of its income and passes it on to the unitholders. So when a Canadian ETF issues a distribution, it lands in investors' hands as dividend, interest or capital gains with their respective tax treatments. This structure permits the manager to optimize an index if desired.

Dividends and Capital Gains Distributions

The current crop of Canadian-based equity ETFs distribute their dividends quarterly and their capital gains annually in December. The iUnits bond funds distribute interest income semi-annually and capital gains income annually in December. U.S. fixed income ETFs distribute income monthly and capital gains at the end of each year, both in cash.

ETF quarterly distributions are made in cash to unitholders. If you find those quarterly cheques a nuisance, ask your brokerage about a dividend reinvestment plan. So far only RBC Investments and Canadian ShareOwner Investments Inc. have dividend reinvestment plans. RBC offers dividend reinvestments for i60s. Canadian ShareOwner offers it on all iUnits. With more demand others will certainly follow. That will save you a commission and allow you to keep your money tracking the total return index.

Capital gains generated from the ETF's own internal buying and selling are distributed at the end of each year. U.S.-based ETFs distribute their capital gains in cash, though they rarely have distributed gains. Canadian-based ETFs distribute their gains in the form of additional ETF units, but only for an instant. In December, a Canadian ETF with a capital gain distribution will issue more units of itself in an amount equal to the value of the capital gain distribution. When this distribution "in-kind" happens, more units are created but the underlying value of the assets remains unchanged. This means that the price of all the ETF units must go down so that when all the units are added up, the total value of all the units still equals the original net asset value. For an instant you own more units at a fractionally lower price. You'll note that this is exactly what happens with conventional mutual funds when they make a distribution: the units are increased by the amount of the distribution, but the value of all the units is decreased by the amount of the distribution. There is no change in the value of your total holdings.

However, the difference with a Canadian ETF is that it immediately "consolidates" all its outstanding shares, knocks the number of units back down to the pre-distribution number and boosts the unit price back to its pre-distribution level. After this, you are left with an unchanged number of shares at the pre-dividend price, but with a higher adjusted cost base. The value and number of your units hasn't changed, but the fund has passed on to you a capital gains tax liability in proportion to the distribution. The good news is that your adjusted cost base increases by the amount of the capital gains distribution so when you subsequently sell your ETF your ultimate capital gain will be less than it would have been without receiving the dividends.

Remember, you are still required to pay tax on this capital gains distribution even though you received it in-kind temporarily, in the form of increased units. The unit consolidation is done so investors aren't left with fractions and odd numbers of shares from distributions. (While you can sell 103 units, it's quite impossible to sell 103.33 shares on a stock exchange.) More importantly, the ETF's divisor would be thrown off if the number of ETF units increased while the share value dropped.

Steve Rive, General Manager of iUnits for BGI Canada Limited, says the capital gains distribution and consolidation confuses many investors and advisors. He points out that the fund is no richer or better off when it has realized a gain. "All that's happened," he says, "is that a tax liability has been generated. Think of a situation where you invested $50,000 in a stock. It goes up to $100,000 and you sell it. You now have $100,000 in cash. The day after you make your sale, you are no richer than before you made the sale but suddenly you owe tax on that $50,000 of capital gain. When these realized gains are distributed by an ETF, there isn't any new wealth in the fund to be passed on to unitholders. All the ETF does is pass on this realized gain." That is why the price and the number of units doesn't ultimately change.

"What a lot of people don't realize," he continues, "is that with a traditional fund, when you get those additional units your price is dropping as well so you're not really any better off than you were before. There's no material difference between what we do and what a traditional fund does. In both cases when the dust settles, the only thing that's happened is that the value of your holdings are unchanged, but the fund's liability for capital gains tax has been flowed through to unitholders on a pro rata basis."

Distributions from U.S.-based ETFs to Canadian residents are most practically treated as income and are therefore taxed at your highest marginal tax rate. (See Chapter Six for an explanation of this.) Distributions from Canadian-based ETFs are more tax-advantaged because they retain their tax character as dividends or capital gains.

Index Construction, Free-Floats

Putting together an index may not seem like a tough job. Take the stocks of 100 companies with the largest market capitalization on a stock exchange and there you've got an index. The bigger a company's capitalization, the greater that company's influence on the index. What could be more straightforward? But take a look at all the listed securities excluded from the Russell U.S. indices:

- foreign stocks and non-U.S. incorporated stocks, ADRs
- closed-end funds
- limited partnerships
- royalty trusts
- stocks trading below $1
- preferred shares

Source: www.russell.com/US/Indexes/US/Methodology.asp

That's a fair number of dance partners ruled out before the music even starts, but this is a big ballroom where every move counts and every discrimination happens for a reason.

Indices are constructed with two primary goals. First, an index should be an accurate representation of a market or market segment, otherwise its fluctuations don't mean much. Second, an index should be investable. In other words, index investors should be able to reproduce the index easily by buying its components. This is where some foreign indices fall short. A company may have a large market capitalization, but when few of the shares are available for trading, it becomes difficult to reproduce the index. This can happen when a company holds many of its own shares or the shares of another company also on the index. Foreign ownership restrictions on stock purchases imposed by some countries further reduces the investability of an index, as does major stock holdings by controlling shareholders, company management or governments.

Most index sponsors have addressed this issue by designing indices and their weightings based on the "free-float" of a company's stock available to foreign investors in the market instead of being based on total market capitalization. Morgan Stanley Capital International, the world's top provider of global stock indices, has converted all its indices from a simple market cap to free-float adjusted weights. This dislodged so many stocks included in major indices that the conversion was done in stages to minimize disruption to the markets. The conversions were completed in June 2002.

At the same time, MSCI aimed to increase the number of companies their indices include in each market, which should give their indices a more accurate representation of those markets. The conversion makes MSCI indices more meaningful benchmarks for investors, but global fund managers are not doing pirouettes in delight: these changes will also fix some notoriously easy to beat indices, such as the MSCI EAFE Index.

The free-float issue isn't as straightforward as it may seem. According to Glenn Doody, Vice President of Canadian Index Services at Standard and Poor's in Toronto, the TSX was one of the first index sponsors to adjust their index to free-float in 1977 when they introduced the TSE 300. S&P has converted almost all its indices to free-float with the exception of the S&P 500 which doesn't require it because of the healthy liquidity of the stocks within that index.

There are, however, degrees of compliance with free-float ideals. Surprisingly, Canada's market is one of the few in which S&P has disregarded ownership restrictions in its index construction. Doody says Canadian restrictions on foreign ownership of media and communication companies, airlines and financial institutions would leave a Canadian index with too few companies to be representative of the market. "Market representation and liquidity are always a trade off," observes Doody. Optimal Canadian market representation requires the inclusion of many companies on which the government has imposed foreign ownership restrictions. S&P's domestic Canadian indices have opted for the best representation rather than for perfect foreign liquidity. The Dow Jones people, at least for the purposes of their global index, do their market cap calculations based on free-float, but the calculations take into account only block holdings of 5% or more. If a country like Japan has many small block holdings, the Dow Jones free-float will not be sensitive enough to adjust for that.

Doody also noted a few other issues in index construction. Exchangeable shares, (shares that can be exchanged for another security either in the same company or in another company), were removed from all S&P Canadian indices two years ago. Multi-class shares were another sore spot recently rectified. A company like Bombardier for instance, has different classes of shares independently listed on different indices. Bombardier B was in the S&P/TSX 60 index and Bombardier A was in the S&P/TSX Small Cap index, but Bombardier itself is a large cap company. With Bombardier and other dual class companies like it, S&P amalgamated the classes into the largest, most liquid class and determined into which index that class should be put. "Securities shouldn't be in the index," says Doody. "Companies should be in the index."

No doubt there will be other refinements to indices as time goes on and their uses become more diverse. "Fifteen or twenty years ago indices were mainly used to measure markets. Today more and more you are seeing indexes with products associated with them—derivatives and ETFs," says Doody.

For investors, knowing something about the problems involved in constructing an index puts their performance—and those of a fund manger—in perspective. All the financial sophistication in the world has yet to make it a science.

What Happens When ETFs Close Down?

In 2002, four ETFs were withdrawn from trading by their sponsor companies. One Canadian-based ETF was withdrawn on November 1, 2002:

SSgA Dow Jones Canada Titans 40

The following three U.S.-based ETFs were withdrawn as of December 13, 2002:

iShares Dow Jones U.S. Chemicals
iShares Dow Jones U.S. Internet
iShares S&P/TSX 60 (U.S.-based)

In all cases the ETFs failed to gain significant assets. Sometimes the popularity of the underlying index was to blame. That may be what hampered State Street Global Advisor's ETF in Canada even though that product had the lowest MER of any Canadian ETF, a noteworthy 0.08%. The Dow Jones Canada Titans 40 Index didn't have much of a following institutionally or with retail investors.

When an ETF is withdrawn from the market, shareholders are first notified of the impending closure. The fund sponsor sets a date for trading to stop and a deadline is given for the units to be redeemed. All investors still holding units or shares in the ETF at that time must redeem their holdings, but no brokerage fees or redemption charges of any kind will be imposed. That at least saves you the expense of a brokerage commission to sell the fund before it wraps up.

Don't worry about getting fair value for your ETF when it is wound down. The fund is liquidated for its net asset value (minus some small expenses) so neither much of a premium nor a discount to NAV will result. Investors are given cash in proportion to their ownership interest in the fund. Institutions and others with holdings of 50,000 units or more can redeem their units for the underlying stocks.

Record Keeping

One of the big reasons ETFs have such low MERs is because they use the established facilities of brokerages to provide the monthly statements for investors and the tax reporting. The brokerage that holds your ETF will issue you a T-3 slip—not the ETF sponsor company. That's using an already established, big and efficient system to great advantage.

Even though ETFs have stock-like qualities, unlike stocks, ETFs don't come in certificate form. No ETF will issue a certificate. Your ownership in an ETF is tracked on an electronic book-based system coordinated through the transfer agent. So don't look to tuck a stock certificate into a safety deposit box or surrender a stock certificate as collateral for a loan, though they can still be used as collateral.

You may be heartened to know that ETFs don't flood you with shareholder information for all the underlying securities. Similar to a conventional mutual fund, retail investors receive shareholder information for the ETF itself and have voting rights only with respect to the business of the ETF and not its underlying securities. Investors with positions of 50,000 units or more of an ETF, typically institutional investors, do have voting rights on the underlying securities.

Smelling the oil yet? Understanding some of the issues in index construction and maintenance will help you choose the right index to track with an ETF. You'll find a complete list of the indices that have ETFs associated with them in the Appendix. There, you'll also find mention of how the indices are constructed and run.

Before you turn back, take a few minutes to review the history of ETFs, where they came from and why. It's been said that history repeats itself. Who knows—maybe some of the failed products that came before ETFs might find the time is finally ripe to reassert themselves. In the next chapter you'll find some predictions about what's next on the scene in exchange traded funds. But before then, here's a global ETF specialist with her vision of the future.

ETFs in the future:
An Interview with Deborah Fuhr

Deborah A. Fuhr is head of ETF and OPALS research for Europe and Asia with Morgan Stanley Equity Research in London. She specializes in the global ETF marketplace.

Donna Green: What developments will fuel the growth of ETFs in the future?

Deborah Fuhr: *There are a number of things that will propel ETFs, but first of all there needs to be more education worldwide. A study last year by Mercer Consulting interviewed something like 728 pension plans in the U.S. and only a third of their managers said they knew what ETFs were.[3] That shows the message has still not made it to the end users even though ETFs have been in the U.S. since 1993. Institutional investors still need education to better understand ETFs and their applications.*

The use of ETFs in wrap accounts seems to be growing and that could be a large growth market for ETFs. Right now in Europe we have a very, very small number of wrap programs and the assets are tiny. Such programs would be good for the traditional independent financial advisors who are supposed to be independent, but actually they are often tied agents and get paid based on selling only certain funds with loads and annual fees. A U.K. government report came out recently saying that's not what we would call an independent financial advisor. An independent advisor should be paid based on doing the job, not promoting one fund over another based on getting paid more money.

Today you don't see ETFs being offered in any 401(k) plans in the U.S. [401(k) plans are a form of defined contribution pension plan in the U.S.] Opening up 401(k) plans to ETFs would be a huge market.

Fixed Income ETFs will also grow the market significantly. A product here in Europe similar to the first four bond ETFs in the U.S. would be very appealing because retail investors don't really have real time prices on fixed income securities right now in Europe. And the ability to achieve your asset allocation goals within a single product class is an appealing proposition.

Having options on ETFs will also further their growth. If you look at the historical growth of the NASDAQ 100 future, the ETF (QQQ) and also NASDAQ 100 options, the future didn't do much until the ETF came along. Then both the future and ETF took off and most days, the option is one of the most actively traded options. Liquidity is enhanced with each related product and they help the traders to price fairly on a real time basis where they should be trading.

I also think firms will continue to look at creating ETFs via new share classes on existing funds as Vanguard has done with VIPERs.

DG: What do you see happening with ETFs in the future?

DF: In the U.S. we'll see more fixed income ETFs on other segments of the fixed income market such as municipal bonds, and the launch of fixed income ETFs in Europe. People are working on this right now so by the first half of 2003 Europe should have some fixed income ETFs.

I also believe MERs will continue to come down in Europe and more sector products will be launched in Europe and Asia. We will also see the advent of options and even futures on ETFs here in Europe. And as assets and trading volumes grow, hedge funds will become more active in using ETFs in Europe. Right now they're a pretty small segment of the market.

DG: What about actively managed ETFs?

DF: It's left to be seen what will happen with active ETFs and traditional funds once the active rules are decided, but they're not going to overtake all mutual funds. Not every fund is going to convert into an ETF. People debated the future of closed-end funds, but they're still around. Each product fills a niche in the market.

September 2002

Notes

1) For the precise calculation method visit *iunits.com/broker/dealer/info/ daily fund values/baskets.*

2) Data on assets and trading volume as of December 31, 2001, Deborah A, Fuhr, "Exchange Traded Funds: A Global Overview," Morgan Stanley Equity Research, Europe, July 16, 2002, p. 25.

3) As of August 2002, Deborah A. Fuhr, "Exchange Traded Funds: A Global Summary," Morgan Stanley Equity Research Europe, September 3, 2002, p. 2.

Chapter Eight

The Past and Future of ETFs

Modern Portfolio Theory and the Efficient Markets Hypothesis together were the intellectual underpinnings of indexing, but indexing as an investment strategy wouldn't have been practical in real life without the technology to make trading a list of stocks all at once possible. In the late 1970s, institutions started taking advantage of new electronic order delivery systems on the NYSE and AMEX that allowed them to trade groups of shares effectively as a single basket. "Program trading" got its name from the computer programs that were designed to generate lists of stocks to be transacted through the electronic order delivery system. The new electronic system made it possible for a large number of different stocks to be bought or sold more or less simultaneously for a fixed commission, and so virtual basket trades began.

Then in 1982, the Chicago Mercantile Exchange introduced an index future on the S&P 500 that proved hugely popular because it was a more efficient way to effectively trade a whole index.[1] A future is a contract promising to buy or sell a stock, commodity, index or other instrument, at a specified price at a set time in the future. An index future is a contract that pays you the cash equivalent of the value of the market at a set time in the future. By buying a contract that promises to pay you the cash value of an index in the future, it is as though you have bought all the stocks in the index, but all you've actually purchased is a contract.

Index futures revolutionized portfolio management. Trading index futures was a pretty good proxy for buying and selling all the stocks in an index and an improvement over doing just that. Futures contracts were dirt cheap to trade and quickly became highly liquid.

Program trading and a heavy use of index futures were the main working parts in something known as "portfolio insurance" that prospered from 1982 to the market crash in October 1987, which some have blamed for the crash itself.[2] Two finance professors at Berkeley, Hayne Leland and Mark Rubinstein, developed software in the late 1970s that was designed to control the risk of an entire portfolio. Their program calculated how much the equity component of a portfolio could go down relative to its cash position before the whole portfolio fell below a specified bottom. When stocks were going down, the software dictated how much money had to be stripped from stocks and plowed into cash. When stocks were going up, more money was taken from cash in favour of equities. Applying this program trading with S&P 500 index futures gave them a dynamic strategy to control the risk of an entire portfolio. By 1986 the professors' company, Leland, O'Brien, Rubinstein Associates, Inc. (LOR) was managing US$60 billion either directly or through software licensing agreements.

"Our computer models worked right on target. It was a really reliable product," said Rubinstein in an interview for this book. "Our simulations showed that even through the great depression that would have disturbed us a little bit. ...[B]ut the results might have been acceptable and in almost all the rest of the time it works like a charm."

The charm lasted until October 19, 1987. That day the market fell so fast and furiously that portfolio insurers couldn't liquidate their positions swiftly enough to protect against losses. The market dropped 20% that dark day and according to Rubinstein, 20% of the sales of stocks and index futures that day were from portfolio insurers who would have sold more if they could have—making it all that much harder for the market to stagger back to its feet.

Regulators had not been impressed with the resilience of futures under stress, so the SEC encouraged the development of low-cost equity basket-type products not associated with the futures market.

Index Participation Shares

That's when a number of equity basket products started being developed in parallel. The first of these was Index Participation Shares (IPS) which came in a few varieties. The most popular was AMEX's "Equity Index Participations," based on the S&P 500 Index. IPS were simply stocks that paid returns linked directly to the underlying index. They could be sold on the secondary market or redeemed for cash—but not for the underlying securities because there weren't any securities behind them. IPS were a claim on the return of a futures contract on the S&P 500 index. The first IPS started trading in May 1989. Not long after, a Chicago court ruled that IPS were actually futures and should trade on a futures exchange and be under the jurisdiction of the Commodity Futures Trading Commission. No futures exchange picked up the innovative product, possibly because they didn't want it competing with their own index futures, and IPS died.[3]

SuperTrust

Meanwhile Leland, O'Brien and Rubinstein were hatching a different portfolio product. In 1988 they made an application to the SEC for something they called a SuperTrust that was to hold a basket of securities identical to the S&P 500 index. It was a complicated product containing SuperShares and SuperUnits. It took LOR five years to painfully maneuver their product through the SEC. By the time it emerged, AMEX was just a few months short of launching its own portfolio product which turned out to be kryptonite for SuperTrust.[4]

Despite having the biggest launch in the history of any fund product to that point, (US$2 billion), SuperTrust failed partly because it was too complicated. AMEX's elegantly simple product, the famous SPDRs, made it to the market three months after SuperUnits, in January 1993, and completely eclipsed LOR's regulatory groundbreaking product—the very first exchange traded fund proper.[5]

TIPS

The demise of IPS in the U.S. was something of a stroke of good fortune for Canada because the Toronto Stock Exchange had an IPS of its own sort in the making. In March 1990 the TSX conducted the first trade on TIPS, Toronto 35 Index Participation Units, based on the Toronto 35 Index, a collection of Canada's biggest and most liquid companies with wide industry representation. Unlike the American IPS, however, TIPS was a trust containing a basket of securities matching the Toronto 35 Index. The trust issued units as a claim on the trust. These units could be bought or sold on the TSX or in sufficiently large numbers, redeemed for the underlying securities in the trust. TIPS was immediately embraced by institutional investors and went on to popularity even among retail investors. So, by some odd reversal of our usual national fortune, the TSX launched a world first—the first successful ETF.

According to Gord Walker, Director of Derivatives, Markets and Marketing at the TSX from 1991 to 1996, TIPS was the model for SPDRs.

He believes a copy of a TIPS prospectus was attached to the SEC application for SPDRs. Walker was responsible for launching and overseeing Canada's second ETF in 1995—HIPs, based on the Toronto Stock Exchange 100 Index. TIPS and HIPs were re-branded into TIPs 35 and TIPs 100 in 1999.

Although TIPS and HIPs were an attempt to bring Bay Street to Main Street, the products were far less popular with retail investors than the TSX expected. They were, however, hugely popular with institutional investors because of their convenience and their penchant to run on nothing more than the smell of an oily rag. TIPS and HIPs did not have a management fee. The funds repaid the TSX for their operating expenses only through interest made from lending the securities of the funds to short sellers, something it could do because of being granted an exemption from the general prohibition for mutual funds against securities lending. That worked out to 0.04% annually, and as it turned out, less than the fund needed to pay its own way. The interest the fund earned on stock dividends was banked before their quarterly distribution to unitholders.

Walker is convinced that more individual Canadian investors would have bought TIPs had the retail investment community had more of a motivation to sell the product. TIPs, like all ETFs, were up against those mutual funds that pay a sales commission and regular trailer fees for as long as the client holds the fund. An ETF sale nets a broker a small stock trading commission nothing like the 5% or so of a typical mutual fund sale (back end load), and usually nothing more thereafter.

Nevertheless, institutional interest in TIPs was strong and they became among the most actively traded securities on the TSX. In a way, TIPs was a victim of its own success. Its vaporous 0.04% forced the TSX to subsidize the operating expenses of the fund and tied up resources that could be directed to its equity listing services, so the exchange decided to off load responsibility for the product onto an outside provider. BGI Canada Limited won the shareholders' permission to manage TIPs by merging it with the already existing i60 Fund. In March 2000, TIPs 35 and TIPs 100 were both merged with BGI Canada's i60 Fund and its comparably robust 0.17% MER. The combined entity made the i60 the largest index fund and one of the largest mutual funds in the Canadian equity category.

SPDRs, of course, went on to great fame and glory, too, even if it did have to crawl over the bodies of a few dead products.

ETFs Today

SPDRs, appropriately enough, spawned WEBS (World Equity Benchmark Shares) in 1996. These ETFs were based on international equity indices and are now known as iShares MSCI Funds. There are now an astonishing 21 of these representing the indices of as many countries. Before there could be eentsy-weentsy ETFs, the arachnid theme was abandoned in favour of more industrial-sounding names like DIAMONDS (January 1998) based on the Dow Jones Industrial Average and Qubes (March 1999) for the NASDAQ 100 Index. There are now 116 U.S.-based ETFs in all and the proliferation is far from over.

U.S. ETF Developments

VIPERs

Perhaps the biggest indication of the irreversible momentum of ETFs was Vanguard Group's launch on May 31, 2001 of its own ETF, the first in what is expected to be a series. Vanguard pioneered index mutual funds for the retail investor, and is the second largest mutual fund company in the U.S. with a staggering US$570 billion under administration. Fidelity Investments still has the distinction of being America's largest mutual fund company, but Vanguard is growing much faster and by the time you read this may have surpassed its rival in "long-term" mutual fund assets.

Vanguard's first ETF is based on an optimized basket of Vanguard's Total Stock Market Index Fund which is itself based on an optimized basket of about 3,400 stocks in the Wilshire 5000 Index. The ETFs in the Vanguard series are called VIPERs which stands for "**V**anguard **I**ndex **P**articipation **E**quity **R**eceipts." The interesting thing about VIPERs is that they are ETFs and simultaneously a new share class of Vanguard's existing index fund. This is a first in the ETF world and will almost certainly be imitated by other fund companies. A second VIPER was introduced in 2002, this one tied to the Wilshire 4500 Index. Vanguard also appears to be positioning itself to launch some ETFs on new MSCI capitaliziation and style indices on the U.S. market. Clearly Vanguard anticipates a promising future for the new version of index funds.[6]

A few other U.S. innovations, including global sector and fixed income ETFs, also deserve mention.

Global Sector ETFs

Global sector ETFs contain stocks from one particular industry sector, but selected from countries around the world. Studies are beginning to show that good timing of sector plays can boost returns, and this applies in big letters to sectors across country boundaries.[7] Given the difficulty in individual stock picking—especially internationally— ETFs are the ideal product for sector plays. You can move in and out of them quickly and because no ETF as yet hedges foreign currencies, you get full exposure to the currency effect on all the international stocks.

So far there are five global sector ETFs, all sponsored by BGI and launched in November of 2001, covering energy, financials, healthcare, technology and telecommunications. (See Appendix C for more details.)

Fixed Income ETFs

The ETF structure can accommodate a vast variety of investments so long as there is a liquid market for them. There are now four bond ETFs in the American market. Three are related to U.S. treasury bond indices and one is pegged to a corporate bond index.

For retail investors, the ability to trade a portfolio of bonds on the open market is a giant advance. Traditionally, bonds are traded through a brokerage's bond desk with little price transparency for the investor. Each trade is charged a commission which is discretely subtracted from the bond's yield and seldom disclosed. Bond ETFs should save investors money on yield spreads lost to implicit commissions and will make building a diversified bond portfolio easier and cheaper. Compared to bond funds, the 0.15% MER on fixed income ETFs is also a bargain.

In July 2002, fixed income ETFs were launched in the U.S. by BGI. At least three other fixed income funds are likely due from them in 2003. A new firm, ETF Advisors, introduced four fixed income ETFs of their own that began trading in November 2002 called Treasury **F**ixed **I**ncome **T**rust **R**eceipts, otherwise known as FITRs (pronounced "fighters").

Pending Developments

Two underdeveloped areas likely to be filled soon are international growth and value ETFs. This will make global style investing far easier than ever before.

Some international regions are not yet well-represented with ETFs. An emerging markets ETF is likely to ameliorate this situation soon. Even in well-covered areas, new ETFs are springing up. ETFs called "Fresco Shares" are soon to be introduced into the U.S. These are offered by UBS and the initial ones will be on the DJ STOXX 50 and the DJ EURO

STOXX 50 indices. These ETFs will hold the 50 largest European and Eurozone stocks respectively.

New indices in the U.S. will probably bring forth new ETFs, also. Brinson Partners, a UBS subsidiary, is working with Morningstar (U.S.) to bring out capitalization and style indices on the U.S. market.

Competition among ETFs exists even among funds not yet launched. With the first leveraged funds snorting at the starting gate, a U.S. fund company, Rydex, has indicated they are going to launch leveraged ETFs similar to ProFunds proposed funds.

These are just some of the products expected out soon. All kinds of variation and permutations await us in the future.

Canadian ETF Developments

Canada's ETF offering has grown from one product in 1999 to 16 products in 2002. Canada boasts one HOLDRS as well. But among all the steps forward, there has been one step back. A Canadian ETF has been withdrawn because it failed to attract much interest: State Street Global Advisors' Dow Jones Canada Titans 40 Index Participation Fund.

Just as State Street was pulling the plug on their product, BGI Canada was launching a REIT iUnits (**R**eal **E**state **I**nvestment **T**rust). The growth of ETFs is hardly likely to stop. In Canada alone, mutual funds lay claim to $400 billion of investors' money. At $5 billion in total assets, ETFs in Canada have a lot of room to expand and innovation will help them forward.

There is no lack of innovation in Canada. The country had fixed income ETFs more than a year before the U.S. rolled theirs out. The iUnits Government of Canada 10-year Bond Fund, and iUnits Government of Canada 5-year Bond Fund are unique in a number of respects. Apart from the fact that they were the world's first fixed income ETFs, they are also the first ETFs not pegged to an index. Both bond funds hold one bond each. As time passes and the maturity shortens, the bond is traded for another government bond closer to the target five and ten-year maturities of the respective funds.

Canada also has two 100% RRSP eligible ETFs tied to foreign markets. This is a unique product specific to Canada and designed to address the foreign content restriction on RRSP savings. They are, in fact, synthetic ETFs in that they do not hold stocks but rather buy exchange traded futures contracts on their targeted index. This is similar to the way 100% RRSP eligible foreign equity mutual funds work. (These funds, often known as clone funds, use private derivatives contracts rather than exchange-traded ones.) The ETFs, however, have MERs that would make their mutual fund counterparts blush: 0.30% and 0.35% compared to well over 2.5% for most clone funds.

The two synthetic ETFs cover the S&P 500 Index and the MSCI EAFE Index. It's likely more of these RRSP eligible foreign equity ETFs will spring up in the next few years, sending clone funds back to the test-tube.

ETFs Internationally

Global markets are introducing ETFs rapidly. As of November 2002, there were 149 ETFs listed on non-North American markets. Domestic or regional ETFs are traded on exchanges around the world—in the United Kingdom, Germany, the Netherlands, France, Finland, Sweden, Switzerland, India, South Africa, Australia, New Zealand, Hong Kong, Singapore, Japan, Israel, Mexico and China.

The trading volume in ETFs increases substantially when options and futures are pegged to them. This is coming soon in Europe. Eurex is a European electronic derivatives trading platform. They are expected to launch futures and options on ETFs in Europe sometime in late 2002, giving ETFs yet another push forward.

Interestingly, Japan has been a particularly successful market for ETFs abroad. Introduced in Japan in 2001, ETFs there have already hit US$16.5 billion with just 18 products. Compare that to Europe's numbers. ETFs have been available in Europe since 2000 and now number 116 in all but with assets of US$8.7 billion—about half of the Japanese total.

According to Deborah Fuhr, global ETF analyst for Morgan Stanley in London, ETFs serve an unusual function in Japan. "In Japan they've created ETFs as a way to facilitate companies selling off their cross-holdings," she notes. "Companies in Japan are pretty cash strapped but they have very significant holdings in affiliated companies. They want to sell off these shares to raise money, but they don't want to have Sony buying Mitsubishi shares, for instance, for fear that when you have proxy and other voting things come up, Sony might vote against Mitsubishi's best interests." Since fund companies there traditionally vote in agreement with the companies they're invested in, cross-holdings can be held in ETFs[8] without giving a competitor the opportunity to take over voting rights. "It's worked successfully," she says. The Japanese market for ETFs is likely to grow even more, says Fuhr, because the Japanese government is implementing some tax changes to make it less onerous to hold ETFs. "Japan taxes people holding funds, but they are going to change that just for ETFs," she says.

Cross-listings

There's also a flurry of cross-listing going on with ETFs globally. Cross-listing allows the securities from one exchange to be traded on another exchange. Institutional investors often have foreign intermediaries through which they can trade foreign securities, but cross-listing gives retail investors the chance to buy and sell stocks that might not otherwise be available to them on a home exchange with lower settlement costs. Cross-listing also increases the liquidity of the cross-listed security. In Europe there are more than 150 ETF cross-listings.

The American Stock Exchange has arranged with Euronext (formed from the merger of the Amsterdam, Brussels and Paris exchanges) and the Singapore Exchange to offer some U.S. ETFs. Talk continues with a number of other countries for similar cross-listing opportunities.

NASDAQ has also announced plans to list Japanese ETFs on its electronic market in both the U.S. and Europe in the future. NASDAQ seems to have plans to provide a global trading platform for ETFs via its network in the U.S., Europe and Japan.

Cross-listing isn't good just for foreign investors. It also has benefits for North American investors when the cross-listing gives reciprocal access. Suppose you own an iShares MSCI Hong Kong and you sell it at 11 a.m. Toronto time. You get a price as of 11 a.m. Toronto time, but the underlying securities are 12 hours away tucked in their beds. Your 11 a.m. price actually reflects the market sentiment about what the Hong Kong market will do when it wakes up, so it is not a perfect tracking device. If, on the other hand, you owned a Hong Kong ETF that tracked the Hong Kong market, your 11 a.m. sell order would be executed the minute the Hong Kong market opened at that exact market price.

The flexibility to trade domestic ETFs in their own time zone will enhance tracking and increase liquidity. It's the financial markets equivalent of free trade.

ETFs may not just be the next generation of mutual funds—they may turn out to be the financial enterprise that boldly goes where no financial instrument has gone before.

The Evolution of ETFs (fig. 41)

1978   Program trading—trading large blocks of different stocks simultaneously based on a computer program's instructions, starts.

1982   LOR's portfolio insurance takes off with the introduction of index futures in the U.S.

1987   October stock market crash puts the lie to portfolio insurance as it was designed. Regulators call for a different kind of stock basket product.

1988   LOR files a proposal to the SEC for a SuperTrust with SuperUnits and SuperShares, the first exchange traded funds.

1989   Index Participation Shares trade on AMEX and the Philadelphia Exchange. Shortly thereafter a Chicago court rules them futures and so eligible for trading on a futures exchange only. No futures exchange picks up the product and it is discontinued.

1990   Toronto 35 Index Participation Units first traded on the TSX, becoming the first successful ETF in the world.

1992   SuperTrust units are traded on AMEX in November but are quickly eclipsed by a simpler product, SPDRs.

1993   Standard and Poor's Depositary Receipts (SPDRs) land on AMEX in January.

1995   HIPs first traded on the TSX.

1996   WEBS (now iShares MSCI Funds) launched.

1998   DIAMONDS (Dow Jones Industrial Average ETF) launched.

1999   Qubes (NASDAQ 100 ETF) launched in March and becomes one of the most heavily traded securities in the U.S.

2000   More than 75 ETFs launched worldwide this year. Canada introduces world's first fixed income ETFs, which are also the first ETFs not related to an index.

2001   May 31 Vanguard Group launches its long awaited initial VIPERs ETF.

2001   July 31 NYSE begins trading SPDRs, DIAMONDS and Qubes.

2002   First U.S. fixed income ETFs (July).

2002   ETFs terminated—one in Canada, three in the U.S.

2002   NYSE adds an additional 34 ETFs; total now trading on NYSE reaches 37.

ETFs in the Future

More Variety

ETFs in general are certain to become far more varied in kind. ETF innovations will not be limited to ordinary stocks and bonds. There's already three real estate investment trust (REIT) ETFs, two in the U.S. and one in Canada. As long as it can be bought and sold with real time pricing, anything can be thrown into an ETF structure. A hedge fund index is being developed in the U.S. now and an ETF associated with that index could easily follow. A Lehman Brothers' report on ETFs as far back as September 2000 predicted a hedge fund of ETFs would follow active and leveraged active fund ETFs.

Passive leveraged ETFs are not far away. In June 2002, ProFund Advisors LLC, a U.S. mutual fund company, made an SEC filing for eight unusual ETFs. The proposed funds are designed to give investors leveraged and short exposure to four indices, the S&P 500, the NASDAQ-100, the Dow and the S&P MidCap 400. The four leveraged funds should return twice the index's return. The short ETFs should profit when the index goes down, by a multiple of two. The funds have not yet been approved for sale, but when they are, another ETF milestone will have been marked.

Pools of ETFs

More immediately, it's not hard to imagine ETFs made up of pools of other ETFs. Spectrum Investment Management Limited in Canada has already done this within a mutual fund. "Tactonics" is Spectrum's global tactical asset allocation fund.[9] It contains as many as 20 ETFs dynamically managed with a proprietary trend-spotting computer model. Clearly ETFs were the best tool the fund managers could find to implement their strategy. Unfortunately, Tactonics' MER at more than 2% will still be as high as any other mutual fund. An ETF holding other ETFs in a dynamic asset allocation could do something very similar without the drawbacks of a mutual fund structure.

ETFs as Product Building Blocks

Right now ETFs are the mutual fund industry's worst nightmare, but I believe that attitude will change once their usefulness within broader investment solutions becomes recognized. The Tactonics fund, which was awarded "Best New Initiative of 2001" by the Canadian Mutual Fund Awards, is a good example of this. ETFolios, the customized asset allocation service offered by Guardian Capital Advisors Inc., is another. These are important first steps because they expand the use of ETFs, and more importantly, allow financial planners to provide ETFs to their clients.

Typically, financial planners are licensed to sell mutual funds only. ETFs, being an exchange traded security, require a securities license which many financial planners do not have. As a result, clients of mutual fund licensed planners are not able to access ETFs through their advisor. The advent of ETFs within the box of a mutual fund will open up ETFs to planning clients.

Even now some prominent figures in the Canadian mutual fund industry and experts in asset allocation are working at establishing a program that integrates ETFs into existing mutual fund portfolios. This service is aimed squarely at planners who, because of licensing restrictions, currently have limited access to ETFs.

Actively Managed ETFs

Germany was the first country to claim to have actively managed ETFs in November 2000. Six months later, Germany had seven index-based ETFs (most run by HypoVereinsbank AG) and 11 actively managed "ETFs" sponsored by DWS Investments, a unit of Deutsche Bank.[10]

Few in the international ETF community, however, consider Germany's actively managed products to be ETFs. The same is true of Australia's so-called active ETFs. The problem rests with the transparency of the underlying portfolios.

Institutional shareholders of Germany's actively managed "ETFs" learn about their portfolio positions with a two-day delay. Retail investors, on the other hand, get one-month-old information. This information lag makes arbitraging impossible. Since the normal arbitraging that keeps index ETF prices in line with their NAVs isn't available for the active funds, the Deutsche Borse of Frankfurt restricts the actively managed "ETFs" on its exchange from trading beyond a set bid/ask spread. According to Deborah Fuhr, global ETF analyst, those restrictions violate the defining characteristics of ETFs:

> "Despite the claims of some European and Australian fund managers, to my mind, we don't yet have actively managed funds. Three things differentiate exchange traded funds from just funds that trade on exchanges. Every day ETFs provide the underlying portfolio to the marketplace. You also have indicative net asset values, and the unique in-kind creation/redemption process. If you look at funds that trade on an exchange, they are normal mutual funds that are just trading on an exchange. You don't know the underlying

portfolio, there are no indicative asset values, and there's no in-kind creation/redemption process. These are not ETFs."[11]

In Canada and the U.S., ETFs are required to provide continuous portfolio disclosure, which poses a problem for active fund managers who don't want to show their hand too flagrantly. There's good reason for that reluctance. If market participants get wind of a manager's intention to buy a security, others will buy it up first and push the price up before the manager has finished establishing his position. Similarly, once its known that a manager is selling a significant position in a stock, others will sell too and grind the price down. That manager's cold sweat is known as "front running." Jurisdictions that permit actively managed ETFs will have to come to some kind of compromise between continuous disclosure and portfolio confidentiality.

So far the North American regulatory hurdle of continuous disclosure is holding back the introduction of actively managed ETFs, but industry sources do not think that will prove insurmountable. The SEC put out a concept paper on actively managed ETFs in November 2001 to solicit comments from industry participants. This is the first step in formulating rules for actively managed ETFs in the U.S., if they are approved at all. It will be interesting to see what develops in other parts of the world.

The appetite for actively managed ETFs may be enormous. Boston-based Financial Research Corporation expects actively managed ETFs to attract as much as US$200 billion in the U.S. alone within five years of their launch.[12] When you think it took nine years for index ETFs to garner US$66 billion, those are serious expectations.

Kevin Ireland, Vice President of ETF Marketing for AMEX is of the opinion that active ETFs are definitely on their way to North America. "The first generation of active funds will be quantitative and rules based, like the leveraged ETFs," he says. "The models being created to price these things effectively on an intraday basis with or without full disclosure are pretty well done. Now it's just a matter of fine-tuning them. Once they get the arbitrage mechanism to work within the trader's realm of risk, then you're going to be able to run an active portfolio and be able to price it effectively during the course of the day."

He believes active ETFs will not have full portfolio disclosure. "No active manager wants everybody to know what he's doing so he can just be copied," says Ireland. "These models that they're creating are going to be able to provide the necessary hedge for liquidity purposes without full disclosure." But he says it isn't going to happen quickly. "It will take baby steps. You aren't going to go from an index fund to a fully non-disclosed portfolio in one leap."

Whether or not actively managed ETFs ever get off the ground, there's still plenty of room for the plain index variety to proliferate. Even with current regulatory restrictions, exchange traded baskets of securities will continue to proliferate here and around the world because they're more efficient and flexible than conventional mutual funds.

Derivatives on ETFs

Mark Rubinstein, who along with his colleagues at LOR was the U.S. ETF pioneer, feels the time is ripe for another generation of ETFs that have options associated with them as did his SuperUnits: "Our product really [was] better than ETFs today because you could break it up and do more with it... I'm going to be quite surprised if some exchange traded funds don't effectively start doing this. In today's context, it's going to be a lot easier to get regulatory approval for things like we were doing. There's a lot more awareness of derivatives and options."

Perhaps Rubinstein's design of options within units won't materialize, but there are other ways to achieve the same end. The Montréal Exchange lists an option on the i60 and is expected to come out with options on a number of BGI Canada's sector ETFs. A futures market in Canada on sector ETFs could develop thereafter.

Options are widely available on a large number of U.S. ETFs. The SEC, as of mid-2002, has approved futures trading on ETFs. Although index futures are well-established, futures on ETFs do not yet exist. At least two companies are developing them now with the first launch expected in early 2003.[13]

The Competition

All good products spur competition and ETFs are no exception. One Internet service in the U.S. allows American investors to buy and sell ready-made portfolios for a flat monthly fee. FOLIO*fn* at *www.foliofn.com* offers over 100 portfolios that cover markets, sectors, risk levels and famous investment strategies like the Dogs of the Dow. Each portfolio can hold up to 50 stocks. The Web site says, "It's as easy as selecting a mutual or index fund." What's more, FOLIO*fn* has the even more remarkable feature of allowing investors to customize the contents of their portfolios with up to two trades a day in as many as three portfolios—all for US$29.95 a month or US$295 a year. That's the equivalent of holding CDN$175,000 of an i60 Unit with an MER of 0.17%—without trading commission. Quite a deal especially when you think of the added flexibility it gives you over a fixed ETF portfolio. Anything less than $175,000, though, and a straight ETF portfolio is considerably cheaper over two years or more even with initial brokerage commissions.

Nancy Smith, Vice President of Investor Education for FOLIO*fn* says there are plans to expand their service to Canada but no official date has been set. She points out that ETFs can be bought through their service and held in their accounts, or an investor can select one of the indices offered at *foliofn.com* and even customize it if desired. There's no MER or any other expenses beyond the monthly or annual fee. Of course, there isn't a big selection of famous name indices to chose from at this point either.

Should these do-it-yourself, ready-made but customizable portfolio service catch on, ETF sponsors might very well be forced to join them at their own game and radically revise the nature of their offering. Time will tell just how active investors ultimately want to become even when they're aiming for a predominantly passive investment approach.

Gavin Quill of Financial Research Corporation is also impressed with the FOLIO*fn* offering. However, his experience and research in the behaviour of retail fund investors puts a damper on his enthusiasm. "It is very commendable and it will be superior for those who want to avail themselves of it," he says. "But I'm skeptical about how many people will want to avail themselves of it. You cannot extrapolate from what the very small minority of techno savvy early adopters do and what the overwhelming majority of busy non-technologically focused, 'happy-with-good-enough' investors are going to do."

He may be right. FOLIO*fn* has already outlived one competitor, netFolio, who shut down a similar service in 2002.

Conventional mutual funds are not likely to lay down and play dead in the face of the ETF threat. Mutual fund companies will almost certainly launch their own ETFs, as Vanguard has done. Sensing the change in the wind, some fund companies might even attempt to convert some of their existing funds to exchange traded funds.[14]

In a move that's got the American Stock Exchange worried, the New York Stock Exchange began trading the three most popular ETFs on its exchange on July 31, 2001. For the first three months of trading in Qubes, DIAMONDS, and SPDRs, the NYSE did not charge transaction fees. ETFs are the mainstay of AMEX which has lost stock listings to NYSE and NASDAQ. This competitive move by NYSE underscores the market importance of these younger U.S. products and the promising future they represent.

We've just entered the third inning of ETF development. Competition among the sponsors and exchanges will continue to spawn more choice and more innovative offerings. The game is only beginning to heat up.

ETFs at Home and Around the Globe:
An Interview with Kevin Ireland

Kevin Ireland is Vice President, ETF Marketing for AMEX and, according to their slogan is, "where ETFs were born, raised, and spend all of their quality time."

Kevin Ireland: *We try to facilitate ETF listings around the world. We're in partnership with Singapore, have an agreement with Euronext, and are in negotiations with several other people where we're going to have the ability to trade these ETFs on a global basis.*

Right now if you want to trade an ETF in Europe you're buying it on a European exchange and you're buying that exchange's version of the ETF. Very soon you're going to be able to buy an ETF in New York, sell it in Singapore, buy it on Euronext and it's all going to be the same ETF. From a global perspective, this is really the first time you can have global access like this to listed equities. This will broaden the exposure of ETFs even more.

Right now Qubes trade off the board [over the counter] in Europe probably as actively as here. This is going to give them a listed venue to trade that one consistent product on an around the clock, global basis.

Donna Green: How will the ETFs be valued when the home market is closed and you can't get a price on the underlying basket?

KI: *With the underlying [fund securities] closed, the ETF will do one of two things: it will track the [index] future or become the price discovery vehicle itself. That will definitely be different. A lot of the success of ETFs on the domestic side has been the ability of ETFs to track the markets so closely.*

Right now we have a 15 minute window where the market is closed and ETFs, along with the futures, become the price discovery vehicle. It gives investors an opportunity to take views on where they think the market is going to go the next day. Now they are going to be able to do that on a 24 hour basis with the understanding, too, that even though the underlying assets aren't trading, the market isn't really static. How often do we come out with news in the underlying securities throughout the course of the evening and the next morning? Now you'll have the capability to act on that.

Obviously, without the arbitrage capability, the price will work a little off supply and demand, but you gain the opportunity to react to market news immediately.

DG: What do you think of fixed income ETFs?

KI: *I think they really enhance the investor's ability to do asset allocation. I think it's even more important than on the equity side to be able to fill in the fixed income portion of your portfolio with a single purchase. You could buy a single treasury, but with an ETF you can get exposure to the entire yield curve. You want to buy corporate bonds? There's obviously tremendous risk right now, but now you can buy a 100 bond basket of high grade corporates all in one shot. These are strategies that only bond traders had before. Not only can you cover the entire yield curve with a single purchase, but you can take active views on which way the yield curve is going to go. You can do this in one or two purchases where you didn't have that kind of capability before.*

Fixed income ETFs will be very important to advisors, but it's going to take a while. There's still a lot of learning which will hamper the immediate growth of fixed income ETFs.

DG: Do you think advisors are interested in selling ETFs?

KI: *Advisors realize the transaction business has been commoditized. The only value added they have is truly as an advisor and that's a fee-based world. Being fee-based allows advisors for the first time to work in conjunction with their customers without a conflict of interest. If an advisor gets 1% on a customer with $100,000, he'll get twice as much when he turns that into $200,000 at 1%. And ETFs are really good parts in the tool box to do the asset allocation.*

If you own a portfolio of 20 fixed income products and 20 stocks and you want to rebalance, effectively you've got to do 40 trades. With ETFs, though not as your entire portfolio, you can make that same adjustment in two, three or four moves. It's simpler, cleaner, and you've lowered your risk with diversification.

The bear market has actually been beneficial to ETFs. We had US$90 billion in assets in May 2002 and four months later we still have $90 billion. When you take away market depreciation which has been substantial, you're talking about significant inflows into these funds. There's been a constant drain from the active side.

The active managers said during the ten-year bull run, when 80% of the active managers underperformed the S&P 500, 'wait until the bear market.' And they didn't prove that true. They're still underperforming their benchmark indexes. I think the active manager poses more risk at this point than just getting into the market. At least you know what you own with an ETF. The proof is in the pudding. Active assets are going down dramatically but inflows into ETFs are continuing.

September 20, 2002.

Notes

1) The history of index futures and other derivative products is instructively and entertainingly told in "The Whence, How and Why of OTC Equity Derivatives: An Introduction to OTC Derivatives for the Financial Investor," by Bruce Collins, Ph.D., Associate Professor of Finance, Western Connecticut State University. The paper is available at *www.wcsu.ct.stateu.edu/finance/newsletter/n/fall98.htm*.

2) For an accessible and entertaining explanation of portfolio insurance see *Capital Ideas, The Improbable Origins of Modern Wall Street*, Peter L. Bernstein, (New York: The Free Press, 1992), pp. 269-294.

3) On the history of equity baskets see *The Handbook of Equity Derivatives*, Revised Edition, Jack Clark Francis, William W. Toy, J. Gregg Whittaker, editors, (New York: John Wiley & Sons, Inc., 2000); "Index Participation Units," Eric Kirzner, pp. 100-120; "Exchange Traded Equity Funds—Genesis, Growth, and Outlook," by Gary L. Gastineau and Clifford J. Weber, pp. 121-141. Also, "Why Financial Instruments Fail or Succeed," by Jack Clark Francis, pp. 631-650.

4) On SuperShares and SuperUnits, a fascinating product that was 15 years ahead of its time, see Mark Rubinstein's extraordinary Web site, *www.in-the-money.com*. Click on articles about SuperShares. Also interesting is his discussion of the development of portfolio insurance.

5) Mark Rubinstein was one of three principals of Leland, O'Brien Rubinstein Associates, Inc. (LOR), the California-based company that invented portfolio insurance, and subsequently SuperTrust, the first ETF in the U.S. The company is no longer active and Rubinstein remains a professor of finance at The University of California at Berkeley. He generously gave an extensive interview for this book. Here is an excerpt from that May 2001 interview, demonstrating so poignantly the heartbreak of pioneers.

Rubinstein:

> *We feel frustrated about the fact that now exchange traded funds are the big deal and even though we had the idea first, at least in terms of applying it, we didn't make it. We were a little company. We feel we've been cheated out of the intellectual credit for this. We were the first people to actually do it.*
>
> *We spent millions of dollars on attorneys trying to convince the SEC to allow us to do this. We were doing something that was obviously right and would be in the interest of investors. If ordinary options are in the interests of investors, these certainly would be. If index funds and mutual funds are in the interest of the investors, these are. So it made no sense to me. They asked*

us to go through all kinds of hoops and we couldn't just sit down at a table and talk to them.

Prime and Scores* had already been approved and our product had an even better reason to exist because we were not trading calls on individual stocks. We were going to make it possible to buy calls on a widely diversified portfolio and generally speaking, that's better for investors than individual stocks.

But the SEC said they were ashamed that they had approved Primes and Scores. They didn't like them and they were going to make us go through a very long procedure instead of a short cut procedure for approval. It ended up taking five years. If the SEC had not done that, our business might be a lot different today.

By the time they ended up approving [SuperShares], index securities in general and options were becoming more popular and there was a variety of them. AMEX ended up going ahead with their own product [SPDRs], but I'm sure if we'd gotten our product out a year or two before they wouldn't have gone ahead and they probably would have helped us more in marketing. We were way ahead of the game in our thinking.

John O'Brien...convinced large companies to buy huge quantities of SuperUnits and then break them up and sell them off to the market. I think we had the largest initial launch of any fund to that point, $2 billion.

Our product was really better than ETFs today because you could break it up and do more with it. Unfortunately, in the practical world there are other things. The SEC won't let you do it, they'll put burdens on you.

The Achilles heel to our product was its complexity. [Because of this] the SEC said every secondary transaction must come with a prospectus. We told the brokerages you can sell [SuperUnits] just like an ordinary stock—but then there was the prospectus problem. Brokerage companies didn't want to change their procedures until the product got popular.

LOR exists as a shell. That's what happened to us. It shows you that when you try to innovate in financial markets you're probably going to fail and you have to get the product just right; otherwise, someone else will come in who makes it just a little bit better and take the whole market which is basically what SPDRs did.

SuperUnits and SuperShares stopped trading in 1995.

*Primes and Scores were a popular but unusual product first introduced in 1983 by a company called Americus. Here's how Prof. Rubinstein explains them in his unpublished paper "SuperTrust" (available on his remarkable site, *www.in-the-money.com* by clicking on "Mark Rubinstein" and scrolling down the list of articles):

"The first trust was based on shares of AT&T. For each share of AT&T a shareholder turned over to Americus, he was issued a trust unit. In turn, the investor could split the unit into a SCORE and a PRIME. At the end of five years, the SCORE received AT&T shares with a market value equal to the capital gains above a preset "termination value" earned over the period (if any). The PRIME received all the cash dividends, AT&T shares equal to the remaining capital value of the trust, and shareholder voting rights" (p. 8). A recombined PRIME and SCORE could be redeemed for a unit at any time and a unit could also be redeemed at any time. There were 28 different stocks being used in these Americus Trusts in 1988. An unfavourable taxing ruling in 1986 made the creation of any more of these trusts impractical. They have all since expired.

6) *Globe and Mail*, "Vanguard about to Beat Fidelity," Aaron Lucchetti, August 2002.

7) See "The Global ETF Investor: Conference Highlights: Slicing the World—The Country versus Sector Allocation Debate," Salomon Smith Barney Equity Research publication, May 22, 2001.

8) In North America, not all fund companies vote with the companies they invest in. Some firms, such as BGI Canada, delegate the proxy voting to an independent third party who objectively assesses the issue at vote. This effectively eliminates any potential conflict of interest between a fund manager and the fund's unitholders.

9) In July 2002, Spectrum's mutual fund family was absorbed by CI Funds and the name was changed to CI Tactonics Fund in September.

10) German institutional investors seem to favour the index products while the actively managed funds are more popular with retail investors. In less than a year and a half, actively managed "ETFs" have attracted over US$16 billion, no doubt owing to the costs of traditional mutual funds in that country which usually carry a sales charge, annual management fees and bank deposit fees. Coleen Moses, SEI Investments, April 24, 2001, e-mail broadcast.

11) Quoted from an interview for this book in September 2002.

12) Gavin Quill, Vice President, Financial Research Corp. in a telephone interview, September 17, 2002.

13) *MAR ETFR*, "How Single Stock Futures will Affect ETFs," Ellise Coroneos, issue no. 23, September 2002, p. 2.

14) An article written by Gary L. Gastineau, Senior Vice President at AMEX, and Clifford J. Weber, Vice President at AMEX, has suggested that even though it is too early to say for certain, it is possible that after a certain date in the future most or all new mutual funds will be exchange traded. "...[T]he facts that exchange traded funds have some attractive

characteristics not available in conventional funds and that these funds are frequently less costly for their sponsors to create and maintain, suggests that substantial gains in market share are likely," p. 140. "Exchange Traded Equity Funds—Genesis, Growth, and Outlook," *The Handbook of Equity Derivatives*, Revised Edition, Jack Clark Francis, et al., Editor, (New York: John Wiley & Sons Inc., 2000).

Part Four
Appendix A

Fact Sheets on All Canadian ETFs

iUnits™ S&P®/TSX™ 60 Index Fund   Large Cap

Pricing and Fund Data

	Oct 31/02	52 Week Range
Price	$35.35	H $45.65
		L $32.05

Fund Ticker Symbol	XIU
Benchmark Ticker	SPTSX60
MER	0.17%
Fund Manager	BGI Canada
Inception Date	Oct. 4/99
Net Assets	$3,114.1MM
Shares Outstanding (000)	88,231
Avg. Daily Trading Vol.	$57.3MM
Underlying Securities	60
Original Index Divisor	1/10
Options Available	Yes
RSP Eligibility	100%

Sector Exposure (%)   Oct 31/02

Sector	%
Financials	35.1
Energy	16.1
Materials	14.2
Consumer Discretionary	7.1
Industrials	6.4
Telecom Services	6.4
Utilities	4.9
Information Technology	3.9
Consumer Staples	3.6
Healthcare	2.5

Distributions

	Income	Cap Gains
Frequency	Qtrly	Yr End

History (per unit)	2000	2001	2002 YTD
Dividends	$0.42	$0.69	$0.50
Return of Capital	$0.06	$0.03	$0.01
Capital Gains	$1.67	$0.41	$ -
Total	$2.15	$1.13	$0.51

Top Ten Holdings (%)

Holding	%
Royal Bank	8.4%
BCE	5.6%
Bank Of Nova Scotia	5.3%
Encana	5.0%
Toronto Dominion Bank	4.3%
Bank Of Montréal	4.3%
Sun Life Financial	3.7%
Manulife Financial	3.6%
Alcan	3.2%
CIBC	3.2%
Top Ten Total (%)	46.6%

iUnits i60 Index Fund vs. Total Return S&P/TSX 60 Index

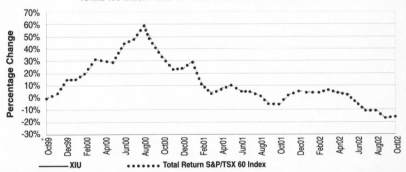

——— XIU   •••••• Total Return S&P/TSX 60 Index

Performance %   Oct 31/02

	1 Mo	3 Mo	6 Mo	1 Yr	3 Yr	5 Yr	10 Yr
Fund NAV	1.93	-4.80	-18.16	-9.99	-5.35	-	-
Benchmark Index	1.95	-4.80	-18.18	-9.90	-5.24	0.42	9.52

Fund Description

The iUnits S&P/TSX 60 Index Fund (i60) is an open-ended mutual fund trust, listed and traded on the Toronto Stock Exchange (TSX), and designed to replicate the performance of the S&P/TSX 60 Index. The index consists of 60 large cap, liquid stocks balanced across 10 industry sectors and represents approximately 60% of the whole market. The index is market capitalized-weighted, float adjusted and rebalanced quarterly.

Source: BGI Canada

iUnits™S&P®/TSX™ 60 Capped Index Fund — Large Cap

Pricing and Fund Data

	Oct 31/02	52 Week Range
Price	$39.35	H $50.55
		L $35.45
Fund Ticker Symbol	XIC	
Benchmark Ticker	SPTSEC	
MER	0.17%	
Fund Manager	BGI Canada	
Inception Date	Feb. 22/01	
Net Assets	$220.36MM	
Shares Outstanding (000)	5,640	
Avg. Daily Trading Vol.	$0.73MM	
Underlying Securities	60	
Original Index Divisor	1/10	
Options Available	No	
RSP Eligibility	100%	

Distributions

Distributions	Income	Cap Gains
Frequency	Qtrly	Yr End
History (per unit)	2001	2002YTD
Dividends	$0.57	$0.56
Return of Capital	$0.02	$0.03
Capital Gains	$ -	$ -
Total	$0.60	$0.59

Sector Exposure (%) — Oct 31/02

Sector	%
Financials	35.1
Energy	16.1
Materials	14.2
Consumer Discretionary	7.1
Industrials	6.4
Telecom Services	6.4
Utilities	4.9
Information Technology	3.9
Consumer Staples	3.6
Healthcare	2.5

Top Ten Holdings (%)

Holding	%
Royal Bank	8.4%
BCE	5.6%
Bank Of Nova Scotia	5.3%
Encana	5.0%
Toronto Dominion Bank	4.3%
Bank Of Montréal	4.3%
Sun Life Financial	3.7%
Manulife Financial	3.6%
Alcan	3.2%
CIBC	3.2%
Top Ten Total (%)	46.6%

iUnits i60C Index Fund vs. Total Return S&P/TSX 60 Capped Index

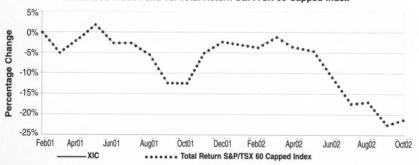

—— XIC   •••••• Total Return S&P/TSX 60 Capped Index

Performance % — Oct 31/02

	1 Mo	3 Mo	6 Mo	1 Yr	3 Yr	5 Yr	10 Yr
Fund NAV	1.93	-4.79	-18.15	-9.98	-	-	-
Benchmark Index	1.95	-4.80	-18.18	-9.90	2.78	5.17	12.08

Fund Description

The iUnits S&P/TSX 60 Capped Index Fund (i60C) is an open-ended mutual fund trust, listed and traded on the Toronto Stock Exchange (TSX) and designed to replicate the S&P/TSX 60 Capped Index. The index consists of 60 large cap, liquid stocks balanced across 10 industry sectors and represents approximately 60% of the whole market. The index is a constrained market capitalized weighted, float adjusted and rebalanced quarterly or when single company exposure exceeds a weighting of 10%.

Source: BGI Canada

iUnits™S&P®/TSX™ Canadian MidCap Index Fund　　　Mid Cap

Pricing and Fund Data

	Oct 31/02	52 Week Range
Price	$40.80	H $51.25
		L $37.85
Fund Ticker Symbol		XMD
Benchmark Ticker		SPTSXM
MER		0.55%
Fund Manager		BGI Canada
Inception Date		Mar. 8/01
Net Assets		$69.7M
Shares Outstanding (000)		1,703
Avg. Daily Trading Vol.		$0.61MM
Underlying Securities		60
Original Index Divisor		1/4
Options Available		No
RSP Eligibility		100%

Distributions	Income	Cap Gains
Frequency	Qtrly	Yr End
History (per unit)	2001	2002YTD
Dividends	$0.17	$0.21
Return of Capital	$0.01	$0.04
Capital Gains	$0.18	$ -
Total	$0.36	$0.25

Sector Exposure (%)　　　Oct 31/02

Sector	%
Financials	29.8
Materials	16.0
Energy	12.2
Information Technology	8.8
Consumer Discretionary	8.3
Industrials	7.9
Consumer Staples	6.0
Utilities	5.4
Telecom Services	4.6
Healthcare	1.0

Top Ten Holdings (%)

Holding	%
Power Corp	6.2%
Cda Life Financial	5.6%
Power Financial	4.5%
Shell Canada	3.6%
Goldcorp	3.2%
Investors Group	3.2%
Onex	3.1%
Brookfield Properties	2.7%
Great-West Life	2.6%
Penn West Petroleum	2.2%
Top Ten Total (%)	36.9%

iUnits iMidCap Index Fund vs. Total Return S&P/TSX Canadian MidCap Index

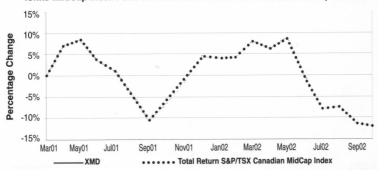

——— XMD　　•••••• Total Return S&P/TSX Canadian MidCap Index

Performance %　　　　　　　　　　　　　　　　　Oct 31/02

	1 Mo	3 Mo	6 Mo	1 Yr	3 Yr	5 Yr	10 Yr
Fund NAV	-0.51	-4.37	-17.00	-6.19	-	-	-
Benchmark Index	-0.47	-4.27	-16.85	-5.72	-	-	-

Fund Description

The iUnits S&P/TSX 60 Canadian MidCap Index Fund (iMidCap) is an open-ended mutual fund trust, listed and traded on the Toronto Stock Exchange (TSX) and designed to replicate the S&P/TSX Canadian MidCap Index. The index consists of 60 mid cap stocks balanced across 10 industry sectors and represents the middle tier of Canadian companies listed on the TSX. The index is market capitalized weighted, float adjusted and rebalanced quarterly.　　*Source: BGI Canada*

iUnits™S&P®/TSX™ Canadian Energy Index Fund

Industry Sector

Pricing and Fund Data

	Oct 31/02	52 Week Range
Price	$29.45	H $33.52
		L $26.15
Fund Ticker Symbol		XEG
Benchmark Ticker		SPTSEN
MER		0.55%
Fund Manager		BGI Canada
Inception Date		Mar. 23/01
Net Assets		$52.30MM
Shares Outstanding (000)		1,774
Avg. Daily Trading Vol.		$0.66MM
Underlying Securities		24
Original Index Divisor		1/4
Options Available		No
RSP Eligibility		100%

Distributions	Income	Cap Gains
Frequency	Qtrly	Yr End
History (per unit)	2001	2002YTD
Dividends	$0.02	$0.06
Return of Capital	$ -	$0.03
Capital Gains	$1.44	$ -
Total	$1.46	$0.09

Sector Exposure (%) Oct 31/02

O&G Exploration & Production	54.8
Integrated Oil & Gas	39.2
O&G Drilling	4.8
O&G Equip. & Services	1.3

Top Ten Holdings (%)

Encana	25.7%
Petro Canada	13.5%
Suncor Energy	12.1%
Talisman Energy	9.2%
Canadian Natural Resources	6.7%
Imperial Oil	5.8%
Nexen	4.9%
Shell Canada	3.7%
Precision Drilling	3.4%
Penn West Petroleum	2.3%
Top Ten Total (%)	87.3%

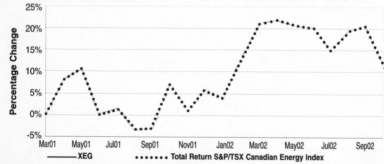

iUnits iEnergy Index Fund vs. Total Return S&P/TSX Canadian Energy Index

—— XEG   •••••• Total Return S&P/TSX Canadian Energy Index

Performance %

	1 Mo	3 Mo	6 Mo	1 Yr	3 Yr	5 Yr	10 Yr
Fund NAV	-7.63	-3.68	-9.27	3.02	-	-	-
Benchmark Index	-7.60	-3.55	-9.05	3.61	-	-	-

Oct 31/02

Fund Description

The iUnits S&P/TSX Canadian Energy Index Fund (iEnergy) is an open-ended mutual fund trust, listed and traded on the Toronto Stock Exchange (TSX) and designed to replicate the performance of the S&P/TSX Canadian Energy Index. The index consists of Canadian energy sector companies selected using Standard & Poor's industrial classifications and guidelines for evaluating company capitalization, liquidity and fundamentals. The index is a constrained market capitalization weighted, float adjusted and rebalanced quarterly or when a single company exposure exceeds a weighting of 25%.

Source: BGI Canada

iUnits™S&P®/TSX™ Canadian Financials Index Fund — Industry Sector

Pricing and Fund Data

	Oct 31/02	52 Week Range
Price	$24.70	H $30.45
		L $22.5
Fund Ticker Symbol	XFN	
Benchmark Ticker	SPTSFN	
MER	0.55%	
Fund Manager	BGI Canada	
Inception Date	Mar. 23/01	
Net Assets	$52.46MM	
Shares Outstanding (000)	2,134	
Avg. Daily Trading Vol.	$0.60MM	
Underlying Securities	23	
Original Index Divisor	1/4	
Options Available	No	
RSP Eligibility	100%	

Distributions

	Income	Cap Gains
Frequency	Qtrly	Yr End
History (per unit)	**2001**	**2002YTD**
Dividends	$0.29	$0.33
Return of Capital	$0.03	$0.08
Capital Gains	$0.06	$ -
Total	$0.38	$0.41

Sector Exposure (%) — Oct 31/02

Sector	%
Banks	64.5
Insurance	23.0
Diversified Financials	11.0
Real Estate	1.6

Top Ten Holdings (%)

	%
Royal Bank	20.1%
Bank of Nova Scotia	12.7%
Toronto Dominion Bank	10.4%
Bank of Montréal	10.3%
Sun Life	8.9%
Manulife Financial	8.7%
CIBC	7.7%
National Bank	3.0%
Power Corp	2.9%
Canada Life Financial	2.6%
Top Ten Total (%)	87.2%

iUnits iFin Index Fund vs. Total Return S&P/TSX Canadian Financials Index

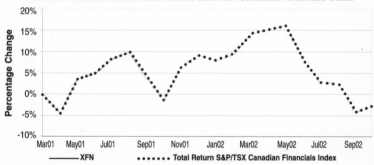

——— XFN   • • • • • • Total Return S&P/TSX Canadian Financials Index

Performance % — Oct 31/02

	1 Mo	3 Mo	6 Mo	1 Yr	3 Yr	5 Yr	10 Yr
Fund NAV	1.33	-5.58	-15.81	-1.93	-	-	-
Benchmark Index	1.37	-5.52	-15.70	-1.44	-	-	-

Fund Description

The iUnits S&P/TSX Canadian Financials Index Fund (iFin) is an open-ended mutual fund trust, listed and traded on the Toronto Stock Exchange (TSX) and designed to replicate the performance of the S&P/TSX Canadian Financials Index. The index consists of Canadian financial sector companies selected using Standard & Poor's industrial classifications and guidelines for evaluating company capitalization, liquidity and fundamentals. The index is a constrained market capitalization weighted, float adjusted and rebalanced quarterly or when a single company exposure exceeds a weighting of 25%.

Source: BGI Canada

iUnits™S&P®/TSX™ Canadian Gold Index Fund — Industry Sector

Pricing and Fund Data

	Oct 31/02	52 Week Range
Price	$40.95	H $57.30 L $32.00
Fund Ticker Symbol		XGD
Benchmark Ticker		SPTSEG
MER		0.55%
Fund Manager		BGI Canada
Inception Date		Mar. 29/01
Net Assets		$140.81MM
Shares Outstanding (000)		3,434
Avg. Daily Trading Vol.		$1.88MM
Underlying Securities		9
Original Index Divisor		1/4
Options Available		No
RSP Eligibility		100%

Distributions

	Income	Cap Gains
Frequency	Qtrly	Yr End
History (per unit)	**2001**	**2002YTD**
Dividends	$0.03	$ -
Return of Capital	$0.03	$0.06
Capital Gains	$ -	$ -
Total	$0.06	$0.06

Sector Exposure (%) — Oct 31/02

Gold	100.0

Holdings (%)

Barrick Gold	26.43%
Placer Dome	24.87%
Goldcorp	14.04%
Meridian Gold	12.42%
Glamis Gold	7.25%
Agnico Eagle Mines	6.73%
Kinross Gold	4.77%
Bema Gold	1.98%
Iamgold	1.51%
Top Ten Total (%)	100.00%

iUnits iGold Index Fund vs. Total Return S&P/TSX Canadian Gold Index

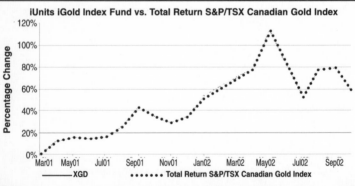

——— XGD   •••••• Total Return S&P/TSX Canadian Gold Index

Performance %   Oct 31/02

	1 Mo	3 Mo	6 Mo	1 Yr	3 Yr	5 Yr	10 Yr
Fund NAV	-11.90	3.32	-11.71	16.66	-	-	-
Benchmark Index	-11.88	3.47	-11.51	17.30	-	-	-

Fund Description

The iUnits S&P/TSX Canadian Gold Index Fund (iGold) is an open-ended mutual fund trust, listed and traded on the Toronto Stock Exchange (TSX) and designed to replicate the performance of the S&P/TSX Canadian Gold Index. The index consists of Canadian Gold sector companies selected using Standard & Poor's industrial classifications and guidelines for evaluating company capitalization, liquidity and fundamentals. The index is a constrained market capitalization weighted, float adjusted and rebalanced quarterly or when a single company exposure exceeds a weighting of 25%.

Source: BGI Canada

iUnits™S&P®/TSX™ Cdn. IT Index Fund

Pricing and Fund Data

	Oct 31/02	52 Week Range
Price	$3.65	H $10.80
		L $2.50
Fund Ticker Symbol	XIT	
Benchmark Ticker	SPTSIT	
MER	0.55%	
Fund Manager	BGI Canada	
Inception Date	Mar. 23/01	
Net Assets	$30.0MM	
Shares Outstanding (000)	7,978	
Avg. Daily Trading Vol.	$0.52MM	
Underlying Securities	18	
Original Index Divisor	1/4	
Options Available	No	
RSP Eligibility	100%	

Distributions Income Cap Gains

Frequency   Qtrly   Yr End

History (per unit)	2001	2002YTD
Dividends	$ -	$ -
Return of Capital	$ -	$0.01
Capital Gains	$ -	$ -
Total	$ -	$0.01

Industry Sector

Sector Exposure (%)   Oct 31/02

Communications Equip.	28.2
Electronic Equip. & Instruments	26.6
Software	17.1
Computer & Peripherals	15.3
IT Consulting & Services	6.9
Internet Software & Services	3.9
Semiconductor Equip. & Products	2.0

Top Ten Holdings (%)

Nortel Networks	28.2%
Celestica	15.6%
Cognos	10.5%
Onex	10.1%
ATI Technologies	9.1%
CGI Group	6.1%
Research In Motion	4.5%
Open Text	2.9%
Zarlink Semiconductor	2.0%
Creo	2.0%
Top Ten Total (%)	91.0%

iUnits iIT Index Fund vs. Total Return S&P/TSX Canadian Information Technology Index

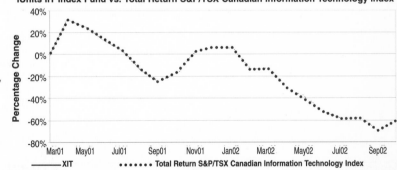

——— XIT   •••••• Total Return S&P/TSX Canadian Information Technology Index

Performance %   Oct 31/02

	1 Mo	3 Mo	6 Mo	1 Yr	3 Yr	5 Yr	10 Yr
Fund NAV	30.30	-5.39	-43.11	-52.42	-	-	-
Benchmark Index	30.45	-5.24	-42.97	-52.17	-	-	-

Fund Description

The iUnits S&P/TSX Canadian Information Technology Index Fund (iIT) is an open-ended mutual fund trust, listed and traded on the Toronto Stock Exchange (TSX) and designed to replicate the perform-ance of the S&P/TSX Canadian Information Technology Index. The index consists of Canadian IT sec-tor companies selected using Standard & Poor's industrial classifications and guidelines for evaluating company capitalization, liquidity and fundamentals. The index is a constrained market capitalization weighted, float adjusted and rebalanced quarterly or when a single company exposure exceeds a weighting of 25%.

Source: BGI Canada

iUnits™S&P®/TSX™ Canadian REIT Index Fund — Real Estate

Pricing and Fund Data

	Oct 31/02	52 Week Range
Price	$9.80	H $9.85
		L $9.65
Fund Ticker Symbol	XRE	
Benchmark Ticker	SPRTRE	
MER	0.55%	
Fund Manager	BGI Canada	
Inception Date	Oct. 22/02	
Net Assets	$12.2MM	
Shares Outstanding (000)	1,253	
Avg. Daily Trading Vol. (MM)	$0.256MM	
Underlying Securities	12	
Options Available	No	
RSP Eligibility	100%	

Distributions

	Income	Cap Gains
Frequency	Qtrly	Yr End

History (per unit)	2002YTD
Dividends	$ -
Return of Capital	$ -
Capital Gains	$ -
Total	$ -

Sector Exposure (%) — Oct 31/02

	Oct 31/02
Real Estate (REITs)	100.0

Top Ten Index Holdings (%)

Riocan REIT	24.1%
H&R REIT	14.3%
Retirement Residences REIT	11.3%
Summit REIT	10.1%
Cdn Real Estate Investment Trust REIT	9.3%
Legacy Hotels REIT	7.6%
Residential Equities REIT	5.5%
Cdn. Apartment Properties REIT	5.5%
Cdn. Hotel Income Properties REIT	3.5%
Cominar REIT	3.2%
Top Ten Total (%)	94.4%

Total Return S&P/TSX Canadian REIT Index

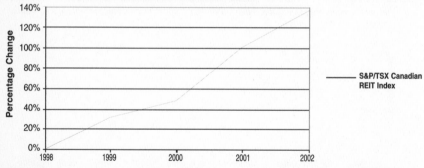

Performance % — Oct 31/02

	1 Mo	3 Mo	6 Mo	1 Yr	3 Yr	5 Yr	10 Yr
Fund NAV	-	-	-	-	-	-	-
Benchmark Index	-1.59	1.34	5.29	18.00	22.00	-	-

Fund Description

The iUnits S&P/TSX Canadian REIT Index Fund (iREIT) is an open-ended mutual fund trust, listed and traded on the Toronto Stock Exchange (TSX) and designed to replicate the performance of the S&P/TSX Canadian REIT Index. The index consists of 12 publically traded investment trusts that invest predominantly in income producing real estate assets, such as retail, residential, office or industrial properties or special purpose properties, including hotels or nursing homes. The index is a constrained market capitalization weighted, float adjusted and rebalanced quarterly or when a single company exposure exceeds a weighting of 25%.

Source: BGI Canada

iUnits™ MSCI International Equity Index RSP Fund   International Equity

Pricing and Fund Data

	Oct 31/02	52 Week Range
Price	$16.62	H $21.25
		L $15.35
Fund Ticker Symbol		XIN
Benchmark Ticker		MXEA
MER		0.35%
Fund Manager		BGI Canada
Inception Date		Sept 11/01
Net Assets		$51.02MM
Shares Outstanding (000)		3,080
Avg. Daily Trading Vol. (MM)		$0.21MM
Underlying Securities*		1,020
Options Available		No
RSP Eligibility		100%

Distributions	Income	Cap Gains
Frequency	Yr End	Yr End

History (per unit)	2001	2002YTD
Dividends	$ -	$ -
Return of Capital	$ -	$ -
Capital Gains	$ -	$ -
Total	$ -	$ -

Sector Exposure (%)   Oct 31/02

Financials	24.4
Consumer Discretionary	13.1
Health Care	10.5
Energy	9.3
Consumer Staples	9.5
Industrials	8.5
Telecom Services	7.0
Materials	6.3
Information Technology	6.3
Utilities	4.7

Top Ten Index Holdings (%)

BP PLC	2.7%
GlaxoSmithKline	2.2%
Vodafone Group	2.1%
Novartis	2.0%
HSBC Holdings	2.0%
Royal Dutch Petroleum	1.8%
TotalFinaElf	1.7%
Nokia	1.7%
Nestle	1.6%
Royal Bank of Scotland	1.2%
Top Ten Total (%)	19.0%

iUnits XIN Index Fund vs. Total Return MSCI EAFE Index

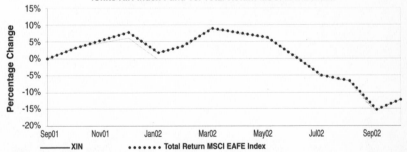

XIN ••••••• Total Return MSCI EAFE Index

Performance % (in CAD$)   Oct 31/02

	1 Mo	3 Mo	6 Mo	1 Yr	3 Yr	5 Yr	10 Yr
Fund NAV	4.51	-8.00	-18.39	-15.98	-	-	-
Benchmark Index	4.00	-7.27	-17.70	-14.44	-12.21	-0.84	6.79

Fund Description

The iUnits MSCI International Equity Index RSP Fund (iIntR) is an open-ended mutual fund trust, listed and traded on the Toronto Stock Exchange (TSX) and designed to track the performance of the MSCI EAFE Index. The MSCI EAFE Index was developed by Morgan Stanley Capital International Inc. as an equity benchmark for international stock performance. The index includes stocks from Europe, Australasia and the Far East.

* underlying securites relates to the index and not the fund. The iIntR maintains 100% RSP eligibility by investing primarily in international country index futures and high quality money market instruments.

Source: BGI Canada

iUnits™ S&P® 500 Index RSP Fund U.S. Equity

Pricing and Fund Data

	Oct 31/02	52 Week Range
Price	$13.90	H $18.85
		L $12.50
Fund Ticker Symbol		XSP
Benchmark Ticker		SPTR
MER		0.30%
Fund Manager		BGI Canada
Inception Date		May 29/01
Net Assets		$109.27MM
Shares Outstanding (000)		7,794
Avg. Daily Trading Vol. (MM)		$0.76MM
Underlying Securities*		500
Options Available		No
RSP Eligibility		100%

Distributions

	Income	Cap Gains
Frequency	Yr End	Yr End

History (per unit)	2001	2002YTD
Dividends	$ -	$ -
Return of Capital	$ -	$ -
Capital Gains	$ -	$ -
Total	$ -	$ -

Sector Exposure (%)

	Oct 31/02
Financials	20.7
Health Care	14.9
Information Technology	14.3
Consumer Discretionary	13.6
Industrials	11.3
Consumer Staples	9.8
Energy	5.8
Telecom Services	4.4
Utilities	2.6
Materials	2.6

Top Ten Index Holdings (%)

Microsoft	3.5%
General Electric	3.1%
Wal-Mart Stores	2.9%
Exxon Mobil	2.8%
Pfizer	2.4%
Citigroup	2.3%
Johnson & Johnson	2.1%
American International Group	2.0%
IBM	1.6%
Merck & Co.	1.5%
Top Ten Total (%)	24.2%

iUnits i500R Index Fund vs. Total Return S&P 500 Index

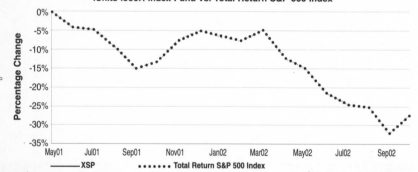

XSP ······ Total Return S&P 500 Index

Performance % (in CAD$) Oct 31/02

	1 Mo	3 Mo	6 Mo	1 Yr	3 Yr	5 Yr	10 Yr
Fund NAV	7.35	-3.68	-17.52	-16.77	-	-	-
Benchmark Index	7.38	-3.55	-17.24	-16.24	-10.50	2.80	12.45

Fund Description

The iUnits S&P 500 Index RSP Fund (i500R) is an open-ended mutual fund trust, listed and traded on the Toronto Stock Exchange (TSX) and designed to track the performance of the S&P 500 Index. The index consists of 500 large cap, liquid stocks balanced across 10 industry sectors and is considered to be the leading barometer of U.S. market activity.

* underlying securites relates to the index and not the fund. The i500R maintains 100% RSP eligibility by investing primarily in S&P 500 Index futures and high quality money market instruments.

Source: BGI Canada

iUnits™ Government of Canada 5-year Bond Fund Fixed Income

Pricing and Fund Data

	Oct 31/02	52 Week Range
Price	$28.60	H $29.05
		L $27.10
Fund Ticker Symbol		XGV
Benchmark Ticker		-
MER		0.25%
Fund Manager		BGI Canada
Inception Date		Nov. 23/00
Net Assets		$112.23MM
Shares Outstanding (000)		3,923
Avg. Daily Trading Vol. (Jun/01)		$0.40MM
Underlying Securities		1
Options Available		No
RSP Eligibility		100%

Distributions	Income	Cap Gains
Frequency	Semi-Annual	Yr End

History (per unit)	2000	2001	2002YTD
Interest Income	$0.12	$1.76	$0.79
Return of Capital	$0.75	$ -	$ -
Capital Gains	$ -	$0.01	$ -
Total	$0.87	$1.77	$0.79

Benchmark Bond Oct 31/02

CAN 7.25% 06/01/07

Benchmark Bond Yield: 4.14%

iUnits iG5 Fund vs. Total Return on Benchmark Bond

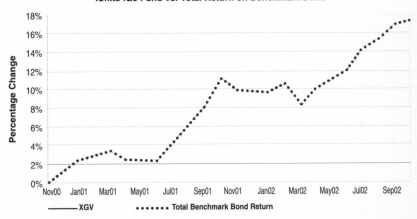

——— XGV   •••••• Total Benchmark Bond Return

Performance % Oct 31/02

	1 Mo	3 Mo	6 Mo	1 Yr	3 Yr	5 Yr	10 Yr
Fund NAV	0.22	2.40	6.43	5.21	-	-	-
Benchmark Index	0.24	2.48	6.63	5.57	-	-	-

Fund Description

The iUnits Government of Canada 5-year Bond Fund (iG5) is an open-ended mutual fund trust, listed and traded on the Toronto Stock Exchange (TSX) and designed to replicate the performance of a 5-year Government of Canada (GOC) bond.   Approximately once a year, the fund will sell the existing holding and select a new 5-year bond to maintain the term to maturity. *Source: BGI Canada*

iUnits™ Government of Canada 10-year Bond Fund   Fixed Income

Pricing and Fund Data

	Oct 31/02	52 Week Range
Price	$27.45	H $27.90
		L $25.60
Fund Ticker Symbol		XGX
Benchmark Ticker		-
MER		0.25%
Fund Manager		BGI Canada
Inception Date		Nov. 23/00
Net Assets		$78.04MM
Shares Outstanding (000)		2,842
Avg. Daily Trading Vol.		$0.24MM
Underlying Securities		1
Options Available		No
RSP Eligibility		100%

Distributions	Income	Cap Gains
Frequency	Semi-Annual	Yr End

History (per unit)	2000	2001	2002YTD
Interest Income	$0.10	$1.51	$0.68
Return of Capital	$0.64	$ -	$ -
Capital Gains	$ -	$0.09	$ -
Total	$0.74	$1.60	$0.68

Benchmark Bond   Oct 31/02

CAN 5.25% 06/01/12

Benchmark Bond Yield: 5.04%

iUnits iG10 Fund vs. Total Return on Benchmark Bond

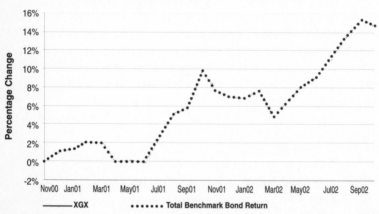

——— XGX   •••••• Total Benchmark Bond Return

Performance %   Oct 31/02

	1 Mo	3 Mo	6 Mo	1 Yr	3 Yr	5 Yr	10 Yr
Fund NAV	-0.52	3.20	7.45	4.33	-	-	-
Benchmark Index	-0.50	3.27	7.60	4.52	-	-	-

Fund Description

The iUnits Government of Canada 10-year Bond Fund (iG10) is an open-ended mutual fund trust, listed and traded on the Toronto Stock Exchange (TSX) and designed to replicate the performance of a 10-year Government of Canada (GOC) bond. Approximately once a year, the fund will sell the existing holding and select a new 10-year bond to maintain the term to maturity. *Source: BGI Canada*

TD S&P/TSX Composite Index Fund — Broad Market

Pricing and Fund Data

	Oct. 31/02	52 Week Range
Price	$20.95	H $26.84
		L $18.88
Fund Ticker Symbol		TTF
Benchmark Ticker		SPTSX
MER		0.25%
Fund Manager		TD Asset Management
Inception Date		Feb. 23/01
Net Assets		$120.76MM
Shares Outstanding		5.77MM
Avg. Daily Trading Vol.		$591M
Underlying Securities		245
Original Index Divisor		1/300
Options Available		No
RSP Eligibility		100%

Distributions

Distributions	Income	Cap Gains
Frequency	Qtrly	Yr End
History (per unit)	**2001**	**2002YTD**
Dividends	$0.23	$0.25
Return of Capital	$ -	$ -
Capital Gains	$0.02	$ -
Total	$0.25	$0.25

Sector Exposure (%) — Oct 31/02

Sector	%
Financials	31.3
Materials	15.3
Energy	14.7
Industrials	8.4
Consumer Discretionary	7.4
Telecom Services	5.4
Utilities	4.9
Consumer Staples	4.7
Information Technology	4.5
Health Care	2.8

Top Ten Holdings (%)

Holding	%
Royal Bank	6.2%
BCE	4.2%
Bank of Nova Scotia	3.9%
EnCana	3.7%
Toronto Dominion Bank	3.2%
Bank of Montréal	3.2%
Sun Life Financial	2.8%
Manulife Financial	2.7%
CIBC	2.4%
Alcan	2.4%
Top Ten Total (%)	34.7%

S&P/TSX Composite Index Fund vs. Total Return S&P/TSX Composite Index

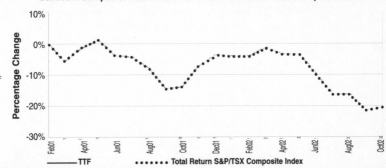

TTF ...... Total Return S&P/TSX Composite Index

Performance % — Oct 31/02

	1 Mo	3 Mo	6 Mo	YTD	1 Yr	3 Yr	5 Yr	10 Yr
Fund NAV	1.18	-5.02	-17.74	-17.71	-7.92	-	-	-
Benchmark Index	1.21	-4.95	-17.69	-17.58	-7.68	-	-	-

Fund Description

The TD S&P/TSX Composite Index Fund is an open-ended mutual fund trust, listed and traded on the Toronto Stock Exchange (TSX), and designed to replicate the performance of the S&P/TSX Composite Index. The S&P/TSX Composite Index comprises approximately 71% of market capitalization for Canadian-based, Toronto Stock Exchange listed companies. The broad economic sector coverage has made the S&P/TSX Composite Index the premier indicator of market activity for Canadian equity markets since its launch on January 1, 1977. *Source: TD Asset Management*

TD S&P/TSX Capped Composite Index Fund   Broad Market

Pricing and Fund Data

	Oct. 31/02	52 Week Range
Price	$24.11	H $31.00
		L $22.85
Fund Ticker Symbol		TCF
Benchmark Ticker		T00CAR
MER		0.25%
Fund Manager	TD Asset Management	
Inception Date		Feb. 23/01
Net Assets		$69MM
Shares Outstanding		2.84MM
Avg. Daily Trading Vol.		$6.6M
Underlying Securities		245
Original Index Divisor		1/300
Options Available		No
RSP Eligibility		100%

Sector Exposure (%) — Oct 31/02

Sector	%
Financials	31.3
Materials	15.3
Energy	14.7
Industrials	8.4
Consumer Discretionary	7.4
Telecom Services	5.4
Utilities	4.9
Consumer Staples	4.7
Information Technology	4.5
Health Care	2.8

Distributions

Distributions	Income	Cap Gains
Frequency	Qtrly	Yr End
History (per unit)	2001	2002YTD
Dividends	$0.27	$0.28
Return of Capital	$ -	$ -
Capital Gains	$0.02	$ -
Total	$0.29	$0.28

Top Ten Holdings (%)

Holding	%
Royal Bank	6.2%
BCE	4.2%
Bank of Nova Scotia	3.9%
EnCana	3.7%
Toronto Dominion Bank	3.2%
Bank of Montréal	3.2%
Sun Life Financial	2.8%
Manulife Financial	2.7%
CIBC	2.4%
Alcan	2.4%
Top Ten Total (%)	34.7%

S&P/TSX Capped Composite Index Fund vs. Total Return S&P/TSX Capped Composite Index

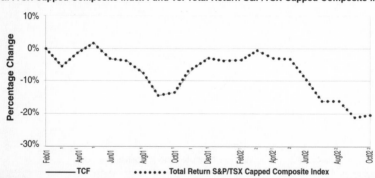

TCF ······ Total Return S&P/TSX Capped Composite Index

Performance %   Oct 31/02

	1 Mo	3 Mo	6 Mo	YTD	1 Yr	3 Yr	5 Yr	10 Yr
Fund NAV	1.21	-4.99	-17.72	-17.69	-7.90	-	-	-
Benchmark Index	1.21	-4.95	-17.70	-17.59	-7.69	-	-	-

Fund Description

The TD S&P/TSX Capped Composite Index Fund is an open-ended mutual fund trust, listed and traded on the Toronto Stock Exchange (TSX), and designed to replicate the performance of the S&P/TSX Capped Composite Index. The S&P/TSX Capped Composite Index includes all of the constituents of the S&P/TSX Composite Index. However, the relative weight of any single index constituent is capped at 10% and readjusted quarterly.   *Source: TD Asset Management*

TD Select Canadian Growth Index Fund   Style-Based

Pricing and Fund Data

	Oct. 31/02	52 Week Range
Price	$5.50	H $10.45
		L $5.50
Fund Ticker Symbol		TAG
Benchmark Ticker		DJCNGT
MER		0.55%
Fund Manager	TD Asset Management	
Inception Date		Dec. 7/01
Net Assets		$11.77MM
Shares Outstanding		2.04MM
Avg. Daily Trading Vol.		$3.1M
Underlying Securities		48
Original Index Divisor		1/100
Options Available		No
RSP Eligibility		100%

Distributions	Income	Cap Gains
Frequency	Qtrly	Yr End
History (per unit)	**2001**	**2002YTD**
Dividends	$ -	$ -
Return of Capital	$ -	$ -
Capital Gains	$ -	$ -
Total	$ -	$ -

Sector Exposure (%) — Oct 31/02

Sector	%
Energy	32.7
Materials	17.7
Industrials	17.0
Information Technology	11.7
Consumer Staples	8.9
Healthcare	6.9
Consumer Discretionary	3.4
Financials	1.6
Telecom Services	0.0
Utilities	0.0

Top Ten Holdings (%)

Holding	%
EnCana	12.8%
Canadian National Railway	7.9%
Barrick Gold	7.6%
Suncor Energy	6.0%
Petro Canada	5.5%
Talisman Energy	4.6%
Nortel Networks	4.3%
Biovail	3.8%
Canadian Natural Resources	3.4%
Loblaw Companies	3.4%
Top Ten Total (%)	59.3%

TD Select Canadian Growth Index Fund vs. Total Return DJ Canada TopCap Growth Index

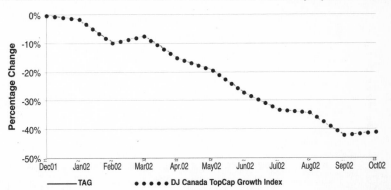

———— TAG   • • • • • DJ Canada TopCap Growth Index

Performance %   Oct 31/02

	1 Mo	3 Mo	6 Mo	YTD	1 Yr	3 Yr	5 Yr	10 Yr
Fund NAV	1.86	-12.14	-30.65	-41.17	-	-	-	-
Benchmark Index	1.82	-12.11	-30.53	-40.99	-	-	-	-

Fund Description

The TD Select Canadian Growth Index Fund is an open-ended mutual fund trust, listed and traded on the Toronto Stock Exchange (TSX), and designed to replicate the performance of the Dow Jones Canada TopCap Growth Index. The index consists of stocks trading on the Toronto Stock Exchange that exhibit strong growth characteristics as determined by Dow Jones. *Source: TD Asset Management*

TD Select Canadian Value Index Fund Style-Based

Pricing and Fund Data

	Oct. 31/02	52 Week Range
Price	$14.55	H $16.84
		L $13.25
Fund Ticker Symbol		TAV
Benchmark Ticker		DJCNVT
MER		0.55%
Fund Manager		TD Asset Management
Inception Date		Dec. 7/01
Net Assets		$20.8MM
Shares Outstanding		1.46MM
Avg. Daily Trading Vol.		$4MM
Underlying Securities		49
Original Index Divisor		1/100
Options Available		No
RSP Eligibility		100%

Distributions

Distributions	Income	Cap Gains
Frequency	Qtrly	Yr End
History (per unit)	**2001**	**2002YTD**
Dividends	$ -	$0.18
Return of Capital	$ -	$ -
Capital Gains	$ -	$ -
Total	$ -	$0.18

Sector Exposure (%) — Oct 31/02

Sector Exposure (%)	Oct 31/02
Financials	55.5
Telecom Services	10.2
Utilities	9.6
Materials	8.6
Consumer Discretionary	5.8
Energy	4.4
Consumer Staples	2.4
Industrials	1.9
Information Technology	0.8
Healthcare	0.0

Top Ten Holdings (%)

Top Ten Holdings (%)	
Royal Bank	12.9%
BCE	8.6%
Bank of Nova Scotia	8.1%
Bank of Montréal	6.6%
Toronto Dominion Bank	6.6%
Sun Life Financial	5.7%
Manulife Financial	5.6%
CIBC	5.0%
Alcan	4.9%
TransCanada Pipelines	3.8%
Top Ten Total (%)	67.8%

TD Select Canadian Value Index Fund vs. Total Return DJ Canada TopCap Value Index

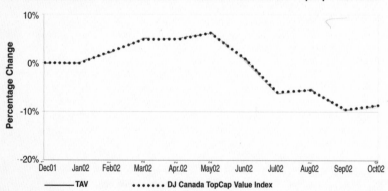

TAV —— ••••••• DJ Canada TopCap Value Index

Performance %

	1 Mo	3 Mo	6 Mo	YTD	1 Yr	3 Yr	5 Yr	10 Yr	Oct 31/02
Fund NAV	0.95	-2.73	-13.21	-8.86	-	-	-	-	
Benchmark Index	1.03	-2.57	-13.03	-8.53	-	-	-	-	

Fund Description

The TD Select Canadian Value Index Fund is an open-ended mutual fund trust, listed and traded on the Toronto Stock Exchange (TSX), and designed to replicate the performance of the Dow Jones Canada TopCap Value Index. The index consists of stocks trading on the Toronto Stock Exchange that exhibit strong value characteristics as determined by Dow Jones. *Source: TD Asset Management*

Appendix B

Making Sense of the Indices: A Reference
Guide to Canadian, U.S., International and
Global Indices Associated with ETFs

A Reference Guide to ETF Indices

You've got to exercise some fundamental selectivity before buying an ETF or you could wind up with something that doesn't suit your basic needs. You shouldn't necessarily want to buy the top performing ETF or the one you believe has the best prospects. Before laying your money on the line, decide which indices are best suited to your portfolio. To do this, understand the indices the ETF universe is related to. Here are some of the key points about the indices used for ETFs in Canada and the U.S. Find the kind of index you need; look at the other indices like it; decide on the index you want; and, then choose an associated ETF.

First let's clarify a few terms. Because indices reflect the market they are trying to measure, they need to be adjusted to market changes. A significant change in the market value of a stock will affect the weighting of that stock in a market capitalization weighted index. Adjusting for stock weightings is called "rebalancing the index." That is just an adjustment to the proportion of the index a company's stock takes up. Deciding what stocks to add or delete from an index is sometimes referred to as "reconstitution" or "constituent rebalancing." Many index sponsors post regular dates for rebalancing and reconstitution, and the criteria for these changes, so money managers who are keenly interested in an index can anticipate changes and work to adjust their holdings in a systematic way. The fewer times an index is adjusted, the more tax efficient its associated ETF will be. The more times it is adjusted, the closer it will pace its market.

Some indices experience more movement within than others. The S&P/BARRA style indices, for example, bump their constituents around from value and growth generally more than the Dow Jones style indices. That is simply a function of the way the styles are defined. If you want a style-related ETF, take a look at how the styles are arrived at. This will give you an idea of how much adjustment within the indices might occur. If tax is an issue you can weigh the anticipated taxable distributions against the style definition you like best. Small cap indices graduate their holdings to mid cap indices frequently, too, so these also have relatively more reconstitution changes than a large cap index for instance.

Also, you will recall from our previous discussion on indexing, the percentage of outstanding shares available for investment—"the float"—affects the investability of an index. Since investability is one of the desiderata of index construction, most contemporary indices are float-adjusted. In other words, the market capitalization weighting is adjusted to reflect the actual market value of the shares available for investment—not just the total number of shares issued by a company. The mechanics of this adjustment are not uniform among index sponsors. For instance, Dow Jones ignores block holdings less than 5% whereas the *Financial Times* index folks who run the FTSE indices in some cases aggregate these small block holdings and adjust the free-float accordingly. The details of free-float calculation are too technical for our purposes here, but you can usually obtain this information from the index sponsor's Web site. We highly recommend a stroll through Dow Jones Indexes site, *www.djindexes.com* and S&P's Web site, *www.spglobal.com*. They are models of fulsome information on their indices and their maintenance methodology. That's especially handy because S&P administers the major Canadian equity indices.

U.S. Indices

Wilshire 5000 Total Market Index
www.wilshire.com

This is the broadest U.S. equity index with approximately 7,000 stocks and covering about 99% of the U.S. equity market capitalization. It is a market capitalization weighted index that does not adjust for free-floats. Companies included must be headquartered in the U.S. and publicly traded. Stocks with no easily available price or shares outstanding data are excluded as are some illiquid stocks. REITs and limited partnerships are not excluded. Reconstitution is done when necessary. Rebalancing is usually done at the end of each month, but may also occur during the month.

ETF: Vanguard Total Stock Market VIPERs*

*This ETF is actually a separate class of the Vanguard Group's Total Stock Market Index Fund, a giant low-cost U.S. index mutual fund. The mutual fund is based on an optimized basket of about 3,400 stocks in the Wilshire 5000 Index. The ETF is a further optimized basket of approximately 1800 stocks out of the 3,400 in the index fund.

Wilshire 4500 Equity Index
www.wilshire.com

Take the Wilshire 5000, subtract the 500 companies in the S&P 500 and you've got the Wilshire 4500. It is a measure of mid and small cap U.S. stocks.

ETF: Vanguard Extended Market VIPERs*
*See note for Vanguard Total Market VIPERs

Dow Jones U.S. Total Market Index
www.djindexes.com/jsp/giMethod.jsp

This index captures about 95% of the total U.S. market capitalization and has no fixed number of stocks. It was designed for investability and its 1,800 or so stocks are liquid. It excludes foreign stocks, thinly traded stocks, closed-end mutual funds, unit trusts and limited partnerships. REITs, however, are not excluded. The index includes all large and mid cap publicly traded stocks but to preserve the index's overall liquidity, only about half of the small cap market is included.

The overall index is divided into the following 10 sectors: basic materials, consumer (non-cyclical), consumer (cyclical), energy, financial, healthcare, technology, industrials, telecommunication services and utilities

Nestled within each of these sectors are various industry groups. For instance, Financials has the following sub-groups: Banks, Insurance, Real Estate and Specialty Finance. Specialty Finance encompasses these subgroups: Savings and Loans, Brokerages and others.

These indices are free-float adjusted and market cap weighted. They are reconstituted quarterly and when extraordinary corporate events occur. Rebalancing is also quarterly unless the number of a company's outstanding shares changes more than 10% in which case the rebalancing is immediate. Delisted stocks are not replaced until a reconstitution date.

ETFs: iShares DJ U.S. Total Market Index Fund

There is also an iShares ETF for each of the 10 Dow Jones U.S. Total Market sectors. A couple of industry sub-group indices also sport iShares ETFs. These are:

iShares DJ U.S. Financial Services Index Fund
iShares DJ U.S. Real Estate Index Fund

Dow Jones U.S. Total Market Style Indices
www.djindexes.com/jsp/tmsMethod.jsp

All the stocks in the DJ U.S. Total Market Index are first separated by class size. As with all Dow Jones country indices, classifying an index component as large, mid or small cap is based on a survey of the country's cumulative capitalization. The top 70% of that total capitalization is automatically classified as large cap. The next 20% is mid cap, and the remaining 10% is screened for trading volume and market capitalization to select a final 5% that comprises the small cap segment. After that basic division, the components are ranked on the basis of six factors: projected price-to-earnings, projected earnings growth, trailing price-to-earnings, trailing earnings growth, price-to-book value, and dividend yield. After some statistical work, each stock emerges identified either as growth, value or neutral, and the style indices are formed. Neutral stocks are excluded, so the resulting indices are a purer representation of growth and value styles than either the Russell or the S&P/BARRA style indices (see below).

The style indices are reviewed at the end of each March and September. Capitalization is reviewed quarterly with immediate changes for extraordinary events.

ETFs: streetTRACKS DJ U.S. Large Cap Growth Index Fund
streetTRACKS DJ U.S. Large Cap Value Index Fund
streetTRACKS DJ U.S. Small Cap Growth Index Fund
streetTRACKS DJ U.S. Small Cap Value Index Fund

Russell 3000, 2000 and 1000 Indices

www.russell.com/US/Indexes/US/Methodology.asp   (You must select "U.S. Resident.")

This index series is constructed by the Frank Russell Company, an investment management firm based in Tacoma, Washington and owned by Northwestern Mutual Life Insurance Company. The index is market capitalization weighted and holds the 3,000 largest stocks in the U.S. It represents around 90% of the U.S. market capitalization and is adjusted for free- float. It excludes stocks under $1, stocks of companies not domiciled in the U.S., and publicly traded entities that are not the stock of an operating company such as Berkshire Hathaway, royalty trusts, limited partnerships, closed-end funds, etc. The index is reconstituted on June 30 and changes are announced in advance. Capitalization rebalancing is done at the end of every month and when corporate activities such as mergers and acquisitions occur. Spin-off stocks may be added to the index when they are issued but deleted stocks are not replaced between reconstitution dates so the number of stocks in the index may fluctuate. Oddly, bankruptcy is not a reason for being dropped from the index.

The largest 1,000 stocks in the Russell 3000 become the Russell 1000. The next 2,000 stocks become the Russell 2000 Index.

ETFs: iShares Russell 1000
iShares Russell 2000
iShares Russell 3000

The Russell Style Indices

www.russell.com/US/Indexes/US/methodology.asp (You must select "U.S. Resident.")

The stocks in the Russell 3000, 2000 and 1000 indices are divided into growth and value styles. There is a Russell 3000 Growth Index, a Russell 3000 Value Index and so on for the thousand series indices. The style decision is based on two variables: the price-to-book ratio (as with the S&P style indices), and the I/B/E/S forecasted long-term growth rate relative to its peers. (I/B/E/S International Inc. is a Thomson Corporation company well- known for its consensus earnings estimates.) The results of these two variables are combined into a score for each stock which, with more fiddling, determines style membership. A total of 70% of the stocks in each index are classified as all value or all growth and 30% are assigned proportionately to value and growth. Growth and value determinations, then, are not mutually exclusive. Some stocks have a little of both. Although this method actively identifies growth stocks as opposed to the S&P/BARRA method that characterizes growth stocks as simply those that aren't value stocks, purists should know the Russell value and growth indices can cause a company's market cap to be divided between both growth and value.

ETFs: iShares Russell 3000 Growth
iShares Russell 3000 Value
iShares Russell 1000 Growth
iShares Russell 1000 Value
iShares Russell 2000 Growth
iShares Russell 2000 Value

Russell Midcap Indices

www.russell.com/US/Indexes/US/methodology.asp

The Russell Midcap indices are a subset of the Russell 1000 indices. The Russell Midcap Index itself is a capitalization weighted index consisting of 800 of the smallest companies in the Russell 1000. These 800 companies make up about 25% of the market cap of the 1000 index. Russell's Web site reported as of July 2001 that the latest reconstitution determined the index's average market capitalization was approximately US$4 billion and its median market capitalization was approximately US$2.9 billion. The largest company in the index was worth US$12 billion in market cap.

The Russell Midcap Growth Index is a subset of the Russell 1000 Growth Index and consists of those companies with higher price-to-book ratios and higher forecasted growth values. Similarly, the Russell Midcap Value Index is also a subset of the Russell 1000 Value Index. It contains companies with lower price-to-book ratios and lower forecasted growth values.

ETFs: iShares Russell Midcap Index Fund
iShares Russell Midcap Growth Index Fund
iShares Russell Midcap Value Index Fund

S&P 500 Composite Index
www.spglobal.com/ssindexmain500.html

This is the most widely followed U.S. stock index for U.S. money managers. The index is constructed by the New York-based firm, Standard & Poor's which is owned by McGraw-Hill, Inc. It is a market capitalization weighted index consisting of 500 large U.S. companies. Contrary to popular belief, the S&P 500 does not contain the 500 largest stocks; rather, it contains leading companies from leading industries which may include relatively small companies. S&P identifies industry sectors within the U.S. equity market, approximates the relative importance of these sectors in terms of market capitalization, and then allocates a representative sample of stocks within each sector. No strict criteria are published. Closely-held companies are typically screened out. The index is rebalanced quarterly for changes to shares outstanding, though share changes in excess of 5% are implemented when they happen. S&P 500 covers about 79% of the U.S. market. With a selection of 500 companies from the U.S. equity market, the S&P 500 is not a broad market index. It is not free-float adjusted.

Deletions from the index occur due to company mergers, financial operating failure, lack of representation or company restructuring. Inclusion, though, is somewhat more subjective and involves the judgment of seven committee members. As a result, changes in index holdings can not necessarily be forecast and can happen at any time. There are no fixed reconstitution dates. In 2000, the S&P index committee added 57 stocks to the respected index, 26 of them high-tech. By mid-April 2001, the 57 stocks were down on average 12.9%. The 23 stocks expelled for reasons other than mergers or acquisitions clocked an average gain of 38.6%. (See Ken Hoover, "Did S&P Get Caught Up In Internet Mania?" *Investor's Business Daily*, April 24, 2001.) This has lead to some criticism that perhaps the S&P 500 is more actively managed than other indices.

ETFs: SPDR
iShares S&P 500
iUnits S&P 500 Index RSP Fund

S&P Sector Indices
www.spglobal.com/indexmain500sector_description.html

Standard & Poor's uses the Global Industry Classification Standard which subdivides the S&P 500 into 10 economic sectors. Separate from this, there are sector ETFs which split the S&P 500 into nine sectors, as determined by the ETF provider. These are the sectors for the Select Sector SPDRs: consumer discretionary, consumer staples, energy, financial, health care, industrial, materials, technology and utilities.

Together the stocks in these nine sectors make up the entirety of the S&P 500 index, so what holds for the S&P 500 index holds for the corresponding sector ETFs.

ETFs: Nine Select Sector SPDRs

S&P MidCap 400 Index
www.spglobal.com/ssindexmain400.html

This index is intended to measure the performance of the mid-sized company segment of the U.S. market. It holds the stock of 400 U.S. mid cap companies selected by market cap, liquidity and industry representation. The median market capitalization of companies in the index as of July 2001 was US$1.8 billion. It is a market capitalization weighted index.

ETFs: MidCap SPDR
iShares S&P MidCap 400

S&P SmallCap 600 Index
www.spglobal.com/indexmain600.html

This index is intended to track the performance of the small cap segment of the U.S. market. It holds 600 U.S. small cap stocks. These stocks must be higher than $1 a share. Their annual trading must exceed 20% of shares outstanding and the company must not be majority owned by another entity. A few other requirements apply. The index is rebalanced quarterly although any share changes greater than 5% are implemented when they happen.

The S&P 500, 400 and 600 together make up the S&P SuperComposite 1500 Index.

ETF: iShares S&P 600

S&P/ BARRA Style Indices
www.spglobal.com/indexmain500growth_description.html

These indices include the S&P 500/BARRA Growth, the S&P 400/BARRA Growth, the S&P 600/ BARRA Growth and the corresponding S&P/BARRA Value indices.

These style indices divide the respective index holdings into value or growth companies by examining their price-to-book (P/B) ratio, a standard yardstick for evaluating the value of a stock. Stocks with a low P/B ratio are designated value stocks and stocks with a high P/B ratio are designated as growth stocks. These divisions are treated as mutually exclusive and the indices are split in half by market capitalization and sorted by price-to-book. Taken together the value and growth stocks always equal the total of their respective index be it the 500, 400 or 600.

This is a pretty simple system. A stock is either value or growth with nothing in between. Critics point out that price-to-book value may be a good indication of a value play, but it doesn't say much about a growth stock except to point out the obvious; namely, that it isn't a value stock.

Reconstitution happens twice a year on January 1 and July 1.

ETFs: iShares S&P 500/BARRA Growth
       iShares S&P 500/BARRA Value
       iShares S&P 400/BARRA Growth
       iShares S&P 400/BARRA Value
       iShares S&P 600/BARRA Growth
       iShares S&P 600/BARRA Value

S&P 100 Index
www.spglobal.com/indexmain100_description.html

A subset of the S&P 500 Index, this index holds 100 large stocks selected from the S&P 500 index. Option contracts are available on this index.

ETF: iShares S&P 100

NASDAQ-100 Index
www.nasdaq.com/indexshares/n100_index.stm

NASDAQ was the world's first electronic stock market, and according to their Web site, home to "over half of the companies traded on the primary U.S. markets." The NASDAQ-100 Index is made up of the 100 largest non-financial companies in the NASDAQ Composite Index. (The NASDAQ Composite Index tracks all the common stocks listed on the NASDAQ Stock Market of which there are more than 5,000.) Major industry groups currently represented include computer hardware and software, telecommunications, retail/wholesale trade and biotechnology. The 100 Index is a modified market capitalization weighted index, which means that it caps the market weightings of its constituents to meet U.S. diversification requirements. No one company's weighting will represent more than 24% of the index, and all the companies with weightings of 4.5%

or more cannot together add up to more than 48% of the index. This is a technology heavy index.

The index is reconstituted on the third Friday of December every year with quarterly reviews for weighting changes.

ETF: NASDAQ-100 Index Tracking Stock, otherwise known as Qubes (QQQ)

Dow Jones Industrial Average
www.djindexes.com/jsp/avgMethod.jsp

This is the oldest continuously published stock index in the world (est. 1896) and is unusual in that it is a price-weighted index. It has another peculiarity, too. Its 30 blue chip constituents are selected by the editors of *The Wall Street Journal*. Rebalancing and reconstitution happen when corporate events dictate them. Because it is not a market cap weighted index, it does not need to take into account free-floats.

ETF: DIAMOND Trust Series 1 (DIAMONDS)

Fortune 500 Index
http://cgi.fortune.com/cgi-bin/fortune/dex/dex.cgi

Fortune is an American business magazine that compiles a list every year ranking the 500 U.S.-based and incorporated companies with the biggest revenue. The Fortune 500 Index takes those companies and adds some additional eligibility criteria: minimum market capitalization, minimum share price, minimum trading volume, and being exchange traded, ranks them according to market capitalization (not free-float adjusted). As a result, the index ranking is different from the list ranking, and because some Fortune 500 companies are private, the index has fewer than 500 companies. The index was launched on December 31, 1999. Its constituents are updated the third Friday in April, naturally after the publication of the Fortune 500 list in *Fortune* magazine, though additions and deletions can happen any time due to corporate actions. Rebalancing is done quarterly or as soon as is practicable after a share change of 5% or more.

ETF: streetTRACKS Fortune 500 Index Fund

Goldman Sachs Technology Index
www.ishares.com

Goldman Sachs is a global investment bank and securities firm. The index is made up of U.S. technology companies across every major sub-sector of technology. It is a modified cap weighted index to limit dominance by a few stocks. To qualify in the index, all stocks must trade on the NYSE, AMEX or NASDAQ and have an annual trading volume of 30% of float. If volume falls to less than 15%, the company is removed. Foreign companies, ADRs, limited partnerships and closed-end funds are excluded. Companies with free-float below 20% are not eligible and companies whose free-float falls below 10% will be removed. Rebalancing takes place semi-annually to reduce portfolio turnover. There is no fixed number of constituents.

ETFs: iShares Goldman Sachs Technology Index Fund

There are now three ETFs based on corresponding Goldman Sachs Technology sub-sector indices:

iShares Goldman Sachs Networking Index Fund

iShares Goldman Sachs Semiconductor Index Fund

iShares Goldman Sachs Software Index Fund

Goldman Sachs Natural Resources Sector Index

www.ishares.com

This is an index designed to reflect U.S. traded, natural resource related stocks. According to the iShares prospectus, the index includes "extractive companies, energy companies, owners and operators of timber tracts, forestry services, producers of pulp and paper, and owners of plantations."

ETF: iShares Goldman Sachs Natural Resources Index Fund

Fortune e-50 Index

www.timeinc.net/fortune/dex/e50/desc.html

This index is made up of 50 publicly traded Internet companies principally based in the U.S. Companies must derive at least 10% of its revenue from Internet activities. Companies must also have minimum share price, trading volume and market value. The index is a modified cap weighted index where weights are modified based on a company's Internet revenue. Weightings are rebalanced quarterly and components are managed so that the index meets diversification requirements: no stock will exceed 10% of the index and no stocks over 4.5% will together add up to more than 50% of the index.

ETF: streetTRACKS Fortune e-50 Index Tracking Stock

Morgan Stanley Internet Index

www.morganstanley.com/mox/index.html

Launched on December 31, 1999 this index comprises American companies involved in Internet usage. Morgan Stanley's Web site says the companies are selected based on "liquidity, borrowability, a demonstration of current leadership, business momentum and market share." There is no fixed number of companies in the index. As of July 2001, it included 30 companies. The index is owned and maintained by Morgan Stanley, a U.S.

financial services company. It is equal-dollar-weighted and rebalanced quarterly.

ETF: streetTRACKS Morgan Stanley Internet Index Fund

NASDAQ Biotechnology Index
http://dynamic.nasdaq.com/dynamic/nasdaqbiotech_activity.stm

This is a cap weighted index that includes the largest and most actively traded biotechnology companies listed on NASDAQ. According to the NASDAQ Web site, the companies "are primarily engaged in using bio-medical research for the discovery or development of novel treatments or cures for human disease." Inclusion requirements include a market cap of at least US$200 million and a price of US$10 or more, good daily trading volume (at least 100,000 shares a day on average) and have been publicly traded for at least six months, except for spin-offs. Securities are reviewed semi-annually and take effect on the third Friday in May and November. There were 72 companies in the index as of November 2002.

ETF: iShares NASDAQ Biotechnology Index Fund

Morgan Stanley High-Tech 35 Index
www.morganstanley.com/msh/structure.htm

This index is made up exclusively of 35 publicly traded electronics-based U.S. technology companies. It was launched on December 16, 1994. It is equal-dollar-weighted and adjustments are made annually on the third Friday of December. The American Stock Exchange calculates this index and Morgan Stanley acts as consultant to AMEX.

ETF: streetTRACKS Morgan Stanley High-Tech 35 Index Fund

Wilshire REIT Index
www.wilshire.com/Indexes/RealEstate/REIT

This index tracks the performance of publicly traded U.S. real estate investment trusts. The index requires the REITs it includes to have a book value of real estate assets of $100 million or more, and a market capital-ization of at least $100 million, and that 75% or more of the company's rev-enue is from real estate assets. Mortgage REITs, Health Care REITS, real estate finance companies, home builders, companies with more than 25% of their assets in direct mortgages, large land owner and subdividers are not included. Additions are made at quarterly intervals. Deletions are done at year-end. The index is a subset of the Wilshire Real Estate Securities Index.

ETF: streetTRACKS Wilshire REIT Index Fund

Cohen & Steers Realty Majors Index

www.cohenandsteers.com

This index tracks the market in large, actively traded U.S. REITs, Real Estate Investment Trusts. There are REITs in many sectors of U.S. real estate. As of November 2002, the Cohen & Steers Index had REITS in apartments, office property, regional malls, warehouse/industrial, shopping centres, health care facilities and hotels.

ETF: iShares Cohen & Steers Realty Majors Index Fund

Bank of New York American Depositary Receipt Indexes
Emerging Markets 50 ADR Index
Developed Markets 100 ADR Index
Europe 100 ADR Index
Asia 50 ADR Index

www.bldrsfunds.com/ and www.adrbny.com/adr_index_landing.jsp

American Depositary Receipts (ADR) are certificates that trade in U.S. markets and represent an interest in shares on a foreign market. The ADR Index tracks all Depositary Receipts, and a similar product called New York Shares, traded on The New York Stock Exchange (NYSE), The American Stock Exchange (AMEX) and NASDAQ. The Bank of New York ADR Index is a composite of many sub-indices, four of which now have ETFs associated with them. The composite index, from which all the other ADR indices are derived, is capitalization weighted and adjusted for free-float utilizing Dow Jones' index methodology.

ETFs: BLDRS* Emerging Markets 50 ADR Index Fund
       BLDRS Developing Markets 100 ADR Index Fund
       BLDRS Europe 100 ADR Index Fund
       BLDRS Asia 50 ADR Index Fund

*pronounced "builders"

U.S. Fixed Income Indices

Lehman Brothers 1-3 Year U.S. Treasury Index
Lehman Brothers 7-10 Year U.S. Treasury Index
Lehman Brothers 20+ Year U.S. Treasury Index

www.lehman.com/fi/indices/index.html

These indices share the same methodology and vary only by the duration of the bonds in the index. All the indices are designed to reflect the public obligations of the U.S. Treasury within their respective duration periods. The indices are market capitalization weighted, pay monthly income, and are rebalanced at the beginning of each month, though changes are permitted intra-month. The index does not include Targeted Investor Notes, state and local government series bonds, inflation-protected treasuries, convertible or stripped bonds.

ETFs: iShares Lehman 1-3 Year Treasury Bond Fund
iShares Lehman 7-10 Year Treasury Bond Fund
iShares Lehman 20+ Year Treasury Bond Fund

GS $ InvesTop Index
www: gs.com/investop/

All 100 bonds in this index are equally weighted at par (face) value. They are all U.S. dollar, highly liquid, investment grade corporate bonds. The index is rebalanced every month, though portfolio changes can occur between rebalancings. Each bond offering included in the index must have at least US$500 million in outstanding face value, be five years old or more and have a minimum of three years to maturity. No strip bonds, callable or convertible bonds are allowed. Distributions from income are paid monthly. This index is run by Goldman Sachs.

ETF: iShares GS $ InvesTop Bond Fund

Ryan On-the-Run Treasury Indexes
Ryan 1 Year Treasury Index
Ryan 2 Year Treasury Index
Ryan 5 Year Treasury Index
Ryan 10 Year Treasury Index
http://www.etfadvisors.com/products/index.html

A treasury is a U.S. government bond. Ryan Labs, a U.S. company, has devised a series of treasury bond indices with fixed maturities. As time passes, you might expect a five-year index to gradually become a four-year index; to prevent this, the Ryan indexes continually refresh the bonds in its portfolio with the most recently auctioned security at each maturity so as to approximate the target maturity. This is called an "on-the-run" (OTR) index.

The index returns are calculated by assuming that the old issue is sold and the new issue is purchased shortly after the U.S. Treasury auction results are announced. Since twelve- month T-bills are no longer issued, the 1 Year Treasury Index is based on two OTR securities, a six-month bill (two-thirds weighting) and a two-year note (one-third weighting).

ETFs: Treasury Fixed Income Trust Receipts (pronounced "fighters") FITRs

Treasury 1 FITRs
Treasury 2 FITRs

Treasury 5 FITRs

Treasury 10 FITRs

These are all sponsored by ETF Advisors.

Global and International Indices

MSCI Indices

www.msci.com

Morgan Stanley Capital International Inc., majority-owned by global financial services firm Morgan Stanley, runs a large series of international indices from broad global indices like the MSCI World Index, to regional indices like the MSCI Europe Index, right down to country-specific indices like the MSCI South Korea Index. MSCI finished revamping their international indices to full free-float weightings in 2002 and with it also achieved greater market coverage from 60% to about 85%. The free-float changes resulted in a lower weighting for telecommunication and utility stocks (commonly owned in some part by governments or with foreign ownership restrictions).

Stocks within each country are sorted by industry and by size in descending order with screens for free-float and liquidity. Rebalancing and reconstitution is done quarterly, one region at a time. All indices are reviewed every 18 months. Extraordinary corporate events affecting weightings and industry representation are addressed as they happen. Changes are announced two weeks in advance.

ETFs: The ETFs on MSCI country indices are extensive; 21 as of fall 2002, all of them iShares. See Directory for a full list.

MSCI EAFE Index

www.msci.com

EAFE (pronounced E-fee) is designed to capture the market performance of developed equity markets in Europe, Australasia and the Far East. It is a free-float adjusted market capitalization index and as of April 2002 the Index included 21 country indices. It encompasses approximately 90% of the world's market capitalization outside of the U.S.

ETFs: iShares EAFE Fund

iUnits MSCI International Equity Index RSP

MSCI EMU Index

www.msci.com

Large and liquid stocks from the 11 countries in the European Economic and Monetary Union make up this index. Like all MSCI indices, it is a free-float adjusted market capitalization index. In addition to being diversified by sector, it is designed to capture approximately 85% of the countries' free-float market capitalization.

ETF: iShares MSCI EMU

S&P Global 1200 Index
www.spglobal.com/indexmain1200_method.html

S&P says this is the first global index to be calculated in real time. It covers 31 countries and is made up of six distinct regional components: S&P 500, S&P/TSX 60, S&P Latin America 40, S&P/TOPIX 150, S&P Asia Pacific 100 and the S&P Europe 350. Each of these components is constituted by the same rules as the S&P 500 with the addition of a float-adjustment factor. The proportion of each regional component is relative to the size of its adjusted market value in the global equity market. Changes of 5% or greater are updated immediately; those less than 5% are reflected on a quarterly basis. Index changes are announced 10 days in advance. The index is divided into 10 sectors according to the Global Industry Classification Standard.

ETFs: iShares S&P Global Energy Sector Fund
iShares S&P Global Financials Sector Fund
iShares S&P Global Healthcare Sector Fund
iShares S&P Global Technology Sector Fund
iShares S&P Global Telecommunications Sector Fund

S&P Global 100 Index
www.spglobal.com/ssindexmainglobal100.html

The S&P Global 100 Index tracks the performance of 100 large multi-national companies. After determining that a company's activities are truly global in nature, each stock is screened for liquidity, sector representation, size and fundamentals. The index is free-float adjusted. Companies are removed from this S&P index for the same four reasons they would be removed from any S&P index: bankruptcy, being bought or merging, corporate restructuring or lack of industry representation. Rebalancing is quarterly or when a change greater than 5% occurs in the outstanding shares. Companies from the S&P Global 100 index are derived from the S&P Global 1200 Index.

ETF: iShares S&P Global 100 Index Fund

Dow Jones Global Titans 50 Index
www.djindexes.com/jsp/gtiMethod.jsp

Calling 50 of the world's largest multinational companies "Titans" is almost as poetic as it is descriptive. These companies are selected from the Dow Jones Global Index and are sorted in descending order by weighted average market value for the last four quarters, with most emphasis on the last quarter. The top 100 companies that survive this screening are then ranked according to fundamental measures that look at assets, profit, foreign sales, book value, sales to revenue and their free-float market capitalization ranking. The top 50 finalists make it into the index. Reconstitution takes place annually, rebalancing quarterly or with a change of more than 10% in the number of a company's outstanding shares.

ETF: streetTRACKS DJ Global Titans Index Fund

S&P Europe 350 Index
www.spglobal.com/indexmaineuro350_method.html

This index is designed to track the performance of stocks in 15 pan-European markets. It has three sub-indices: the S&P Euro (holding stocks from the 10 Eurozone countries) the S&P Euro Plus (adds Denmark, Norway, Sweden and Switzerland), and the S&P United Kingdom. It is intended to cover about 70% of the market capitalization of its target markets. Inclusion depends on liquidity, sector representation, fundamental analysis and market capitalization. It has 350 stocks adjusted for free-float. Free-float adjustments are reflected in market capitalization calculations and take into account the number of shares a company has freely available outside of control blocks, government holdings, and other situations that restrict the number of shares available for investment.

Additions to the index generally occur when there is a vacancy arising from an index deletion. Float weights are reviewed annually, in the third week of June, or as soon as a change of 5% or greater occurs due to a major corporate event.

ETF: iShares S&P Europe 350 Fund

S&P/TOPIX 150 Index
www.spglobal.com/indexmaintopix_method.html

Described by S&P as the Japanese counterpart to the S&P 500, this index includes 150 stocks from each major sector of the Tokyo market. According to S&P's Web site, the index "...represents approximately 70% of the market value of the Japanese equity market." Only highly liquid stocks from large Japanese companies are included.

ETF: iShares S&P/TOPIX 150 Fund

Dow Jones STOXX 50 Index
www.stoxx.com/indexes/bluechip.html

One of Dow Jones' blue chip indices, the STOXX Web site describes it as consisting of 50 stocks covering the market sector leaders in the Dow Jones STOXX™ 600 Index. The Dow Jones STOXX 600 Index is derived from the largest 600 stocks in the Dow Jones STOXX Total Market Index, which is a European index.

STOXX indices are intended to reflect stock market activity in the European Monetary Union and the Eurozone. They are designed in accordance with Dow Jones Global indices and are free-float adjusted and market capitalization weighted.

ETF: DJ STOXX 50

This ETF is sponsored by UBS and is one of two in what is expected to be a series of ETFs known as Fresco Shares.

Dow Jones EURO STOXX 50 Index
www.stoxx.com/indexes/bluechip.html

Like the Dow Jones STOXX 50 Index immediately above, this is another blue chip Dow Jones index based on the Dow Jones STOXX Total Market Index. The EURO STOXX 50 contains 50 market sector leading stocks from the Dow Jones EURO STOXX Index, a Eurozone index. These indices adhere to the methodology of Dow Jones Global indices.

ETF: DJ EURO STOXX 50

Sponsored by UBS, one of their Fresco series of ETFs.

Canadian Indices

S&P/TSX Composite Index
www.spglobal.com/indexmaintse300_method.html

This index is the broadest measure of the Canadian equity market. To be included in the index, companies must have been listed on the TSX for at least 12 months (though IPOs can be considered in certain cases) and must meet certain size and liquidity requirements. The volume, value and number of transactions taken together must be at least 0.025% of the same sum done for all the companies trading on the TSX to be considered for the index. To stay in the index, that figure can go as low as 0.020%. A stock must not have had more than 25 non-trading days in the previous 12 months to get into the index, but can have as many as 50 non-trading days once in the index. At least 25% of the companies free-float shares must turnover in one year to be included in the index and turnover must be no lower than 20% to continue in the index.

A company must have a minimum weight of 0.05% of the index on a float adjusted basis (0.025% to stay in) and a minimum trade-weighted average price of $1 over the previous three months.

Generally only common stocks of operating companies are allowed in the index which means limited partnerships, royalty trusts, REITs, preferred shares and exchangeable shares are excluded. The index is float adjusted for companies with purchase restrictions on 20% or more of outstanding shares. Stocks are ranked on a float quoted market value (QMV) basis. The S&P's Web site defines QMV as "the close price of that security on that day multiplied by the number of float shares." Reconstitution happens quarterly though deletions and a subsequent replacement can occur at any time. Rebalancings occur as soon as possible with a capitalization change of 0.05% or more of relative weight.

ETF: TD S&P/TSX Composite Index Fund

S&P/TSX Capped Composite Index
www.spglobal.com/TSX_method.pdf

This index holds all the stocks of the TSX Composite but their weights are limited (capped) to 10% of the index. This is to ensure diversification, and was a response to the heavy weighting of Nortel Networks Corp. in early 2000. Weights are adjusted quarterly but changes of relative weights greater than 0.05% are adjusted "on the first practical date." Share capitalization changes are announced one business day before being reflected in the index.

ETF: TD TSX 300 Capped Index Fund

Dow Jones Canada TopCap Growth Index
Dow Jones Canada TopCap Value Index
www.djindexes.com.jsp/tmsMethod.jsp

For these indices, stocks are selected from among all the stocks in the Dow Jones Canada Total Market Index which, according to Dow Jones, covers 95% of Canada's market capitalization. Stocks can be judged to be either growth, value or declared neutral. Neutral stocks are not included in either style index unless they have a market capitalization equal to at least 2% "of its size segment capitalization." The size segments are "large cap, mid cap, small cap, top cap and low cap" in both growth and value. The style indices are free-floated and are reviewed twice a year in March and September.

According to the Dow Jones Web site, "A stock's style classification is determined by the company's performance in terms of six measures—two

projected, two current and two historical:
Projected Price-to-Earnings Ratio (P/E)
Projected Earnings Growth
Price-to-Book Ratio (P/B)
Dividend Yield
Trailing P/E
Trailing Earnings Growth
ETFs: TD Select Canadian Growth Index Fund
TD Select Canadian Value Index Fund

S&P/TSX 60 Index
www.spglobal.com/indexmaintse_method.html

This index comprises 60 of Canada's largest and most liquid companies selected from the TSX Composite Index. The 60 Index is balanced across 10 sectors and float adjusted. Stocks are selected based on liquidity, size, sector representation and stability. Because this is an S&P index, the same four reasons for deleting a company from the index apply: acquisition by another company, bankruptcy, company restructuring and lack of industry representation.   Additions are made to replace deleted companies as required. Index rebalancing is quarterly and market capitalization adjustments are made to exclude block holdings of 20% or more. Stock weight changes greater than 0.05% are implemented when they occur.   Index changes are announced three days in advance. This large cap index was launched December 31, 1998 and is included in the S&P Global 1200.

ETF: iUnits S&P/TSX 60 Index Participation Fund

S&P/TSX 60 Capped Index
www.spglobal.com/indexmaintse_method.html

This index is a capped version of the S&P/TSX 60. No one company in the index will be greater than 10%. Weights are adjusted quarterly unless components' relative weights change by more than 0.05%. In that case, the adjustment will be made when the change in weight occurs. Additions or deletions to the index due to rebalancing are announced a month in advance. See the S&P/TSX Composite index description for rules.

ETF: iUnits S&P/TSX 60 Capped Index Fund

S&P/TSX Canadian Midcap Index
www.spglobal.com/indexmaintsemc_method.html

This index includes Canadian mid-size companies with their weightings adjusted across economic sectors. Capitalization, liquidity and fundamentals determine inclusion. Acquisition by another company, bankruptcy, restructuring or lack of sector representation can knock a component out of the index. Additions will be made to fill deletions. Float is adjusted for changes of 20% or more. Stock weightings are updated quarterly or with a change of 0.05% or more on the basis of the TSX Composite Index. Reconstitution changes are announced one month in advance. Other changes are announced three days ahead of time. This index was launched in May 1999.

ETF: iUnits S&P/TSX Canadian MidCap Index Fund

S&P/TSX Sector Indices
www.spglobal.com/indexmaintsesector_method.html

Stocks included in these sector indices are drawn from the pool of stocks listed in S&P/TSX Composite Index. The same inclusion and ranking criteria apply as for the S&P/TSX Composite, but the weighting of any one component stock is capped at 25% of the index. Sectors are defined according to the S&P/MSCI Global Industry Classification Standard (GICS), but so far only four sector indices have been restructured to reflect that classification. All the sub-indices should be fully revised by the end of March 2003.

The sector indices currently are:

> Canadian Financials
> Canadian Information Technology
> Canadian Energy
> Canadian Gold

ETFs: iUnits S&P/TSX Canadian Energy Index Fund
iUnits S&P/TSX Canadian Financials Index Fund
iUnits S&P/TSX Canadian Gold Index Fund
iUnits S&P/TSX Canadian Information Technology Index Fund

S&P/TSX Canadian Real Estate Income Trust Index
www.spglobal.com/indexmaintseincome_description.html

With a similar construction methodology to the S&P/TSX sector indices, this index is a sub-index of the S&P/TSX Canadian Income Trust Index. All trusts in the Trust Index must derive their income from an actual underlying business. To be considered for inclusion in the REIT index, a REIT must generally have been listed on the TSX for 12 months, be among the larger trusts of its kind, and be regularly and actively traded. No one REIT in the index can exceed a 25% weighting. Weightings are adjusted quarterly except for capped weightings falling below 20% or uncapped weightings rising above 30%. In these cases the adjustments will be done as soon as possible.

This is a float adjusted index to exclude the value of concentrated holdings of 20% or more. Deletions from the index can occur due to bankruptcy, restructuring or lack of representation within the REIT industry.

ETF: iUnits S&P/TSX Canadian REIT Index Fund

Appendix C

ETF Directory:
Vital Statistics on International ETFs,
both Existing and Pending

U.S. ETFs: Classified by Market Cap and Style

Exchange Traded Funds	Trading Symbol	Intraday NAV Symbol	Approx # of Positions	Original Index Divisor	Inception Date	Expense Ratio (%)	◊Total Assets ($ Mil)	Avg Daily Volume (1000/shrs)	Dividend /Income Distrib.	†Listed Options (O) LEAPS® (L)
U.S. EQUITY: MAJOR MARKET FUNDS										
Broad Market										
Extended Market VIPERs	VXF	EAH	3,067	1/6	12/27/01	0.20	19	6	Q	-
iShares DJ US Total Market Idx Fd	IYY	NLA	1,625	1/5	06/12/00	0.20	106	23	Q	O
iShares Russell 3000 Idx Fd	IWV	NMV	2,950	1/10	05/22/00	0.20	907	379	Q	O
Total Stock Market VIPERs	VTI	TSJ	3,542	1/100	05/31/01	0.15	1,025	152	Q	O
Large Cap										
DIAMOND Trust Series 1	DIA	DXV	30	1/100	01/20/98	0.18	3,333	6,088	M	O
iShares Russell 1000 Idx Fd	IWB	NJB	997	1/10	05/15/00	0.15	546	119	Q	O
iShares S&P 100 Idx Fd	OEF	OEV	100	1/10	10/23/00	0.20	148	40	Q	O
iShares S&P 500 Idx Fd	IVV	NNV	500	1/10	05/15/00	0.09	5,087	265	Q	-
NASDAQ-100 Idx Tracking Stock	QQQ	QXV	100	1/40	03/10/99	0.20	16,354	88,626	Q	L
Standard & Poors Depositary Receipts	SPY	SXV	500	1/10	01/29/93	0.12	26,545	25,392	Q	-
streetTRACKS Fortune 500 Idx Fd	FFF	FFY	453	1/10	10/10/00	0.20	61	24	Q	O
Mid Cap										
iShares Russell Midcap Idx Fd	IWR	NIZ	797	1/10	07/16/01	0.20	54	17	Q	O
iShares S&P MidCap 400 Idx Fd	IJH	NJH	400	1/5	05/22/00	0.20	541	50	Q	O
Standard & Poors MidCap 400 Dep Rec	MDY	MXV	400	1/5	05/04/95	0.25	5,420	1,372	Q	L
Small Cap										
iShares Russell 2000 Idx Fd	IWM	NJM	1,990	1/5	05/22/00	0.20	2,348	919	Q	O
iShares S&P SmallCap 600 Idx Fd	IJR	NIR	600	1/2	05/22/00	0.20	979	200	Q	O

STYLE FUNDS

Exchange Traded Funds	Trading Symbol	Intraday NAV Symbol	Approx # of Positions	Original Index Divisor	Inception Date	Expense Ratio (%)	◊Total Assets ($ Mil)	Avg Daily Volume (1000/shrs)	Dividend /Income Distrib.	†Listed Options (O) LEAPS® (L)
Broad Market Growth										
iShares Russell 3000 Growth Idx Fd	IWZ	NBE	1,867	1/10	07/24/00	0.25	39	18	Q	O
Broad Market Value										
iShares Russell 3000 Value Idx Fd	IWW	NNW	2,072	1/10	07/20/00	0.25	48	10	Q	O
Large Cap Growth										
iShares Russell 1000 Gr Idx Fd	IWF	NBF	575	1/5	05/22/00	0.20	452	144	Q	O
iShares S&P 500/BARRA Gr Idx Fd	IVW	NJG	166	1/10	05/22/00	0.18	413	76	Q	-
streetTRACKS DJ US Large Cap Gr Idx Fd	ELG	FLG	60	1/20	09/29/00	0.20	13	8	S	-
Large Cap Value										
iShares Russell 1000 Val Idx Fd	IWD	NJU	754	1/5	05/22/00	0.20	677	225	Q	O
iShares S&P 500/BARRA Val Idx Fd	IVE	NME	337	1/10	05/22/00	0.18	510	114	Q	-
streetTRACKS DJ US Large Cap Val Idx Fd	ELV	FLV	110	1/20	09/29/00	0.20	32	2	S	-
Mid Cap Growth										
iShares Russell Midcap Growth Idx Fd	IWP	NIW	455	1/4	07/16/01	0.25	55	20	Q	O
iShares S&P MidCap 400/BARRA Gr Idx Fd	IJK	NNK	161	1/2	07/24/00	0.25	216	55	Q	O
Mid Cap Value										
iShares Russell Midcap Value Idx Fd	IWS	NIV	545	1/8	07/16/01	0.25	72	17	Q	O
iShares S&P MidCap 400/BARRA Val Idx Fd	IJJ	NJJ	241	1/2	07/24/00	0.25	494	66	Q	O

Exchange Traded Funds	Trading Symbol	Intraday NAV Symbol	Approx # of Positions	Original Index Divisor	Inception Date	Expense Ratio (%)	◊Total Assets ($ Mil)	Avg Daily Volume (1000/shrs)	Dividend /Income Distrib.	†Listed Options (O) LEAPS® (L)
Small Cap Growth										
iShares Russell 2000 Gr Idx Fd	IWO	NLO	1,297	1/5	07/24/00	0.25	364	227	Q	O
iShares S&P SmallCap 600/BARRA Gr Idx Fd	IJT	NLT	244	1/2	07/24/00	0.25	221	35	Q	O
streetTRACKS DJ US Small Cap Gr Idx Fd	DSG	PSG	356	1/20	09/29/00	0.25	15	7	S	-
Small Cap Value										
iShares Russell 2000 Val Idx Fd	IWN	NAJ	1,345	1/5	07/24/00	0.25	736	175	Q	O
iShares S&P SmallCap 600/BARRA Val Idx Fd	IJS	NJS	359	1/2	07/24/00	0.25	457	111	Q	O
streetTRACKS DJ US Small Cap Val Idx Fd	DSV	PSV	336	1/10	09/29/00	0.25	44	9	S	-
U.S. Equity ETFs Classified by Sector										
Consumer Discretionary										
Consumer Discretionary Select Sector SPDR Fd	XLY	YXV	87	1/10	12/22/98	0.28	105	250	Q	-
iShares DJ US Cons Cyc Sector Idx Fd	IYC	NLL	266	1/5	06/12/00	0.60	139	50	Q	-
Retail HOLDRS	RTH	IRH	20	-	05/02/01	*	95	189	R	O
Consumer Staples										
Consumer Staples Select Sector SPDR Fd	XLP	PXV	34	1/10	12/22/98	0.28	219	161	Q	L
iShares DJ US Cons Non-Cyclical Sector Fd	IYK	NMJ	97	1/5	06/12/00	0.60	131	29	Q	-
Energy										
Energy Select Sector SPDR Fd	XLE	EXV	25	1/10	12/22/98	0.28	233	475	Q	L
iShares DJ US Energy Sector Idx Fd	IYE	NLE	58	1/5	06/12/00	0.60	82	22	Q	O
Oil Service HOLDRS	OIH	OXH	18	-	02/07/01	*	254	1,291	R	O

Exchange Traded Funds	Trading Symbol	Intraday NAV Symbol	Approx # of Positions	Original Index Divisor	Inception Date	Expense Ratio (%)	◊Total Assets ($ Mil)	Avg Daily Volume (1000/shrs)	Dividend /Income Distrib.	†Listed Options (O) LEAPS® (L)
Financials										
Financial Select Sector SPDR Fd	XLF	FXV	81	1/10	12/22/98	0.28	423	1,907	Q	L
iShares DJ US Financial Sector Idx Fd	IYF	NLF	283	1/5	05/22/00	0.60	106	18	Q	O
iShares DJ US Financial Services Idx Fd	IYG	NAG	157	1/5	06/12/00	0.60	30	7	Q	-
Regional Bank HOLDRS	RKH	XRH	18	-	06/23/00	*	282	89	R	O
Healthcare										
Biotech HOLDRS	BBH	IBH	19	-	11/23/99	*	1,043	1,506	R	L
Health Care Select Sector SPDR Fd	XLV	NXV	46	1/10	12/22/98	0.28	108	76	Q	L
iShares NASDAQ Biotechnology Idx Fd	IBB	IBF	72	1/10	02/08/01	0.50	475	440	Q	O
iShares DJ US Healthcare Sector Idx Fd	IYH	NHG	181	1/5	06/12/00	0.60	286	51	Q	O
Pharmaceutical HOLDRS	PPH	IPH	19	-	02/01/00	*	432	396	R	O
Industrials										
Industrial Select Sector SPDR Fd	XLI	TXV	69	1/10	12/22/98	0.28	123	169	Q	L
iShares DJ US Industrial Sector Idx Fd	IYJ	NIJ	247	1/5	06/12/00	0.60	46	14	Q	-
Materials										
iShares DJ US Basic Mat Sector Idx Fd	IYM	NLB	65	1/4	06/12/00	0.60	88	38	Q	-
Materials Select Sector SPDR Fd	XLB	BXV	37	1/10	12/22/98	0.28	186	391	Q	L
Natural Resources										
iShares Goldman Sachs Natural Resources	IGE	NGJ	112	1	10/22/01	0.50	19	2	Q	-

Exchange Traded Funds	Trading Symbol	Intraday NAV Symbol	Approx # of Positions	Original Index Divisor	Inception Date	Expense Ratio (%)	◊Total Assets ($ Mil)	Avg Daily Volume (1000/shrs)	Dividend /Income Distrib.	†Listed Options (O) LEAPS® (L)
Real Estate										
iShares Cohen & Steers Realty Majors Idx Fd	ICF	ICG	31	1/4	01/29/01	0.35	128	27	Q	-
iShares DJ US Real Estate Idx Fd	IYR	NLR	68	1/2	06/12/00	0.60	136	39	Q	-
streetTRACKS Wilshire REIT Idx Fd	RWR	EWR	92	1/1	04/27/01	0.25	28	6	S	-
Technology-Broad Based										
iShares DJ US Technology Sector Idx Fd	IYW	NJW	298	1/10	05/15/00	0.60	99	51	Q	O
iShares Goldman Sachs Tech Idx Fd	IGM	IPM	217	1/4	03/13/01	0.50	24	45	Q	O
streetTRACKS MS High-Tech 35 Idx Fd	MTK	JMT	35	1/10	09/29/00	0.50	44	76	S	-
Technology Select Sector SPDR Fd	XLK	KXV	90	1/10	12/22/98	0.28	656	1,252	Q	L
Technology-Internet										
B2B Internet HOLDRS	BHH	BUX	14	-	02/24/00	*	18	24	R	O
Internet HOLDRS	HHH	HHI	14	-	09/23/99	*	77	79	R	L
Internet Architecture HOLDRS	IAH	XAH	20	-	02/25/00	*	76	37	R	O
Internet Infrastructure HOLDRS	IIH	YIH	15	-	02/25/00	*	8	156	R	-
streetTRACKS Fortune e-50 Idx Tkg Stock	FEF	FEY	50	1/10	10/10/00	0.20	4	4	Q	O
streetTRACKS Morgan Stanley Int Idx Fd	MII	MMI	26	1/1	09/29/00	0.50	3	9	S	-
Technology-Other										
Broadband HOLDRS	BDH	XDH	20	-	04/06/00	*	45	139	R	O
iShares Goldman Sachs Networking Idx Fd	IGN	NVK	32	1/4	07/10/01	0.50	12	178	Q	O
iShares Goldman Sachs Semiconductor Idx Fd	IGW	NVW	53	1/4	07/10/01	0.50	37	46	Q	O
iShares Goldman Sachs Software Idx Fd	IGV	NVV	44	1/4	07/10/01	0.50	16	134	Q	O
Semiconductor HOLDRS	SMH	XSH	20	-	05/05/00	*	421	4,757	R	O
Software HOLDRS	SWH	XWH	20	-	09/27/00	*	68	356	R	O

Exchange Traded Funds	Trading Symbol	Intraday NAV Symbol	Approx # of Positions	Original Index Divisor	Inception Date	Expense Ratio (%)	◊Total Assets ($ Mil)	Avg Daily Volume (1000/shrs)	Dividend /Income Distrib.	†Listed Options (O) LEAPS® (L)
Telecommunications										
iShares DJ US Telecom Sector Idx Fd	IYZ	NJZ	32	1/5	05/22/00	0.60	35	38	Q	O
Telecom HOLDRS	TTH	ITH	15	-	02/01/00	*	95	147	R	O
Wireless HOLDRS	WMH	IWH	20	-	11/01/00	*	28	40	R	O
Utilities										
iShares DJ US Utilities Sector Idx Fd	IDU	NLU	75	1/2	06/12/00	0.60	142	62	Q	O
Utilities HOLDRS	UTH	XUH	19	-	06/23/00	*	117	86	R	O
Utilities Select Sector SPDR Fd	XLU	UXV	37	1/10	12/22/98	0.28	123	99	Q	L
International										
Broad Based Global										
iShares S&P Global 100 Idx Fd	IOO	OON	98	1/20	12/05/00	0.40	33	13	Q	-
Market 2000+ HOLDRS	MKH	XKH	58	-	08/30/00	*	91	33	R	O
streetTRACKS DJ Global Titans Idx Fd	DGT	UGT	50	1/3	09/20/00	0.50	21	2	Q	O
Global Sectors										
iShares S&P Global Energy	IXC	XGC	45	-	11/12/01	0.65	13	7	Q	-
iShares S&P Global Financial	IXG	XGG	194	-	11/12/01	0.65	8	2	Q	-
iShares S&P Global Healthcare	IXJ	XGJ	71	-	11/12/01	0.65	14	3	Q	-
iShares S&P Global Technology	IXN	XGN	124	-	11/12/01	0.65	4	13	Q	-
iShares S&P Global Telecommunications	IXP	XHP	45	-	11/12/01	0.65	9	7	Q	-
Broad Based										
iShares MSCI EAFE	EFA	EFV	787	-	08/14/01	0.35	3,541	303	S	O

Exchange Traded Funds

Exchange Traded Funds	Trading Symbol	Intraday NAV Symbol	Approx # of Positions	Original Index Divisor	Inception Date	Expense Ratio (%)	◊Total Assets ($ Mil)	Avg Daily Volume (1000/shrs)	Dividend /Income Distrib.	†Listed Options (O) LEAPS® (L)
Regional										
BLDRS Asia 50 ADR Idx	ADRA	ADRAI	50	1/15	11/13/02	0.30	19	1	Q	-
BLDRS Developed Markets 100 ADR Idx	ADRD	ADRDI	100	1/15	11/13/02	0.30	18	1	Q	-
BLDRS Emerging Markets 50 ADR Idx	ADRE	ADREI	50	1/15	11/13/02	0.30	21	1	Q	-
BLDRS Europe 100 ADR Idx	ADRU	ADRUI	100	1/15	11/13/02	0.30	18	2	Q	-
Europe 2001 HOLDRS	EKH	EKI	47	-	01/18/00	*	14	5	R	O
Fresco Dow Jones EUROSTOXX 50	FEZ	FEZIV	50	1/100	10/21/01	0.30	193	51	Q	-
Fresco Dow Jones STOXX 50	FEU	FEUIV	50	1/100	10/21/01	0.30	30	6	Q	-
iShares MSCI EMU	EZU	WWE	271	-	07/25/00	0.84	108	27	S	-
iShares MSCI Pacific ex-Japan	EPP	EPK	136	-	10/25/01	0.50	99	19	Q	-
iShares S&P Europe 350 Idx Fd	IEV	NJG	342	-	07/25/00	0.60	478	85	Q	-
iShares S&P Latin America 40	ILF	NIH	38	-	10/25/01	0.50	7	3	Q	-
Country Specific International										
Asia/Pacific										
iShares MSCI Australia Idx Fd	EWA	WBJ	71	-	03/18/96	0.84	74	43	S	-
iShares MSCI Hong Kong Idx Fd	EWH	INH	29	-	03/18/96	0.84	90	109	S	-
iShares MSCI Japan Idx Fd	EWJ	INJ	286	-	03/18/96	0.84	608	939	S	-
iShares MSCI Malaysia (Free) Idx Fd	EWM	INM	69	-	03/18/96	0.84	85	108	S	-
iShares MSCI Singapore Idx Fd	EWS	INR	35	-	03/18/96	0.84	79	79	S	-
iShares MSCI South Korea Idx Fd	EWY	WWK	78	-	05/12/00	0.99	83	88	S	-
iShares MSCI Taiwan Idx Fd	EWT	WWM	90	-	06/23/00	0.99	116	123	S	-
iShares S&P/TOPIX 150	ITF	NIT	151	-	10/23/01	0.50	29	3	S	-

Exchange Traded Funds	Trading Symbol	Intraday NAV Symbol	Approx # of Positions	Original Index Divisor	Inception Date	Expense Ratio (%)	◊Total Assets ($ Mil)	Avg Daily Volume (1000/shrs)	Dividend /Income Distrib.	†Listed Options (O) LEAPS® (L)
Europe										
iShares MSCI Austria Idx Fd	EWO	INY	16	-	03/18/96	0.84	13	15	S	-
iShares MSCI Belgium Idx Fd	EWK	INK	19	-	03/18/96	0.84	9	6	S	-
iShares MSCI France Idx Fd	EWQ	WBF	55	-	03/18/96	0.84	41	26	S	-
iShares MSCI Germany Idx Fd	EWG	WDG	48	-	03/18/96	0.84	69	55	S	-
iShares MSCI Italy Idx Fd	EWI	INE	42	-	03/18/96	0.84	25	10	S	-
iShares MSCI Netherlands Idx Fd	EWN	INN	24	-	03/18/96	0.84	16	7	S	-
iShares MSCI Spain Idx Fd	EWP	INP	36	-	03/18/96	0.84	15	10	S	-
iShares MSCI Sweden Idx Fd	EWD	WBQ	38	-	03/18/96	0.84	7	14	S	-
iShares MSCI Switzerland Idx Fd	EWL	INL	39	-	03/18/96	0.84	29	17	S	-
iShares MSCI United Kingdom Idx Fd	EWU	INU	133	-	03/18/96	0.84	110	67	S	-
Americas										
iShares MSCI Canada Idx Fd	EWC	WPB	80	-	03/18/96	0.84	58	76	S	-
iShares MSCI Brazil Idx Fd	EWZ	WWC	40	-	07/14/00	0.99	68	370	S	-
iShares MSCI Mexico Idx Fd	EWW	INW	30	-	03/18/96	0.84	66	192	S	-
Fixed Income										
iShares Lehman 1-3 Year Treasury Idx Fd	SHY	SHZ	9	-	03/26/02	0.15	769	246	M	-
iShares Lehman 7-10 Year Treasury Idx Fd	IEF	IEN	7	-	03/26/02	0.15	755	74	M	-
iShares Lehman 20+ Year Treasury Idx Fd	TLT	TLZ	20	-	03/26/02	0.15	670	316	M	-
iShares GS $ InvesTop Corporate Bond Fd	LQD	DLL	101	-	03/26/02	0.15	1,072	174	M	-
Treasury 1 FITR ETF	TFT	TFZ	6	-	11/01/02	0.15	9	1	M	-
Treasury 2 FITR ETF	TOU	TOG	6	-	11/01/02	0.15	9	7	M	-
Treasury 5 FITR ETF	TFI	TFV	7	-	11/01/02	0.15	9	2	M	-
Treasury 10 FITR ETF	TTE	TTY	6	-	11/01/02	0.15	9	3	M	-

* Expenses for HOLDRS consist of a custody fee of $2 per round lot (100 shares) per quarter. However, according to the HOLDRS prospectus, the trustee will waive that portion of the fee which exceeds the total cash dividends and other cash distributions.

◊ Total Assets as of October 31, 2002
† Listed Options
O=Options, L=LEAPS®
LEAPS® — Long-term Equity AnticiPation Securities®
LEAPS® are put and call options on underlying stocks that have January expirations up to three years from their time of listing. Conventional options with expirations up to nine months are also traded on all stocks for which LEAPS® are available. LEAPS®, which have their own ticker symbols, meld into conventional options each January when their expirations fall to one-year out.

Dividend/Income Distribution
Q — Quarterly
R — As Received
S — Semi-Annually
M — Monthly

INTERNATIONAL EXCHANGE TRADED FUNDS

Trading Symbol	Exchange Traded Fund	Sector/ Country	Inception Date	Expense Ratio (%)
Europe (Euro denominated unless otherwise specified)				
Australia (AUD denominated)				
AXSBAE AU	Access BNP Paribas AU Equity	Active Australia	Jul-01	1.90%
AXSMGE AU	Access BNP Paribas Global	Active Global	Jul-01	2.10%
AXSBMD AU	Access BNP Paribas Managed	Active Balanced	Jul-01	1.90%
AXSBSC AU	Access BNP Paribas Small Co.	Active Small Cap	Jul-01	2.15%
CDF	Commonwealth Div. Share Fund	Active Australia	Jun-98	0.95%
IDX AU	Indexshares Fund	Broad Market	Mar-01	0.95%
STW	streetTRACKS ASX S&P 200 Idx	Large Cap	Aug-01	0.29%
SFY	streetTRACKS ASX S&P 50 Index	Large Cap	Aug-01	0.29%
SLF	streetTRACKS ASX S&P 200 Prty.	Australian Real Estate	Aug-01	0.40%
WHTMAE	Wilson HTM Australian Equities	Active Australia	Sep-99	0.99%
WHTMFI	Wilson HTM Fixed Interest	Aus. Fixed Interest	Dec-00	0.55%
WHTMOS	Wilson HTM Overseas Share	International Equity	Oct-98	0.99%
DeutscheBorse				
SX5E	DJ EURO STOXX 50 Ex Anteile	EMU Large Cap	Dec-00	0.50%
SX5P	DJ STOXX 50 Ex Anteile	Europe Large Cap	Dec-00	0.50%
EUN2	DJ EURO STOXX 50 LDRS	EMU Large Cap	Apr-00	0.50%
EUN1	DJ STOXX 50 LDRS	Europe Large Cap	Apr-00	0.50%
SXAP	DJ STOXX 600 Autos	Europe Automotive	Jul-02	0.50%
SX7E	DJ EURO STOXX Banks	EMU Financials	May-01	0.50%
SX7P	DJ STOXX 600 Banks	Europe Financials	May-01	0.50%
SXPP	DJ STOXX 600 Basic Resources	Europe Resources	Jul-02	0.50%
SX4P	DJ STOXX 600 Chemicals	Europe Chemicals	Jul-02	0.50%
SXOP	DJ STOXX 600 Construction	Europe Construction	Jul-02	0.50%
SX2P	DJ STOXX 600 Cyclical Goods	Europe Cyclical Goods	Jul-02	0.50%
SXEP	DJ STOXX 600 Energy	Europe Energy	Jul-02	0.50%
SXFP	DJ STOXX 600 Financial Services	Europe Financial Services	Jul-02	0.50%
SX3P	DJ STOXX 600 Food	Europe Food	Jul-02	0.50%
SXDE	DJ EURO STOXX Healthcare	EMU Healthcare	May-01	0.50%
SXDP	DJ STOXX 600 Healthcare	Europe Healthcare	May-01	0.50%
SXNP	DJ STOXX 600 Industrial Goods	Europe Industrial Goods	Jul-02	0.50%
SXIP	DJ STOXX 600 Insurance	Europe Insurance	Jul-02	0.50%
SXMP	DJ STOXX 600 Media	Europe Media	Jul-02	0.50%
SXHP	DJ STOXX 600 Non-Cyclical	Europe Non-Cyclical	Jul-02	0.50%
SX1P	DJ STOXX 600 Retail	Europe Retail	Jul-02	0.50%
SX8E	DJ EURO STOXX Technology	EMU Technology	May-01	0.50%
SX8P	DJ STOXX 600 Technology	Europe Technology	May-01	0.50%
SXKE	DJ EURO STOXX Telecom.	EMU Telecoms	May-01	0.50%
SXKP	DJ STOXX 600 Telecom.	Europe Telecoms	May-01	0.50%
SX6P	DJ STOXX 600 Utilities	Europe Utilities	Jul-02	0.50%
DAXEX	DAXEX Anteile	German Large Cap	Dec-00	0.50%
FRC6	Fresco DJ UK Titans 50	U.K. Large Cap	Mar-02	0.50%
FRC1	Fresco EURO STOXX 50	EMU Large Cap	Mar-02	0.50%
EX14	FTSE 100 Share Index Fund	U.K. Large Cap	Jan-02	0.50%
MDAXEX	MDAX EX	German Mid Cap	Apr-01	0.50%

INTERNATIONAL EXCHANGE TRADED FUNDS

Trading Symbol	Exchange Traded Fund	Sector/ Country	Inception Date	Expense Ratio (%)
NDQ GR	NASDAQ 100 QQQ	U.S. Large Cap	Mar-99	0.18%
NMKXEX	NEMAX 50 EX	German Large Cap	Apr-01	0.50%
SMIEX	SMI EX Anteile	Swiss Large Cap	Mar-01	0.50%
SRD	SPDRs SPY	U.S. Large Cap	Jan-93	0.12%
UNO4	Unico MSCI Cons Discretionary	Europe Cons Discretionary	Mar-02	0.50%
UNO7	Unico MSCI Europe Cons Staples	Europe Cons Staples	Mar-02	0.50%
UNO5	Unico MSCI Europe Energy	Europe Energy	Mar-02	0.50%
UNO2	Unico MSCI Europe Financials	Europe Financials	Mar-02	0.50%
UNO3	Unico MSCI Europe Health Care	Europe Healthcare	Mar-02	0.50%
UNO6	Unico MSCI Europe Telecom	Europe Telecoms	Mar-02	0.50%
DJGTE	DJ Global Titans EX	Global Large Cap	Aug-02	0.50%
FRC2	Fresco DJ Industrial Average	U.S. Industrials	Mar-02	0.50%
FRC4	Fresco DJ US Tech	U.S. Technology	Mar-02	0.60%
LDRA	FTSE Global Autos LDRS	Global Autos	Jan-02	0.50%
LDRB	FTSE Global Banks LDRS	Global Banks	Jan-02	0.50%
LDRC	FTSE Global Cyclicals LDRS	Global Cyclical	Jan-02	0.50%
LDRE	FTSE Global Energy LDRS	Global Energy	Jan-02	0.50%
LDRF	FTSE Global Financials LDRS	Global Financials	Jan-02	0.50%
LDRG	FTSE Global Industries LDRS	Global General Industries	Jan-02	0.50%
LDRI	FTSE Global Basic Indus LDRS	Global Basic Industries	Jan-02	0.50%
LDRM	FTSE Global Media LDRS	Global Media	Jan-02	0.50%
LDRN	FTSE Global Non-Cyclicals LDRS	Global Non-Cyclicals	Jan-02	0.50%
LDRP	FTSE Global Pharmaceuticals LDRS	Global Pharmaceuticals	Jan-02	0.50%
LDRQ	FTSE Global Tech LDRS	Global Technology	Jan-02	0.50%
LDRT	FTSE Global Telecom LDRS	Global Telecommunications	Jan-02	0.50%
LDRU	FTSE Global Utilities LDRS	Global Utilities	Jan-02	0.50%

Euronext (Amsterdam)

Trading Symbol	Exchange Traded Fund	Sector/ Country	Inception Date	Expense Ratio (%)
AEXT	streetTRACKS AEX Index Fd	Netherlands Large Cap	May-01	0.30%
EUE	DJ EURO STOXX 50 LDRS	EMU Large Cap	Apr-00	0.50%
EUN	DJ STOXX 50 LDRS	Europe Large Cap	Apr-00	0.50%
ISFAi	Shares FTSE 100	U.K. Equities	Apr-00	0.35%
IERA	iShares FTSE Euro 100	Europe Large Cap	Dec-00	0.50%
IETA	iShares FTSE EuroTOP 100	Europe Large Cap	Oct-02	0.50%
ICYC	iShares FTSE European Consumer Cyclicals	European Consumer Cyclicals	Jul-01	0.40%
IUTL	iShares FTSE European Utilities	European Utilities	Jul-01	0.40%
ITEK	iShares FTSE European Technology	European Technology	Feb-01	0.40%
ISEE	iShares FTSE European Media	European Media	Feb-01	0.40%
IBKS	iShares FTSE European Banks	European Banks	Feb-01	0.40%
IBIO	iShares FTSE European Pharma & Biotech	European Pharma & Biotech	Feb-01	0.40%
IOIL	iShares FTSE European Oil & Gas	European Oil & Gas	Jul-01	0.40%
IUSE	iShares FTSE European Consumer Non Cyclicals	Euro Consumer Non Cyclicals	Jul-01	0.40%
STUK	streetTRACKS MSCI UK Index	U.K. Broad Market	Jul-01	0.30%
TGA	FTSE Global Autos LDRS	Global Autos	Jan-02	0.50%
TGB	FTSE Global Bank LDRS	Global Banks	Jan-02	0.50%
TGC	FTSE Global Cyclical LDRS	Global Cyclicals	Jan-02	0.50%
TGE	FTSE Global Energy LDRS	Global Energy	Jan-02	0.50%

INTERNATIONAL EXCHANGE TRADED FUNDS

Trading Symbol	Exchange Traded Fund	Sector/ Country	Inception Date	Expense Ratio (%)
TGF	FTSE Global Financials LDRS	Global Financials	Jan-02	0.50%
TGG	FTSE Global General Industries LDRS	Global General Industries	Jan-02	0.50%
TGI	FTSE Global Basic Indus LDRS	Global Basic Industries	Jan-02	0.50%
TGM	FTSE Global Media LDRS	Global Media	Jan-02	0.50%
TGN	FTSE Global Non-Cyclical LDRS	Global Non-Cyclicals	Jan-02	0.50%
TGP	FTSE Global Pharmaceuticals LDRS	Global Pharmaceuticals	Jan-02	0.50%
TGQ	FTSE Global Tech LDRS	Global Technology	Jan-02	0.50%
TGT	FTSE Global Telecom LDRS	Global Telecommunications	Jan-02	0.50%
TGU	FTSE Global Utilities LDRS	Global Utilities	Jan-02	0.50%

Euronext (Paris)

Trading Symbol	Exchange Traded Fund	Sector/ Country	Inception Date	Expense Ratio (%)
ERO	streetTRACKS MSCI Pan-Euro	Broad Market	Jun-01	0.30%
SPO	SPDR Euro	EMU Large Cap	Feb-02	0.35%
SPE	SPDR Europe 350	Europe Large Cap	Nov-02	0.35%
CAC	Master Share CAC 40	French Large Cap	Jan-00	0.30%
MSE	Master DJ EURO STOXX 50	EMU Large Cap	Mar-01	0.40%
ETT	Easy ETF Global Titans 50	Global Large Cap	Apr-01	1.00%
DJE	DJIA Master Unit	U.S. Industrials	Apr-01	0.50%
UST	MSCI US Tech Master Unit	U.S. Technology	Dec-01	0.50%
EUE	DJ EURO STOXX 50 LDRS	EMU Large Cap	Apr-00	0.50%
EUN	DJ STOXX 50 LDRS	Europe Large Cap	Apr-00	0.50%
GXN	DJ STOXX 50 SM EX	Europe Large Cap	Jan-01	0.40%
ETE	Easy ETF EURO STOXX 50	EMU Large Cap	Apr-01	1.00%
ETN	Easy ETF STOXX 50 Europe	Europe Large Cap	Apr-01	1.00%
EUE	DJ EURO STOXX 50 LDRS	EMU Large Cap	Jan-01	0.40%
GXE	DJ EURO STOXX 50 SM EX	EMU Large Cap	Jan-01	0.40%
SYV	EasyETF ASPI Euro	Europe Large Cap	Feb-02	0.60%
ICYC	iShares FTSE European Consumer Cyclicals	European Consumer Cyclicals	Jul-01	0.40%
IUTL	iShares FTSE European Utilities	European Utilities	Jul-01	0.40%
ITEK	iShares FTSE European Technology	European Technology	Feb-01	0.40%
ISEE	iShares FTSE European Media	European Media	Feb-01	0.40%
IBKS	iShares FTSE European Banks	European Banks	Feb-01	0.40%
IBIO	iShares FTSE European Pharma & Biotech	European Pharma & Biotech	Feb-01	0.40%
IOIL	iShares FTSE European Oil & Gas	European Oil & Gas	Jul-01	0.40%
IUSE	iShares FTSE European Consumer Non Cyclicals	Euro Consumer Non Cyclicals	Jul-01	0.40%
STV	streetTRACKS MSCI Euro Cons Disc	EMU Consumer Disc.	Sep-01	0.50%
STS	streetTRACKS MSCI Euro Cons Stap	EMU Consumer Staples	Sep-01	0.50%
STN	streetTRACKS MSCI Euro Energy	EMU Energy	Aug-01	0.50%
STZ	streetTRACKS MSCI Euro Fin.	EMU Financials	Aug-01	0.50%
STW	streetTRACKS MSCI Euro Health	EMU Healthcare	Sep-01	0.50%
STQ	streetTRACKS MSCI Euro Indust.	EMU Industrials	Sep-01	0.50%
STK	streetTRACKS MSCI Euro IT	EMU Information Tech.	Aug-01	0.50%
STP	streetTRACKS MSCI Euro Materials	EMU Materials	Sep-01	0.50%
STT	streetTRACKS MSCI Euro Telecom	EMU Telecom	Sep-01	0.50%
STU	streetTRACKS MSCI Euro Utilities	EMU Utilities	Sep-01	0.50%

INTERNATIONAL EXCHANGE TRADED FUNDS

Trading Symbol	Exchange Traded Fund	Sector/ Country	Inception Date	Expense Ratio (%)
Finland				
IHEX25	HEX 25 Index Share	Large Cap	Feb-02	0.25%
Hong Kong (Asset & price values in USD)				
2800	SSgA TraHK	H.K. Large Cap	Nov-99	0.10%
2801	iShares MSCI-China Tracker	China	Nov-01	0.99%
4363	iShares MSCI-South Korea Idx Fd	South Korea	May-00	0.99%
4362	iShares MSCI-Taiwan Index Fd	Taiwan	Jun-00	0.99%
Israel				
TALI IT	TALI 25	Israeli Large Cap	May-00	0.80%
Japan (Tokyo & Osaka) (U.S. denominated)				
1320 OS	Nikkei 225 Daiwa	Broad Cap	Jul-01	0.23%
1329	Nikkei 225 iShares	Broad Cap	Sep-01	0.22%
1330	Nikkei 225 Nikko	Broad Cap	Jul-01	0.23%
1321 OS	Nikkei 225 Nomura	Broad Cap	Jul-01	0.24%
1305	S&P/TOPIX 150 Daiwa	Large Cap	Jul-01	0.20%
1307	S&P/TOPIX 150 iShares	Large Cap	Aug-01	0.22%
1315	S&P/TOPIX 150 iShares	Large Cap	Aug-01	0.29%
1308	S&P/TOPIX 150 Nikko	Large Cap	Dec-01	0.11%
1306	S&P/TOPIX 150 Nomura	Large Cap	Jul-01	0.24%
1612	TOPIX Banking Daiwa	Japan Banking	Mar-02	0.22%
1615	TOPIX Banking Nomura	Japan Banking	Apr-02	0.22%
1310	TOPIX Core 30	Large Cap	Apr-02	0.22%
1311	TOPIX Core 30 Nomura	Large Cap	Apr-02	0.22%
1610	TOPIX Electrical Appliances Daiwa	Japan Appliances	Mar-02	0.22%
1613	TOPIX Electrical Appliances Nomura	Japan Appliances	Apr-02	0.22%
1611	TOPIX Transportation Equipment Daiwa	Japan Trans Equip.	Mar-02	0.22%
1614	TOPIX Transportation Equipment Nomura	Japan Trans Equip.	Apr-02	0.22%
New Zealand				
WIN	AMP Investments World Index	Global	Aug-97	0.80%
OZY	Australian 20 Leaders Index Fund	Large Cap	Feb-97	0.60%
MDZ	NZ MidCap Index Fund	Mid Cap	Jun-97	0.75%
TNZ	NZSE 10 Index Fund	Large Cap	Jun-96	0.40%
OM Sweden (SEK denominated)				
XACT	XACTOMX	Swedish Large Cap	Oct-00	0.30%
Peru Stock Exchange				
QQQ	NASDAQ 100 QQQ	U.S. Large Cap	Mar-99	0.20%
Singapore				
DIA	DIAMONDS Trust Series 1	U.S. Large Cap	Jan-98	0.18%
IYW	iShares DJ US Tech. Index Fd	U.S. Technology	May-00	0.60%
EWS	iShares MSCI-Singapore Idx. Fd	Singapore Large Cap	Mar-96	0.84%

INTERNATIONAL EXCHANGE TRADED FUNDS

Trading Symbol	Exchange Traded Fund	Sector/Country	Inception Date	Expense Ratio (%)
IVV	iShares S&P 500 Index Fd	U.S. Large Cap	May-00	0.09%
SPY	SPDRs	U.S. Large Cap	Jan-93	0.12%
STTF	streetTRACKS STRAITS TIMES	Broad Market	Apr-02	0.30%

South Africa (SAR denominated)

STX40	SATRIX 40	S.A. Large Cap	Nov-00	0.30%
STXIND	SATRIX Industrial Index	S.A. Industrials	Feb-02	0.80%
STXFIN	SATRIX Financial Index	S.A. Financials	Feb-02	0.80%

Switzerland

EUN	DJ STOXX 50 LDRS	Europe Large Cap	Apr-00	0.50%
EUNE	DJ EURO STOXX 50 LDRS	EMU Large Cap	Apr-00	0.50%
FDJ100	Fresco DJ Japan Titans 100	Japan Large Cap	Nov-01	0.70%
FDUK50	Fresco DJ UK Titans 50	U.K. Large Cap	Nov-01	0.50%
FDUSIA	Fresco DJ Industrial Average	U.S. Large Cap	Nov-01	0.50%
FDUSLC	Fresco DJ US Large Cap	U.S. Large Cap	Nov-01	0.50%
FDUSTC	Fresco DJ US Tech 40	U.S. Technology	Nov-01	0.60%
FSEU50	Fresco DJ EURO STOXX 50	EMU Large Cap	Nov-01	0.50%
SMIEX	IndEXchange SMI	Swiss Large Cap	Aug-01	0.50%
XMSMI	SMI-XMTCH	Swiss Large Cap	Mar-01	0.35%

United Kingdom (GBP denominated)

ISF	iShares iFTSE 100 Index	U.K. Large Cap	Apr-00	0.35%
ITMT	iShares iFTSE TMT	Tech/Media/Telecom	Oct-00	0.50%
IEUR	iShares iFTSE Ex-UK 100	Europe Non-U.K.	Dec-00	0.50%
IEUT	iShares FTSE Eurotop100	Euro Large Cap	Oct-02	0.50%
IUSA	iShares S&P 500 ETF	U.S. Large Cap	Mar-02	0.40%
ICYC	iShares FTSE European Consumer Cyclicals	Euro. Consumer Cyclicals	Jul-01	0.40%
IUTL	iShares FTSE European Utilities	European Utilities	Jul-01	0.40%
ITEK	iShares FTSE European Technology	European Techn.	Feb-01	0.40%
ISEE	iShares FTSE European Media	European Media	Feb-01	0.40%
IBKS	iShares FTSE European Banks	European Banks	Feb-01	0.40%
IBIO	iShares FTSE European Pharma & Biotech	European Pharma & Biotech	Feb-01	0.40%
IOIL	iShares FTSE European Oil & Gas	Euro. Oil & Gas	Jul-01	0.40%
IUSE	iShares FTSE European Consumer Non Cyclicals	Euro. Consumer Non Cyclicals	Jul-01	0.40%
EUN	DJ STOXX 50 LDRS	Europe Large Cap	Apr-00	0.50%
EUE	DJ EURO STOXX 50 LDRS	EMU Large Cap	Apr-00	0.50%
QQQ	NASDAQ 100 QQQ	U.S. Large Cap	Mar-99	0.20%

Virt-X

EUN	DJ STOXX 50 LDRS	Europe Large Cap	May-02	0.50%
EUNE	DJ EURO STOXX 50 LDRS	EMU Large Cap	May-02	0.50%
FSEU50	Fresco EURO STOXX 50	EMU Large Cap	May-02	0.50%
ISF	iShares FTSE 100	U.K. Equities	May-02	0.35%
IEUR	iShares FTSE Euro 100	EMU Large Cap	May-02	0.50%
IEUT	iShares FTSE Eurotop 100	EMU Large Cap	May-02	0.50%
FTGA	FTSE Global Autos LDRS	Global Autos	Jan-02	0.50%

INTERNATIONAL EXCHANGE TRADED FUNDS

Trading Symbol	Exchange Traded Fund	Sector/ Country	Inception Date	Expense Ratio (%)
FTGB	FTSE Global Banks LDRS	Global Banks	Jan-02	0.50%
FTGI	FTSE Global Basic Ind LDRS	Global Basic Ind.	Jan-02	0.50%
FTGC	FTSE Global Cyclicals LDRS	Global Cyclicals	Jan-02	0.50%
FTGE	FTSE Global Energy LDRS	Global Energy	Jan-02	0.50%
FTGF	FTSE Global Financial LDRS	Global Financials	Jan-02	0.50%
FTGG	FTSE Global Gen Ind LDRS	Global General Ind.	Jan-02	0.50%
FTGM	FTSE Global Non-Cyclical LDRS	Global Non-Cyclicals	Jan-02	0.50%
FTGP	FTSE Global Pharmaceutical LDRS	Global Pharm.	Jan-02	0.50%
FTGQ	FTSE Global Technology LDRS	Global Technology	Jan-02	0.50%
FTGT	FTSE Global Telecoms LDRS	Global Telecom.	Jan-02	0.50%
FTGU	FTSE Global Utilities LDRS	Global Utilities	Jan-02	0.50%
iUSA	iShares S&P 500	U.S. Large Cap	Jan-02	0.35%
FDUSIA	Fresco DJ Industrial Average	U.S. Large Cap	May-02	0.50%
FDUSLC	Fresco DJ US Large Cap	U.S. Large Cap	May-02	0.50%
FDUSTC	Fresco DJ US Technology	U.S. Technology	May-02	0.60%

Source: Managed Account Reports, LLC, Barclays Global Investors, Morgan Stanley

Pending ETFs*

ASSET CLASS
Small Cap
Vanguard SmallCap VIPERs (VB)

Fixed Income
iShares Lehman Bros Gov't/Credit
iShares Lehman Brothers Treasury

International
BoNY International 100 100 ADR
BoNY International Telecom 35 ADR
BoNY Latin America 35 ADR
FTSE/Xinhua China 25
iShares MSCI Regionals — ACWI
iShares MSCI Regionals — All Country Far East
iShares MSCI Regionals — Emerging Markets
iShares S&P Asia Pacific 100 Index Fund
iShares S&P Global 1200 Index Fund
iShares MSCI South Africa Index Fund
NETS (New Era Trust Securities)
SSgA/Nomura ETFs
Van Eck Economex Metals
Van Eck Economex Natural Gas
Van Eck Economex Petroleum
VIPERs — Asia Pacific
VIPERs — Emerging Markets
VIPERs — European

Leveraged ETFs
ProFunds Airline Ultra Sector — DJ x1.5
ProFunds Banking Ultra Sector — DJ x1.5
ProFunds Basic Materials Ultra Sector — DJ x1.5
ProFunds Bear — S&P 500 x-1
ProFunds Biotechnology Ultra Sector — DJ x1.5
ProFunds Bull — S&P 500
ProFunds Consumer Cyclical Ultra Sector — DJ x1.5
ProFunds Consumer Non-Cyclical Ultra Sector — DJ x1.5
ProFunds Energy Ultra Sector — DJ x1.5
ProFunds Entertainment & Leisure Ultra Sector — DJ x1.5
ProFunds Financial Ultra Sector — DJ x1.5
ProFunds Healthcare Ultra Sector — DJ x1.5
ProFunds Industrial Ultra Sector — DJ x1.5
ProFunds Internet Ultra Sector — DJ x1.5
ProFunds Oilfield Equip & Services Ultra Sector — DJ x1.5
ProFunds OTC — NASDAQ 100
ProFunds Pharmaceuticals Ultra Sector — DJ x1.5
ProFunds Precious Metals Ultra Sector — DJ x1.5

ProFunds Real Estate Ultra Sector — DJ x1.5
ProFunds Semiconductor Ultra Sector — DJ x1.5
ProFunds Technology Ultra Sector — DJ x1.5
ProFunds Telecom Ultra Sector — DJ x1.5
ProFunds Ulta OTC — NASDAQ 100 x2
ProFunds Ultra MidCap — S&P 400 x2
ProFunds Ultra Smallcap — Russell 2000 x2
ProFunds UltraBear — S&P 500 x-2
ProFunds UltraBull — S&P 500 x2
ProFunds UltraShort OTC — NASDAQ 100 x-2
ProFunds Utilities Ultra Sector — DJ x1.5
ProFunds Wireless Ultra Sector — DJ x1.5
Rydex Arktos — NASDAQ 100 x-1
Rydex Nova — S&P 500 x1.5
Rydex OTC — NASDAQ 100
Rydex Tempest 500 — S&P 500 x-2
Rydex Titan 500 — S&P 500 x2
Rydex Ursa — S&P 500 x-1
Rydex Velocity 100 — NASDAQ 100 x2
Rydex Venture 100 — NASDAQ 100 x-2

Style ETFs
Morningstar Large Cap Growth
Morningstar Large Cap Value
Morningstar Mid Cap Growth
Morningstar Mid Cap Value
Morningstar Small Cap Growth
Morningstar Small Cap Value
VIPERs Growth
VIPERs Value

Source: Managed Account Reports, LLC, Barclays Global Investors
* List of planned ETF products as of October 2002
Some or all of these ETFs may or may not be subsequently launched.

Appendix D
Web Directory

For Canadian ETF Products
www.iunits.com

Covers information on the BGI Canada Limited iUnits family of ETFs including daily NAV and related information.

www.me.org

Montréal Exchange site. Options on the i60s are traded at the Montréal Exchange. Offers outstanding explanation of options and futures in their Derivatives Institute section (*www.derivatives-institute.com/accueil_en.htm*)

www.tdassetmanagement.com

Deals with ETFs, closed-end funds and pooled indexed and quantitative funds. Includes daily NAV and related information.

www.tsx.com

Toronto Stock Exchange site. All Canadian-based ETFs are traded on the TSX.

For U.S.-Based ETF Products
www.amex.com

Information on all AMEX-listed ETFs with quotes and graphing.

www.amextrader.com

Outstanding ETF section with distribution history on all AMEX-listed ETFs from inception. Gives volumes, premiums/discounts, last trade to NAV and arranges for delivery of paper or electronic prospectus.

www.bldrsfunds.com

Information on BLDRS, the NASDAQ sponsored family of ETFs based upon The Bank of New York ADR Index.

www.cboe.com

Chicago Board Options Exchange: Major U.S. marketplace trading equity, index, interest rate and ETF options.

www.etfadvisors.com

Home of Treasury Fixed Income Trust Receipts, FITRS, (pronounced "fighters"): indexed to on-the-run treasury securities.

www.frescoshares.com

Overview of Fresco Index Shares funds.

www.holdrs.com

Devoted to news and market information on HOLDRS, a Merrill Lynch exchange traded basket security.

www.ishares.com

Information on BGI U.S.-based ETF offering, iShares. NAV information, tracking against the index, and numerous other tools helpful with portfolio construction.

www.morningstar.com

Information and research from the mutual fund ranking giant.

www.nasdaq.com

Listed under investment products, coverage includes the NASDAQ ETF family and the ETF Dynamic Heatmap (A colour-coded guide ranking 100 ETFs by their daily percentage price change (updated every minute).

www.nyse.com

The "Big Board" site provides data on their listed and traded ETFs.

www.spdrindex.com

Information and data on select Sector SPDRs.

www.streettracks.com

Information on State Street Global Advisors' ETF offerings.

www.vipers.vanguard.com

Information on the share class of Vanguard index funds that trade on an exchange.

General ETF and Indexing Sites

www.bylo.org

Site run by a Canadian private investor about do-it-yourself mutual fund investing and indexing.

www.exchangetradedfunds.com

This site is attempting to become the premier information source for ETFs. It has partnered with the ETFR, the only industry newsletter devoted exclusively to ETFs.

www.indexfunds.com

Excellent site for news, articles and information on index funds, indexing and ETFs. Comprehensive listing of available ETFs.

www.indexinvestor.com

Information to help investors improve investment performance through enhanced asset allocation and indexing.

www.journalofindexes.com

An open discussion of index issues based upon a cooperative effort between Index Funds International and Financial Advisor magazine.

www.marhedge.com

Site of the ETFR, the ETF industry newsletter. News on alternative investments like ETFs, hedge funds, HOLDRs, etc.

Index Providers

www.barra.com

Detailed information on the S&P/BARRA family of indices.

www.bnyadr.com

The Bank of New York depositary receipts site.

www.cgi.fortune.com

Information on Fortune indices.

www.djindexes.com

Revamped site full of information on methodology and maintenance of Dow Jones indices.

www.lehman.com

Listing of Lehman Brothers global family of fixed income benchmarks.

www.morganstanley.com

Morgan Stanley indices site.

www.msci.com

Site specific to MSCI international indices (U.S. indices coming soon).

www.russell.com

Site for information on Russell indices.

www.ryanindex.com

Ryan Labs bond indices methodology.

www.spglobal.com

Site for extensive information on S&P indices, their methodology and maintenance.

www.stoxx.com

Provider of Dow Jones STOXX indexes.

www.wilshire.com

Wilshire index information.

Mutual Fund Sites

www.globefund.com

Exceptionally good site for information about all Canadian mutual funds with benchmark comparisons.

www.ici.org

Offers a monthly assets report on ETFs not including HOLDRS. This is the site of the Investment Companies Institute, the American trade organization for mutual fund companies.

www.ific.ca

The Investment Funds Institute of Canada. Provides information and services for its members, investors and the media.

www.morningstar.ca

Canadian mutual fund site with the famous five star rating system. Extensive articles commissioned for the site.

Miscellaneous

www.cef.com

Closed-end funds site.

www.financialengines.com

Nobel prize winning economist, William Sharpe's site.

www.in-the-money.com

Site run by Mark Rubinstein, inventor of portfolio insurance.

www.vanguard.com/bogle_site/bogle_speeches.html

Archived speeches and information from the founder of the Vanguard Group, John Bogle.

ETF Portfolio Services

www.agileinvesting.com

AgileInvesting is an investment advisory service based on the use of Exchange Traded Funds to construct cost-efficient, diversified investment portfolios.

www.ETFolios.com

Guardian Capital Advisors' asset allocation service offering customized ETF portfolios directly to investors or through accredited investment advisors.

www.foliofn.com

Low cost FOLIOtrade^{sm} brokerage service allows you to trade individual stocks or to build a diversified portfolio with a single click.

Technical Analysis

www.barchart.com

On-line financial quotes, charts and technical analysis for stock and commodity traders.

www.bigcharts.com

Provides free comprehensive and easy-to-use investment research like interactive charts, quotes, industry analysis, intraday stock screeners, as well as market news and commentary.

www.clearstation.com

ClearStation, subsidiary of E*TRADE Group, is an investment Web site and community offering portfolio management with investment education and the essentials of technical and fundamental analysis.

www.decisionpoint.com

Technical analysis site offering education and prepackaged chart books covering over 1,800 stocks, mutual funds and market/sector indexes including ETFs.

www.dorseywright.com

A leading source of information and education on the point and figure charting methodology.

www.globeinvestorgold.com

Canadian site offering investment information including news, portfolio tracking, technical analysis and instant alerts.

www.stockcharts.com

Provides dynamic financial information such as investors' interactive charting tools, stock quotes, analysis and education for on-line investors.

www.stockmarkettiming.com

Stock Market Timing is a financial service for investors that offers a system for trading the popular ETFs: DIA, SPY and QQQ.

www.traders.com

Home of the *Technical Analysis of Stocks & Commodities* magazine, one of the longest running monthly publication for traders.

Appendix E

Recommended Reading

Why Smart People Make Big Money Mistakes—and How to Correct Them, Gary Belsky and Thomas Gilovich, Simon & Schuster, New York, 1999.

Against the Gods: The Remarkable Story of Risk, Peter L. Bernstein, John Wiley & Sons, New York, 1996.

Capital Ideas, Peter L. Bernstein, The Free Press, New York, 1993.

The Four Pillars of Investing: Lessons for Building a Winning Portfolio, William J. Bernstein, McGraw-Hill, New York, 2002.

The Intelligent Asset Allocator: How to Build Your Portfolio to Maximize Returns and Minimize Risk, William J. Bernstein, McGraw-Hill, New York, 2000.

Bogle On Mutual Funds: New Perspectives for the Intelligent Investor, John Bogle, McGraw-Hill, New York, 1994.

Common Sense on Mutual Funds, John Bogle, John Wiley & Sons, New York, 1999 .

John Bogle on Investing, John Bogle, McGraw-Hill, New York, 2001.

The Power of Index Funds, revised edition, Ted Cadsby, Stoddart Publishing Co., Toronto, 2001.

So You Want More Money... second edition,, George Caners, B.Sc., CA., M.B.A., C.F.P, Estate Services Inc., Brockville, 2001.

The Wealthy Boomer: Life After Mutual Funds, Low Cost Alternatives in Managed Money, Jonathan Chevreau, Michael Ellis and S. Kelly Rodgers, Key Porter Books, Toronto, 1998.

Point and Figure Charting: The Essential Application for Forecasting and Tracking Market Prices, second edition, Thomas J. Dorsey, John Wiley & Sons, New York, 2001.

Investment Policy: How to Win the Loser's Game, second edition, Charles D. Ellis, Irwin Professional Publishing, Chicago, 1993.

Classics: An Investor's Anthology, Edited by Charles D. Ellis and James R.Vertin, Business One Irwin, Homewood, Illinois, 1989.

Classics II: Another Investor's Anthology, Edited by Charles D. Ellis and James R. Vertin, Business One Irwin, Homewood, Illinois, 1991.

The Index Fund Solution, Richard E. Evans, Simon & Schuster, New York, 2000.

The Handbook of Equity Derivatives, revised edition, Edited by Jack Clark Francis, William Toy and J. Whittaker, John Wiley & Sons, New York, 2000.

How to be an Index Investor, Max Isaacman, McGraw-Hill, New York, 2000.

A Random Walk Down Wall Street, revised edition, Burton G. Malkiel, W.W. Norton & Company, New York, 1996.

Money Logic, Moshe A. Milevsky, Michael Posner, Stoddart Publishing Co., Toronto, 2000.

Technical Analysis of the Financial Markets: A Comprehensive Guide to Trading Methods and Applications, John J. Murphy, Prentice Hall Press, New York, 1999.

The Visual Investor: How to Spot Market Trends, John J. Murphy, John Wiley & Sons, New York, 1996.

Technical Analysis Explained: The Successful Investors Guide to Spotting Investment Trends and Turning Points, third edition, Martin J. Pring, McGraw-Hill Trade, New York, 1997.

Stocks for the Long Run, Jeremy J. Siegel, McGraw-Hill, New York, 1998.

What Wall Street Doesn't Want You To Know: You Can Build Real Wealth Investing in Index Funds, Larry E. Swedroe, Truman Talley Books, New York, 2001.

The Only Guide to a Winning Investment Strategy You'll Ever Need, Larry E. Swedroe, Truman Talley Books/Dutton, New York, 1998.

Fooled By Randomness: The Hidden Role of Chance in the Markets and in Life, Nassim Nicholas Taleb, Texere LLC, New York, 2001.

Time In, Time Out, Brooke Thackray & Bruce Lindsay, Upwave Media Inc., Toronto, 2000.

Core and Explore: The Investing Rush Without the Ruin, Duff Young, Prentice Hall Canada, Toronto, 2000.

Glossary

Actively managed Portfolios can be actively managed or passively managed. Actively managed portfolios employ an investment manager to make investment decisions according to investment objectives, usually with the goal of beating a benchmark index.

Asset allocation The practice of dividing a portfolio into investment categories known as asset classes such as cash, fixed income, equities, real estate, tangibles, etc. Strategic asset allocation places investment in asset classes for the long-term. Tactical asset allocation positions some or all of the asset classes temporarily to capture expected short or intermediate term market movements.

Authorized participant A U.S. term for large investors, institutions, exchange specialist and arbitrageurs who place creation/redemption unit orders with an exchange traded fund.

Basis point One one-hundredth of a percentage point or 0.01%. 100 basis points equals 1 percentage point.

Benchmark Something against which to measure performance. The S&P/TSX 60 Index, for instance, is a benchmark for the performance of large cap Canadian equity managers.

Cap or Capitalization Refers to market capitalization: the value of a public corporation's outstanding shares. It is calculated by multiplying the current market price of a company's shares by all its outstanding shares.

Capped An index or a fund is capped when there is a limit to the concentration of its holdings. For instance, the S&P/TSX Capped Composite Index limits all constituents to no more than 10% of the index. This ensures diversification in a market situation in which a few large companies can dominate an index.

Cash drag Underperformance due to cash in a portfolio.

Closed-end funds A fund that has a fixed number of issued shares and is traded on a stock exchange. Often trades at a discount or premium. Is opposed to an open-end fund that continually issues shares (units) and doesn't trade on a stock exchange.

Correlation How the movement of two variables is related. When asset classes respond similarly to market conditions, they are said to be "positively correlated." When they respond differently they are said to be "negatively correlated."

Creation unit The smallest number of securities that can be cashed in for exchange traded fund (ETF) shares. Correspondingly, a redemption unit is the smallest number of ETF units that can be cashed in for the underlying securities. Most ETFs require a minimum of 50,000 of their own shares in order to exchange them for the underlying securities.

Derivatives Contracts whose value is based on the performance of another asset or index. Derivatives include forwards, futures and options.

Designated broker (Cdn.) Registered brokers and dealers who enter into agreements with an exchange traded fund to perform certain brokerage related funtions.

Dividends Earnings paid out to shareholders.

Diversification In portfolio management, spreading investments among different asset classes to mitigate risk.

Distributions Payments by a mutual fund to unitholders of earnings within the fund.

Enhanced index fund An index fund that overweights or underweights index constituents with the goal of achieving returns superior to the index.

Efficient frontier In Portfolio Theory, the curve that depicts the points which maximize expected return for a pre-determined level of risk.

Exchange traded funds (ETFs) A basket of securities that trades on a stock exchange.

Ex-dividend A stock is said to be ex-dividend during the time a dividend is declared and the time it is issued. Anyone buying a stock during this ex-dividend period will not be entitled to the forthcoming dividend.

Forward contracts A promise to buy or sell a specific investment at a set time in the future for the current price when the contract is made. This is different from a futures contract, which is a promise to buy or sell at the future price at a set time in the future.

Futures A promise to buy or sell a specific investment at a set time in the future for the then current price.

HOLDRS A fixed and mostly unchanging basket of investments traded on a stock exchange. Issued by Merrill Lynch. Stands for 'Holding Company Depositary Receipts.' Some consider HOLDRS a kind of exchange traded fund (ETF), but they are more properly known as exchange traded baskets.

Index A collection of stocks designed to be reflective of a market.

Indexing An investment management strategy that tries to track an index.

Liquidity The ease and speed with which an investment can be sold without affecting the price of the investment.

Margining Borrowing money from a brokerage to buy securities. Done through a margin account that charges interest on borrowings, collateral must be kept in the account to cover some percentage of the margined stock.

Market timing The practice of darting in and out of investments with the aim of catching them only during their upward movement.

Marginal tax rate The tax rate at which your next dollar of income is taxed.

Management Expense Ratio (MER) Fees charged by a manager of a fund, and other expenses (excluding security commissions), divided by the assets of the fund to arrive at a percentage of costs to assets.

Modern Portfolio Theory A study of the relationship between investments and asset classes and their expected risk and return.

Mutual fund A pool of securities managed on behalf of unitholders that is bought or redeemed by the fund company. Units are continually offered (open-ended).

Net Asset Value (NAV) The value of an individual unit in a fund. It is calculated by taking the total value of the fund including cash and dividing it by the number of outstanding shares.

Optimization In index management, the practice of buying selected components of an index to as closely match the movement of the index as possible without actually buying all the index constituents. This is opposed to replication of the index.

Options Contracts granting the right to buy or sell an investment at a set price by a specified date.

Over-the-counter (OTC) A market for securities that is apart from a stock exchange. Bonds are sold OTC. Transactions are arranged over the phone or through computer networks connecting dealers.

Passively managed An investment style in which a portfolio is structured to track a specific index. See 'Actively managed.'

Price limit order An order to buy a stock that specifies a price or better.

Rebalancing In portfolio management, adjusting back to an optimal asset allocation.

REITS Real Estate Investment Trusts

Replication An indexing strategy that involves buying everything in the index; i.e., replicating the index. This is one of a few indexing strategies. Also see "optimization."

Reversion to the mean The habit of investment manager performance to revert to the mean performance over time.

Secondary market The market in which shares are bought and sold after their initial public offering. All stock exchanges and over-the-counter markets are secondary markets.

Secular Long-term, not seasonal or cyclical.

Tracking error The deviation from the index's price or return of any investment whose purpose is to keep pace with an index.

Short selling Selling a stock without owning it. This is done by those who expect the price of the stock to fall before the borrowed shares must be returned.

Segregated 1) In mutual funds, a fund in which all or most of the principal is guaranteed. 2) With respect to investment accounts, this refers to keeping an investor's holdings separate from those of other investors as opposed to commingling them.

Stop loss An order to sell a stock when the price goes below a designated threshold.

Style drift In mutual funds, style drift occurs when a fund manager makes investments not completely in keeping with the fund's declared investment style or bias. A value fund loaded with a popular growth stock to boast returns would be an example of a fund experiencing style drift.

Underwriters Registered brokers and dealers who subscribe for and buy units of an exchange traded fund as they are issued.

Table of Figures

Index